SAY IT AGAIN

Also by Dorothy Uris

TO SING IN   EVERYBODY'S BOOK OF   A WOMAN'S
ENGLISH   BETTER SPEAKING   VOICE

SAY IT AGAIN

,, ,, ,,
,, ,, ,,
,, ,, ,,

DOROTHY URIS' PERSONAL ""'" "COLLECTION OF QUOTES,""""" !!!!!!! COMMENT & ANECDOTES *

 A SUNRISE BOOK · E.P. DUTTON · NEW YORK

Note: Where the quotation comes from the *New York Times,*
the credit is abbreviated—*NYT.*

For information contact:
E.P. Dutton, 2 Park Avenue, New York, N.Y. 10016

Library of Congress Cataloging in Publication Data
Uris, Dorothy.
  Say it again.

  1. Anecdotes. 2. Quotations, English. I. Title.
PN6261.U7 808.88'2 78-14909
ISBN: 0-87690-308-1

Published simultaneously in Canada by
Clarke, Irwin & Company Limited, Toronto and Vancouver

10 9 8 7 6 5 4 3 2 1

First Edition

For MICKEY—
and his legacy of love and laughter

THE MANY TO THANK

As the collector of these quotables, I am indebted beyond measure to the host of contributors from the distant past to the present whose words alone make such a book a reality.

I am forever grateful to the splendid librarians who can spot just the right book such as R. L. Marquard's *That Brings to Mind*, a fond compilation of old and retold anecdotes; to my friends who sent clippings or books from their own shelves or offered their professional writings; and to my son Joe who, among others, would phone to ask, "Have you heard the one about . . . ?"

For the nitty-gritty of tireless cutting and pasting, there was Naomi Robison who also contributed the zingy *Say It Again* for the title. And finally, my thanks to Marian Skedgell the editor for her unflagging enthusiasm and guidance.

Dorothy Uris

CONTENTS

“”‖**
...

BEFORE YOU "SAY IT AGAIN"...

I was a fledgling actress attending a technique class in *The Method* (Stanislavski's of course) when the director gave a student actor this scene to improvise: "You are marooned on a desert island—not a human being in sight for weeks. You are asleep under a tree. You awaken and there in the clearing you see a young woman, deep in slumber. You run towards her. Startled, she jumps to her feet. You throw your arms around her and hold her close. . . . That's the scene." The young actor nodded thoughtfully, then frowned. "But what's my motivation?" he asked.

Apparently, what is obvious to one is not to another.

Why did I embrace the chance to publish this collection of quotables? The answer lies in the books, the so-called treasuries of quotations, that take up library shelf space.

Remember the old vaudeville gag, "That's no lady—that's my wife," the classic putdown of women? Well, without exception, the "Wife Joke" in dressier guise is still around in these very books. At first I could not believe the extent of stereotyped humor directed at women. But the joke is on the jokers. The truth is that this old chestnut, however refurbished, doesn't work so well today. The same goes for those ethnic jokes about Poles or Jews or blacks—they bomb more often than not. Thanks to the heightened sensibility of our time, what once passed for humor has begun to sour in the mouth of the speaker. The moribund jests that persist on the printed page will, we hope, be speedily interred.

A glance at the index of *Bartlett's Familiar Quotations,* the respected source and granddaddy of them all, speaks volumes. Herewith alphabetically under the heading *Woman,* are entries from *a* to *g:*

1

WOMAN

accurate about her age,
always has revenge ready,
bad-tempered,
beautiful, cooking dinner,
clamours of a jealous,
contentious,

discovers she has a soul,
dissimulation innate in,
frailty thy name is,
fury of a disappointed,
grieve to be overmastered,

Had enough? The listing goes on through the letter *w*. As for the worthier quotes and comment in collections, it would seem that men have written nearly all that is memorable. Thus my aim was to compile a non-sexist (though not non-sexual) collection, geared toward women but by no means exclusively. I found it exhilarating to dig about in obvious and odd places, gathering nuggets, witty and wise, from females through the centuries. An exploration like that can change lives.

Reaching for a quote has become a reflex. Why bother cogitating when quoting saves time and says it better? De Montaigne bears me out: "I quote others the better to express myself."

Here's one from Thucydides, historian of antiquity: "History is an everlasting possession." (If you can find it!) Following his lead, I was the one possessed, for I could hardly pry myself from the past. The "glory of classical Athens" and the "grandeur of Rome" remain intact. Who cannot recall the names of pagan goddesses, those super-role models and counterparts of gods? But where are the names of real women? Except for some dazzlers like Sappho, they have remained obscure.

The historian, Sarah P. Pomeroy, has rescued from oblivion the sandaled maidens and matrons in classic robes. In her book, *Goddesses, Whores, Wives and Slaves,* she writes: "Despite the perspective of some 2000 years, the women of classical antiquity evoke an emotional response . . . the ancient views of women remain valid for the modern world." Indeed, their concerns so nearly resemble ours that at one point I was almost impelled to dash off a letter to the *New York Times* in their defense.

Especially riveting were chronicles by and about American women in the colonial and revolutionary periods. The New York Historical Society placed in my hands the surviving pages of Mercy Otis Warren's play, *The Group,* written in 1775. This satire on disloyalty is a living testament to her wit and courage. The piecing together of names and deeds became a patchwork of glorious color, designed, as it were, by Mercy, Abigail, Patience, Phyllis, Martha, Dolley. The many who came after them made equally stunning history, though largely neglected by historians.

Nonetheless I began to miss the men. After all, how could I ignore my teachers both in and out of school? And what about Shakespeare, the remembered resonances of his syllables? I had played Juliet in high school and later Jessica on Broadway. Or how do without Mark Twain whose complete works had spent so many years in my bookcase? Or the leather-worn edition of Thoreau? Or Thurber? And yes, even Mailer—if *Ms* magazine will forgive me. Besides, literature abounds in male aphorisms, pithy thoughts expressed in a sentence, and in epigrams, sharp and terse, that are indispensable to a collection. And of course, on closer acquaintance, I fell in love with Benjamin Franklin, the universal man whose observations, uncannily current, emit flashes of light through these pages.

What with women's past works resurrected, and the present literary boom, we have more of women's words to choose from, while men's literary output, profuse and accessible as always, adds breadth to the collection. Thus a necessary balance for me and the book was restored. I trust that men will find this new mix useful and entertaining. The section "Men on Women, Women on Men," a series of both feisty and flattering exchanges, should cool some anger, rather than invite any. As Oscar Wilde, that wielder of one-liners, said, "Laughter is not at all a bad beginning for a friendship."

A definition to guide any collector of droll stories that do not put anyone down is William Thackeray's; "Humor is a mixture of love and wit." Endearing anecdotes call for retelling. The listener remembers and smiles. "I like the way you told that," someone will usually say. Agnes Repplier sums it up: "On the preservation of the comic spirit depends in some measure the ultimate triumph of civilization."

From where or whom do today's yarns originate, those that spring from our own time and mores to race across the country faster than the speed of sound? Louis Untermeyer reminds us that although the central figures change and one famous name substitutes for another, the twist, the tag line, the point of the joke remains constant. Yet humorists such as Dorothy Parker place their own mark upon a quip. Even the virtually all-male collections concede to an occasional thrust of hers. Somerset Maugham wrote: "Dorothy Parker can no more help being amusing than a peach tree can help bearing peaches. She seems to carry a hammer in her handbag to hit the appropriate nail on the head."

Spilling from the presses, the written word provides a primary source for gatherers of humor. Often unconscious howlers pop up in the straight stuff of news and articles.

Martin Grotjahn, psychiatrist, tells us in *Beyond Laughter:* "Women are traditionally supposed to be incapable of even retelling a joke. This, of course, is true only for the woman who submits to the socially conditioned demands of our time. . . . The woman has as much natural intelligence . . . to enjoy wit as her male counterpart. But if she is clever, she will not show it."

Wrong, dear doctor. Women are "showing it," their enjoyment and practice of wit, and not just together in purdah but out in the open. Fearlessly they have joined the ranks of raconteurs, traditionally male.

More women write humor now: Lois Gould, Nora Ephron, Erma Bombeck, Eve Merriam, Judith Viorst, Fran Lebowitz; and more women perform comic routines on TV and in clubs. I recall Mae West in one of her old movies, intoning with phoney elegance, "Beulah, peal me a grape," and just the other day, Lily Tomlin summed up the seventies with, "Remember, we're all in this alone." None of this is unprecedented, however; witty females have dispensed humor through the ages. Jane Austen's humor bridges the centuries. Nora Ephron comments, "There have been very few Jane Austens. You could count them on the fingers of one hand —male and female."

J. B. Priestley says, in *English Humour*, "Women on the whole have sharper eyes and ears . . . quick to notice pretensions, dubious motives, and all manner of social absurdities."

What makes a good storyteller?—an appetite for recounting the daily run of laughable incident and a good ear for anecdotes to pass around. Women reading to children and ad-libbing the choice parts have been rehearsing all along. With a four-year-old critic to keep me on track, I dare not stray for a moment.

I have been fortunate in my teachers. Jane Dorsey Zimmerman, my epigrammatic professor of speech at Teachers College, coined many sharp ones in her classes. I recall two that apply specifically to our discussion: "Practice makes permanent," and "All speaking is public."

Consider a cassette your best friend and severest critic. Practice, practice the content and language of anecdotes. From *Say It Again,* choose selections that spark your interest. Your cassette, the little monster, will at first deliver a low blow to the ego, but persevere. Practice will make permanent. Once you've overcome shyness with a quick quip or narration, especially in mixed company, you can try your wings anywhere. To amuse is fun and an asset from livingroom, to office, to platform.

"I tell the best stories I have—I tell them the best way I know—and what do people do? They laugh," that wonderful clown, Bobby Clark, once remarked.

Say It Again and yet again. A quote becomes yours once you have transformed it from reading to speaking by giving it voice. Under the forty-five subject headings that follow, you have a wide choice from past to present. Each section begins with a selection from the distant past that comes alive with amazing gusto. Buffeted as we are in today's whirl of events, history acts as an anchor. From way back then to now, the years between also contribute their share of humanity and literary genius.

Take your pick from the rich assortment of short jests, anecdotes, aphorisms, epigrams, one-liners, comment from myriad sources, quotes and quotations, short verses and longer poems. The old illuminates the new as the new the old. Relatedness is all. Under each subject, the arrangement of the diversity of materials creates an impact of impressions, stirring the imagination. The juxtaposition of names and words and deeds will never cease to astonish me.

Louis Untermeyer in *Great Humor* points out that "No sharp line separates the anecdote from the jest or the jest from the joke." Purists, however, insist that a joke is only the bare bones of a story. Whether bare or covered, the story should relate to the situation at hand—an approach to be followed in both private and public speaking.

"Apt is a small but healthy word," says Millett Wood, authority on speechmaking. Watch when you take off with a borrowed thought. Has your quote branched out, hanging loose from your subject? Apt quotations, amusing or serious, tied to the content will show no sign of breaking away.

To lend a homey touch to an anecdote, speakers have indulged for ages in the ploy of substituting an aunt, uncle or themselves for the characters in a story, a kind of game in which the listener suspends disbelief. The hackneyed device by now fools no one and downgrades the humor. By all means let your imagination ride with the anecdote, embellishing with new detail and prolonging the fun, but keep your relatives out of it.

Another banality is the advice to begin your talk always with an anecdote for the purpose of putting the audience in a receptive mood. The result? Many listeners react instead with impatience. "Well, get on with it," their expressions seem to be saying. Why not wait until interest outfront flags (the attention span diminishes yearly), then take time out for some verbal refreshment, not necessarily of a comic nature. Revive interest by quoting some passage to lift the spirit, a short piece from a play, or a poem—in tune, of course, with your subject. But please don't announce your selection with that trite convention: "And I quote . . ."

Rigid rules invite us to break them. Time was when emotions and gestures were prescribed in detail for use on the platform. *"Fear*—the mouth opens; the eyes are expanded and gaze upon the fearful object . . . the hands, outspread, are held with the palms outward" ("Women's Gesture in Oratory and Elocution," from *Hill's Manual,* 1873). I guess the first woman who refused to outspread her palms was considered a radical.

Should we say to "give a talk" or to "make a speech"? I vote for the first since the second has acquired an aura of stuffiness. Besides, the verb *to give* sounds just right. The bland noun, *speaker,* doesn't do much and *talker* won't do at all, suggesting *talkativeness* which we want to avoid. *Orator* is not only antique, but also, it seems, mendacious. "Even when he is doing his best to tell the truth, the successful orator is *ipso facto* a liar," said Aldous Huxley. Undoubtedly, we need new words for the doing and the doer of this act of communication.

The soothing syrup served up in speech books instructs us that fear comes from adrenaline rushing to your glands and stirring you up. More to the point: you must shake yourself loose from the "star" syndrome that handicaps more women than men. I mean the illusion of that lone figure, the speaker-performer, exhorting thousands—what I call the "colosseum complex." People who have never set foot on stage or platform will fantasize a recurrent nightmare of forgetting their lines. Far from the illusion is the reality—talking with people about some matter of mutual interest, which is the essence of the good talk, anywhere, anytime. "Speaking is essentially a responsible, friendly conversation between two, one being the listener," says Millett Wood in *The Art of Speaking.*

What do you *want* to talk about? No matter how well-intentioned, your effort won't mean much unless the subject moves *you* to inform, convince, protest, raise a smile or laugh, to shine and yes, to win. And if at first, you do succeed, try, try again. With your feet once wet, you'll find that the water, while cold, is bracing.

Make no mistake, *informal,* a good word for the style of speaking in our time, never means *unprepared.* But, you ask, what about those after-dinner wits called upon for "impromptu" remarks, suitable to the occasion? While everyone is at the chicken and peas, the wits have noted which notables sit on the dais. Reaching into their well-used stock of memorized anecdotes to select the best for the occasion, they make deft changes of name and place. They rise to applause and follow with what sounds like instant humor. Jessie Haver Butler, long-time teacher, tells us in her book, *Time To Speak Up,* "It might truly be said—as with Chauncey Depew, the great after-dinner speaker of the 19th century—that Eleanor Roosevelt has spent her entire lifetime preparing her impromptu speeches."

It was the custom only yesterday to poke fun at clubwomen. Those cartoons of large-busted women in ludicrous hats have at last disappeared from the magazines. And women, as they have these two hundred years, have gone right on (with or without hats) pursuing and refining the fine art of organizing. Today this valuable talent takes many forms.

Do you have to chair a meeting of the Committee to Save Our Parks? See *Environment,* p. 68 for that pertinent quip or quote. Or will you preside at a political rally to elect your aunt, the judge and candidate for the senate? See *Politics,* p. 173.

You've been tagged *to say a few words,* a common euphemism for a short talk, to present an award or accept one yourself, perhaps as Woman of the Year in your hometown (see *Feminism,* p. 93 and *Work,* p. 251); to laud your boss at a surprise birthday party for three hundred close friends (*Money* p. 145 and *Age* p. 15); to make a toast at your college chum's wedding—third time around (*Sex* p. 195 and *Marriage* p. 131).

When you catch the sound of laughter, refrain from talking through it or giggling yourself unless the joke's on you. Remind your family and friends to restrain their over-compensating hilarity; they may be the only ones laughing. Pretend to lose yourself in narration as if trying to recollect the incident, even though actually you've been rehearsing for a week. I've always said, "Scratch a woman, find an actress."

Introducing speakers is another assignment that needs planning. Play a modest role in setting the stage for the star-speaker. Keep the biographical data down to a minimum and shun the clichés: "It gives me great pleasure" or "I have the honor," etc. Substitute what comes naturally: "How pleased (delighted, proud) I am at this moment..." Or "To perform this assignment is no chore." Or start right off with an *àpropos* story that enhances the moment. Look under *Law, Government, Medicine, Science,* etc., depending on the speaker's profession.

Much more frequent today, in place of one person soloing on a platform is the reasoning together of a small body of people with a common cause. At meetings, conferences, conclaves, caucuses they unite to get things done. Must we always have unmitigated solemnity with our bread-and-butter reports? Is there a law that the papers delivered at conventions country-wide must be dreary? Some listeners may wish that the founding fathers had included freedom *from* speech in the Bill of Rights. They drowse through the papers and stay up all night.

If you work at it, even a large dose of straight information can be yawn-free. Interject a restorative from literature or dust off some anecdotes applicable to your field. Robert Louis Stevenson remarked: "You could read Kant by yourself, if you wanted; but you must share a joke with someone else."

Among its many possible applications, this collection can be used to brighten the process of educating, offering first aid to my colleagues, the teachers. Whenever I pull off a witticism to dissipate the doldrums that descend on the classroom, my students overrespond with guffaws. "Is she for real?" once came across in a stage whisper and at another time I heard, "Someone must have spiked her Geritol!" a sally much funnier than mine.

As for the PR people, they have been known to dress up interviews with epigrams put into the mouths of their clients. In advertising copy, writers often feature quotations. Some perfume ads fairly drip with poetic imagery. Everybody's doing it.

And though the *art* of conversation may have gone, we still manage to do a lot of talking. What we have lost perhaps in the elegant turn of a phrase we have gained in frankness and informality. Might we describe the new elegance as the ability to say what we mean in clearcut, straight-forward language? To which I would add, the ability to laugh.

Some pointers: Don't tell a story you can't finish. "I can't remember the tag, but it went something like this . . ." will write finis to your effort.

Watch the advance sales pitch for the "terrific" one you've just heard. A boost like that will turn everyone into a critic.

Take care not to give away the punch line at the start—"did you hear the one about the elephant's footprints in the aspic?"

Sex as comedy enjoys ever wider circulation among storytellers. Make sure your contribution reveals more wit than smut.

Conversing openly with few taboos brings a mutual release of tensions. The best anecdotes mirror our manners and mores and deflate pretenses —a boon to our health and our lives.

I chose a poem of Marianne Moore's to grace the final page. But for me there is no end, only a pause, in the treasure hunt. For tomorrow or the day after, I know there will surely surface an excerpt of wit and beauty unsurpassed. And my fingers will reach for the scissors.

Meanwhile, I'll take my cue from a master storyteller. "I remember a good story when I hear it, but I never invented anything original. I am only a retail dealer," said Abraham Lincoln.

—DOROTHY URIS

SAY IT AGAIN

,, ,, ,,

,, ,, ,,

,, ,, ,,

ADVERTISING

The New York Central stands at the head for the speed and comfort of its trains. A ride over its line is the finest one-day railroad ride in the world.

—*Harper's Weekly* (1894)

Laughter Lends a New Charm to Beauty when it discloses a pretty set of teeth. Whiteness, when nature has supplied this element of loveliness, may be retained through life by using the fragrant
SOZODONT
This popular dentifrice is now a recognized essential of every toilet table.

—*Harper's Weekly* (1894)

The enthusiasm Jenny Lind, the Swedish Nightingale, provoked in this country was called Lindmania. Her face was used on every conceivable object: medals, coins, cigars, busts, bottles, books, sheet music, paper dolls with costumes, a flower, a theater, innumerable statues and, of course, a cow.

—THE NEW YORK HISTORICAL MUSEUM

Chlorosis, or greensickness, is a disorder noted in young girls about a year after the first menses. The symptoms are a heavy, tired condition and a dislike of wholesome food. Dark greenish circles appear round the eyes, the patient seems bloodless, is apt to be dizzy, the heart palpitates, fainting spells occur, the menses are irregular, the head aches, there are pains in the back and hips, dyspepsia appears, and there is gas in the bowels.

Take *Lydia E. Pinkham's Blood Purifier* alternately with her *Vegetable Compound* and be cured. (c. 1889)
—CARROLL CARROLL: *Variety*

Is it sick to love a pen?
Is it crazy to love marker pens that give you the smoothest, thinnest line in town?
Is it kinky to go buggy over pens that feel so right in your hand?
Is it mad to worship pens with clever little metal "collars" to keep their plastic points from getting squishy?
Is it neurotic to adore pens that will never skip out on you?
It's only normal.
—ADV.

. . . those ubiquitous full-color double-page spreads picturing what to serve on those little evenings when you want to take it easy.
You wouldn't cook that much food for a combination Thanksgiving and Irish wake. (Equally discouraging is the way the china always matches the food. You wonder what you're doing wrong; because whether you're serving fried oysters or baked beans, your plates always have the same old blue rims.)
—PEG BRACKEN, *The I Hate to Cook Book*

Toys are designed to make good thirty-second messages, not to make good toys. That's why you have all these dolls that walk, talk, roll over, and so on. They can each do one thing, which looks great on TV. But you can't even hug the dolls because of all that machinery in their middle. . . . Television has taken a child from the age of two and entered into a kind of contractual agreement with him. The advertiser is saying, in effect, "You're going to help us sell our product."
—PEGGY CHARIN, president, co-founder, Action for Children's Television

A consumer is born every ten seconds.
—EDWIN NEWMAN

Advertisers of rich cake mixes, desserts, and other calorie-packed indulgences actually fight to place their colorful, mouth-watering ads, loaded with subliminal triggers, in close proximity to articles on dieting and weight reduction.
—WILSON BRYAN KEY, *Media Sexploitation*

I remember well the time when a cabbage could sell itself just by being a cabbage. Nowadays it's no good being a cabbage—unless you have an agent and pay him a commission. Nothing is free anymore to sell itself or give itself away.
—JEAN GIRAUDOUX

"[This product] is rich in polyunsaturates, elements with a unique action that helps increase the moisture-holding capacity of the skin to produce a fresher, smoother look."

The comparative tense is a great gift to the cosmetics industry. Who is to say that a fresher, smoother look might not mean fresher and smoother than a prune?

—EVE MERRIAM, *Figleaf*

I see my own role as precisely that of an artist. But my kind of art has nothing to do with putting images on canvas. My concern is with creating images that catch people's eyes, penetrate their minds, warm their hearts, and cause them to act.

Maybe there's something wrong with selling *anything,* but I live in America, not on the moon. So let the process unfold.

—GEORGE LOIS, *The Art of Advertising*

Mr. Sinatra and his wife were lunching at the beach club in Southampton with friends in celebration of their first wedding anniversary. An airplane flew by and wrote "Happy First, Barbara and Frank" in the sky. The only other products merchandised in the sky over Southampton this way are Noxema and Coppertone, and so many people at the beach club were unhappy.

"There goes the neighborhood," one man said bitterly.

—JOHN CORRY

Gertrude Stein warned me in the late 1930s of the emergence of the "publicity saint—someone who just got publicity; they didn't have to do anything or say anything that changed anything or meant very much."

—ERIC SEVAREID

Because people like Steve McQueen, Barbra Streisand, and Jacqueline Onassis are so instantly recognizable, their fame presents the risk to an advertiser that they will be better remembered than the product or service being advertised. . . . What's really lucky is to have people with a blander look but whose acting ability is so sharp that people don't remember them.

—JANE BRINKER, casting director

Reproduction
of the World-Famous
MONA LISA
Original Value
$1,000,000
Now only 99¢

KOSHER RESTAURANT
featuring
African Cuisine

MERCY ANIMAL CLINIC
office guarded
by attack dog

—LEE BOLTIN, street adv., *Smithsonian*

Arms that flutter and turn to wing.
Air that clouds and turns to plumage.
Swan that turns . . . there! swan-to-raven.
White that's pierced and turns to red.
Pavlova to swan to legend to fragrance.
—PERFUME ADV.

. . . We grew up founding our dreams on the infinite promise of American advertising. I still believe that one can learn to play the piano by mail and that mud will give you a perfect complexion.
—ZELDA FITZGERALD, *Save Me the Waltz*

It's a blend of carefree Orlon and lighthearted polyester.
—CLOTHING ADV.

Congratulations, darling, to the loveliest and best vice-president ever promoted. And the best wife a man ever had.
—ADV. FOR A DIAMOND NECKLACE

Sponsors obviously care more about a ninety-second commercial and *want* to pay you more than any guest star gets for a ninety-minute *acting* performance.
—BARBARA STANWYCK, *McCall's*

Listening to another exhibitor's complaints about the pastel content of a poster, I lightly suggested that we could gory it up by throwing a bucket of blood across it. His eyes brightened with enthusiasm and admiration. "That's it," he exclaimed, "that's just what it needs. That'll bring 'em in."
    I confined myself to red paint, however; paint is cheaper, holds its color longer, and smells better. Anyhow, it brought 'em in.
—ARTHUR MAYER, *Merely Colossal*

Unmentionables—those articles of ladies' apparel that are never discussed in public, except in full-page, illustrated ads.
—*Changing Times*

The car dealer, of course, is only a metaphor for the entire plague of pitchmen who infest the [late late] movie. There is the carpet king, incessantly walking to his gigantic warehouse. The suit salesman. The party with the fantastic new vegetable slicer. It dices, slices, cubes, chops, peels, and all for the incredibly low price of——
    And now, back to Gary Cooper after this fantastic record bargain.
    I never make it to the end of the great movies. It's a case of low tolerance to torture. At 1:15 A.M. you may get ten minutes of movie and two minutes in the bargain basement. By 2 A.M. you get two minutes of movie and ten minutes of the world's most resistible salesmanship.
—RUSSELL BAKER, *NYT Mag.*

I think our data shows that women's liberation or women's organizations in general have really had a very significant effect on the values of women, which perhaps we don't fully realize. . . .

How good her coffee is is important to her, just as it's important to you or me or anybody in this room, male or female. But it's not the center of the universe. How white her sheets are is not the center of the universe. There are other things more important.
> —EXCERPT FROM YANKELOVICH PRESENTATION, "Research on
> Current Trends in America"

Patient on the operating table to the surgeon: "Fifteen hundred dollars for everything . . . and that's my final offer."
> —ADV. FOR A HOSPITAL PLAN

The youngster who surreptitiously begins smoking fears demonstrating ineptitude in the handling of a cigarette or otherwise compromising his image as a suave, experienced smoker.

The advertising companies know this well and capitalize on it extensively. . . . Once the target is "hooked" in the teens, the industry's job has been done and a high percentage of such youngsters can be relied upon to remain addicted for years.
> —RICHARD A. GARDNER, M.D., in letter to *NYT*

When Mark Twain edited a paper in Missouri, one of his subscribers wrote him that he had found a spider in the paper and wanted to know whether it meant good luck or bad. Mark Twain replied: "Old Subscriber: Finding a spider in your paper was neither good luck nor bad luck for you. The spider was merely looking over our paper to see which merchant is not advertising so that he can go to that store, spin his web across the door, and lead a life of undisturbed peace ever afterward."
> —RALPH L. WOODS, *A Third Treasury of the Familiar*

AGE

It gives me great pleasure to converse with the aged. They have been over the road that all of us must travel, and know where it is rough and difficult and where it is level and easy.
> —PLATO, *Republic*

How foolish was my hope and vain That age would conquer sin.
> —CHARLES WESLEY, *In Advancing Age*

. . . you and I are old;
Old age hath yet his honor and his toil.
Death closes all. But something ere the end,
Some work of noble note, may yet be done . . .
The long day wanes; the slow moon climbs; the deep
Moans round with many voices. Come, my friends
'Tis not too late to seek a newer world.
Push off, and sitting well in order smite
The sounding furrows; for my purpose holds
To sail beyond the sunset, and the paths
Of all the western stars, until I die. . . .
Though much is taken, much abides; and though
We are not now that strength which in old days
Moved earth and heaven, that which we are, we are;
One equal temper of heroic hearts,
Made weak by time and fate, but strong in will
To strive, to seek, to find, and not to yield.
　　　　　—ALFRED, LORD TENNYSON, *Ulysses*

If I had my life to live over again, I would start barefoot earlier in the spring. . . .
　　　　　—EIGHTY-FIVE-YEAR-OLD WOMAN, in "Woman's Almanac," *Good*
　　　　　　　Housekeeping

You are beautiful and faded,
Like an old opera tune
Played upon a harpsichord.
　　　　　—AMY LOWELL, "A Lady"

In early America, the young were often victims of the old. In modern America, the old have been victims of the young. We might try to build a future without victims altogether.
　　　　　—DAVID HACKETT FISCHER, *Growing Old in America*

Seventy is wormwood
Seventy is gall
But it's better to be seventy
Than not alive at all.
　　　　　—PHYLLIS MCGINLEY

Three aged men—seventy, eighty, and ninety—were asked whom they would like to be buried with. George Washington, said one. Abe Lincoln, said another. The third one said, Elizabeth Taylor.
　　"She ain't dead yet," his friends said.
　　"Neither am I," the dreamer shot back.
　　　　　—CHARLES LINDNER

WIFE (toasting her husband on his eighty-fifth birthday): May you live to be 119.

HE: Why not 120?

SHE: For one year, I want to be a widow.

After his appearance at a nursing home, a woman asked Charles Lindner, "Bob Hope, can I have your autograph?"

"I'm not Bob Hope," he said.

"I know, but what's the difference?" she answered. "My grandson, who is two and a half years old and will get it, won't know, either."

My talent, of which there is a great deal, has just been training itself for seventy years.
—RUTH GORDON, actress

A physician was conducting a standard geriatric test on a woman of eighty-three. He asked her: her name, address, his name, what year it was, what month. All these she answered promptly. When he asked her what day it was, she stumbled, "It's Tuesday—no, it's Friday. No, it's Tuesday." She paused. "You know, Doctor, when you wake up in the morning, sometimes you can't remember—there's so much not to do."
—FROM A DOCUMENTARY FILM BY DAVID ROBISON

How old would you be if you didn't know how old you was?
—SATCHEL PAIGE

Woman in convalescent home: "When you come here, nobody knows where you are."
—IMOGEN CUNNINGHAM, *After Ninety*

No one grows old by living—only by losing interest in living.
—MARIE RAY

OK—you can come out of the closet now. You don't have to pretend to be young anymore. Gray chic is in. Those pushy kids who spawned the youth culture of the sixties and seventies are déclassé now. Medical science is increasing the life-span even as the sagging birthrate holds down the young. Chortle—you're winning the numbers game.
—JANE OTTEN, *Newsweek*

The life insurance office was shocked by the ninety-seven-year-old man who wished to take out a policy. His application was turned down. Whereupon the old gentleman said with annoyance, "You folks are mak-

ing a big mistake. If you look over your statistics, you'll find that mighty few men die after ninety-seven."
—*N.Y. Post*

David and Lena, in the sunset of their lives, their children and grandchildren scattered to all parts of the country, were discussing what remained of their future.

"We've had a good life together," said Lena contentedly.

"Yes, it has been good," agreed David. "And I'll tell you something, Lena. If, God forbid, one of us should die first, I have made up my mind to spend the rest of my life in Israel."
—*Encyclopedia of Jewish Humor*

I wake up every morning at nine and grab for the morning paper. Then I look at the obituary page. If my name is not on it, I get up.
—HARRY HERSHFIELD

A seventyish wife came home to find her husband making love to a neighbor. Furious, she slapped him; he lost his balance and rolled down the stairs. The family doctor phoned her to ask why she'd hit her husband —the poor guy had suffered a sprained shoulder. "Well, Doc," she said, "if he can do what he did at seventy-five, I figured he could fly."
—*The Tonight Show*

Cousin Martha Matheny looked out a window and was dismayed to see Dr. Beall walking about in the snow in his bare feet. She told him that he would catch his death tramping around in the snow at his age—he must have been eighty then. He explained that nothing was so good for opening the pores of the feet as a walk in the snow. The human foot, he added, was intended by God Almighty to come in contact with the good earth from time to time.
—JAMES THURBER, *Thurber Album*

There is no such thing as an old woman. Any woman of any age, if she loves, if she is good, gives a man a sense of the infinite.
—JULES MICHELET, *L'Amour* (1859)

How can I die? I'm booked.
—GEORGE BURNS

The image is created and it's up to you to keep fitting that image. If you try too hard—and I did for several years—you look like a plastic caricature of yourself. I was waiting for an elevator and I actually heard one woman beside me saying to another: "See her? She used to be Joan Crawford," and it had taken me two hours that morning to put on the makeup that made me look like Joan Crawford.
—JOAN CRAWFORD, *McCall's*

Youth is a gift of nature, but age is a work of art.
    —GARSON KANIN

Age-based retirement arbitrarily severs productive persons from their livelihood, squanders their talents, scars their health, strains an already overburdened Social Security system, and drives many elderly persons into poverty and despair. Ageism is as odious as racism or sexism.
    —CLAUDE PEPPER, chairman, House Committee on Aging

All sorts of allowances are made for the illusions of youth; and none, or almost none, for the disenchantment of age.
    —ROBERT LOUIS STEVENSON

Three boy scouts had been sent out from the scout meeting to perform their good deed for the day. "We helped a little old lady across the street," they reported.
    The scoutmaster was dumbfounded. "You mean to tell me that all three of you helped the same little old lady across the street? It certainly didn't take all three of you."
    "Oh, yes, it did," one of the scouts said, "because she didn't want to cross the street."
    —WINSTON PENDLETON, *How to Win Your Audience with Humor*

We grow neither better nor worse as we get old, but more like ourselves.
    —MAY LAMBERTON BECKER

One of the many things nobody ever tells you about middle age is that it's such a nice change from being young.
    —DOROTHY CANFIELD FISHER

There is beauty in extreme old age—Do you fancy you are elderly enough?
    —W.S. GILBERT, *The Mikado*

At a crossing in the city, a red Chevelle waits at a red light. Behind it, a yellow Checker cab. Enter: old lady with a cane. She begins to hobble across the street. At the moment she finds herself midway between the headlights of the Chevelle, the light changes to green. Simultaneously, the cabbie leans on his horn. The driver of the Chevelle turns off his engine, removes his keys from the ignition switch, emerges from the car, walks back to the cab, and presents the cabbie with the keys.
    "Here," he says. "You run her over. I haven't got the stomach for it."
    —*NYT*

Three Ages of Man/Woman
        Youth
     Middle Age
        and
  You Look Great!
        —ANON.

Old and new make the warp and woof of every moment. There is no
thread that is not a twist of these two strands.
        —RALPH WALDO EMERSON

Can I still make myself useful? That one may legitimately ask, and I
think that I can answer "yes." I feel that I may be useful in a more
personal, more direct way than ever before. I have, though how I do not
know, acquired much wisdom. I am better equipped to bring up children.
. . . It is quite wrong to think of old age as a downward slope. One climbs
higher and higher with the advancing years, and that, too, with surprising strides.
        —LETTER FROM GEORGE SAND TO A FRIEND, quoted in André
        Maurois, *Lélia, the Life of George Sand*

Death is simply nature's way of telling us to slow down.
        —*Encyclopedia of Jewish Humor*

In every animal that walks upright the deficiency of the fluids that fill
the muscles appears first in the highest part. The face first grows lank
and wrinkled; then the neck; then the breast and arms; the lower parts
continuing to the last as plump as ever; so that the covering all above
with a basket, and regarding only what is below the girdle, it is impossible of two women to tell an old one from a young one.
        —BENJAMIN FRANKLIN, "Eight Reasons to Marry an Older
        Woman"

A seventy-six-year-old man was hospitalized for heart failure. Once his
heart trouble was checked, he kept saying that he would have his mother
drive over and fetch him! So the physicians decided to keep him hospitalized a few weeks longer until his mental state improved. That turned out
to be unnecessary. One day his mother, age ninety-five, drove over from
a town one hundred miles away, accompanied by her ninety-seven-year-
old sister, and they took him home.
        —LAWRENCE GALTON, *Don't Give Up on an Aging Parent*

We're recycling ourselves. Young people didn't invent activism. We were
active in our day in the peace movement, the labor movement, the cooperative movement. The young seem to feel that old people descended
from outer space. They forget we have a past.
        —DORIS MENDEZ, Gray Panther

The elderly are the only outcast group that everyone eventually expects to join. I wonder what Archie Bunker would say about Puerto Ricans if he knew he was going to become one on his next birthday.
—ALEX COMFORT, *A Good Age*

Today's sexually inhibited elderly women are yesterday's good girls now grown older in a world that has never recognized their full sexual potential. I see a trend in the making that could lead to a parity with older men, which is to say, the emergence of the sensuous grandmother.
—DR. NANCY DATAN, psychologist

If God had to give a woman wrinkles, He might at least have put them on the soles of her feet.
—NINON DE LENCLOS

Two silver-haired, genteel females rumbled down the main street in their aged coupe, made an illegal turn, and ignored the traffic cop's efforts to stop them. Catching up with them, he demanded angrily, "Didn't you hear my whistle?"

The octogenarian at the wheel glanced at him coyly. "Yes, I did, Officer," she said, "but I never flirt when I'm driving."

"You win, lady!" answered the cop, grinning. "Drive on!"

Susan Sontag writes that getting older is "a crisis that never exhausts itself, because the anxiety is never really used up. Being a crisis of the imagination rather than of 'real life,' it has the habit of repeating itself again and again. . . . Aging is a movable doom." Perhaps. But thanks to the persistence of human desire and to the powers of the human spirit, it is also a movable feast. Precisely because aging is a "crisis of the imagination," our attitudes can transform the experience.
—JANE O'REILLY, *MS*

The eighty-year-plus lady went to the doctor for her checkup and she complained of her aches and pains. He listened sympathetically. "You must understand, my dear, I'm a doctor, not a magician. I cannot make you any younger."

"Younger?" she said. "No, I'm asking you to make me older, Doctor."

Old age and poverty are two heavy burdens. Either is enough.
—GERMAN PROVERB

Retirement takes all the fun out of Saturdays.
—DUKE GMAHLE, quoted by Jack Rosenbaum

We don't grow older, we grow riper.
—PABLO PICASSO

Old age is like climbing a mountain. You climb from ledge to ledge. The higher you get, the more tired and breathless you become, but your view becomes much more extensive.
—INGMAR BERGMAN

You know you're getting old when the candles cost more than the cake.
—BOB HOPE

ANIMALS

A righteous man regardeth the life of his beast.
—PROVERBS 12:10

I tend to be suspicious of people whose love of animals is exaggerated; they are often frustrated in their relationships with humans.
—YLLA (CAMILLA KOFFLER)

I think I could turn and live with animals, they're so placid and self-contain'd,
I stand and look at them long and long.
—WALT WHITMAN

Humpback whales sing in different accents. You can tell where they come from by listening to them—there is a southern accent and a northern and middle accent. When the banks become crowded with whales the water may be literally saturated with the sound and the whale reproductive system may be upset.
—DR. HOWARD E. WINN, oceanographer, *UPI*

Some female fireflies are able to mimic the illuminated mating signals of other species of fireflies, luring would-be suitors into what quickly becomes a deadly embrace.
   When a flying male is attracted by the flashing signal from the perched female and comes close enough, she grabs him and eats him.
—DR. LLOYD, biologist

A city colleague found a new way of coping with [the problem of] pigeons. His system is to trap them and drive them out to the suburbs.
—BETSY BROWN, *NYT*

Male lions are not as fast as the females who stalk and kill.
—CYNTHIA MOSS, *Portraits in the Wild*

The lion and the calf shall lie down together, but the calf won't get much sleep.
—WOODY ALLEN

I had a hamster in the movie I was in—and one of the things that the crew would say to tease me was: "Oh, goodie, we're going to have hamster and eggs this morning." I just don't have the stamina for this sort of thing.
—QUINN CUMMINGS, child actress

"Goodness! It would be cheaper to buy a horse and just be kind to it!"
—WOMAN SEEING THE TICKET PRICE FOR AN ASPCA THEATER BENEFIT

The ritual of his fertility
Is simple; he was bred only to breed,
The homely husband to a score of cows.
Yet monstrous as a myth, his front denies
His humbled horns, as, hugely male, he stands
Hung with endurance as with iron weights.
Clustering flies mate round his red-rimmed eyes.
—BABETTE DEUTSCH, "A Bull"

The cow is a mammal. At the back it has a tail on which hangs a brush. With this he sends flies away so they don't fall into the milk. The head is for the purpose of growing horns and so his mouth can be somewhere. ... Under the cow hangs milk. It is arranged for milking. How the cow does it I have not yet realized, but it makes more and more. The cow has a fine sense of smell and one can smell it far away. This is the reason for fresh air in the country. .... The cow does not eat much but what it eats it eats twice so that it gets enough.
—from a child's essay, "Birds and Beasts" in Casey Miller and Kate Swift, *Words and Women*

Depend on the rabbit's foot if you will, but remember it didn't work for the rabbit!
—R. E. SHAY

On the Japanese island of Koshima, a female macaque monkey called Imo, a genius among monkeys, invented a method for cleaning unpalatable sand from the sweet potatoes that the group of scientists observing the monkeys had been scattering on the beach since the previous year. She dipped each potato into the water of a brook with one hand and brushed away the sand with another. During the following two years this

habit of washing potatoes spread to 90 percent of the members of Imo's troop: Only the youngest infants didn't know it, and the oldest males steadfastly refused to adopt it.
—*NYT Mag.*

Veterinarian to cat owner: Give him one of these pills every four hours. Then use this to stop your bleeding.
—GEORGE WOLFE in *The Saturday Evening Post*

Of all God's creatures, there is only one that cannot be made the slave of the leash. That one is the cat. If man could be crossed with the cat, it would improve man, but deteriorate the cat.
—MARK TWAIN

These fat scotenas were all different shapes and colors, black, white, tabby, ginger, tortoiseshell, and of all ages, too, so that there were kitten fillying about with each other and there were pussies full-grown and there were real dribbling starry ones very bad-tempered.
—ANTHONY BURGESS, *A Clockwork Orange*

Chows, while a riddle,
Are tempting to coddle.
Yet, kit and caboodle,
No peer has the Poodle.
For Poodle
     Thinks highly of Me.
—PHYLLIS MCGINLEY, "Raddled Rhyme in Praise of Poodles"

The boy next door was complaining because his folks wouldn't allow him to have a dog. "I've begged and begged and they always say no." And my boy said to him, "You just didn't go about it in the right way. You keep asking for a puppy. The best way to get a puppy is to beg for a baby brother—and they'll settle for a puppy every time."
—WINSTON PENDLETON, *How to Win Your Audience with Humor*

I am secretly afraid of animals—of all animals except dogs, and even of some dogs. I think it is because of the *us-ness* in their eyes, with the underlying *not-usness* which belies it.
—EDITH WHARTON

Posted on the bulletin board of a professional dog training academy:
The dog is possibly the best available vehicle for parents to use in the sex education of their children. Promiscuity and its results for the female

dog present a natural opportunity to discuss similar tendencies and problems in the human female.

—"NO COMMENT," *MS*

The duchess de La Rochefoucauld's dog is getting awfully thin. . . . But what can I do? She bought that dog full grown from a kennel where they didn't know his right name. A dog without his right name is bound to get thin.

—JEAN GIRAUDOUX, *The Madwoman of Chaillot*

ART

Women in general have no love of art; they have no proper knowledge of any; and they have no genius.

—JEAN JACQUES ROUSSEAU

In 1554 in Cremona, Italy, Sofonisba signed one small self-portrait of herself seated at the spinet, with a luminous and confident gaze. If she had been playing the lute, the painting would have been considered obscene (the "feminine" shape of the lute was a well-known symbol for wantonness), but the spinet (often called the virginal) is her way of conveying to the world her learning and accomplishment. In a long career, she later exchanged drawings with Michelangelo.

—KAY LARSON, *Village Voice*

She has made an illustration for which I paid one guilder—it is a wonder that a woman can do so much.

—ALBRECHT DÜRER, on one of his sixteenth century colleagues

Artemisia Gentileschi (1590–1642), a disciple of Caravaggio who helped to spread his influence throughout Italy, had—as we say now—a lot going for her: great talent, strong drive, sexual independence, and the respect of her male peers. . . .

Aware of herself as a female in a male profession ("You will find the spirit of Caesar in the soul of this woman," she wrote to a patron later in her illustrious life), Artemisia liked to depict heroic women and portrayed herself as the embodiment of "La Pittura" (Painting).

—GRACE GLUECK, *NYT Mag.*

In the admirably, vigorous, inexcusably forgotten work of Artemisia Gentileschi, the stereotype of a nebulous soft and tender "feminine style" is shattered.

—FRANCINE DU PLESSIX GRAY

For most of history, as Virginia Woolf put it, "anonymous was a woman." Pliny describes several women who, like Thamyris, daughter of the painter Micon, "scorned the duties of women and practiced her father's art."

—KAY LARSON, *Village Voice*

The beautiful "Portrait of Charlotte du Val d'Ognes" at the Metropolitan, which for a century and a half was claimed as a David, is now widely attributed to David's pupil, Constance Marie Charpentier; recent cleaning reveals that one of Frans Hals's famous versions of "The Jolly Toper" was painted by his nineteen-year-old follower Judith Leyster; and the "Portrait of Marco dei Vescovi," long attributed to Tintoretto, has been judged by Lionello Venturi to be the work of the painter's gifted daughter, Marietta.

—ANN SUTHERLAND HARRIS and LINDA NOCHLIN, *Women Artists 1550–1950*

The first American of either sex to become a professional sculptor was Patience Lovell Wright (1725–1786). Wright took models from life and reproduced their features in wax so accurately that they appeared real. Mrs. John Adams once watched an old clergyman reading a newspaper for ten minutes before she realized he was made of wax. Patience had a forceful personality, talked constantly, and spoke to her models—who were some of the most important people in English and American society —as equals, sprinkling her conversation with profanity, . . . considered amusing rather than offensive.

In London with letters of introduction, her career prospered, and she was soon sending advice to the king and queen addressed to them as "George" and "Charlotte."

—LINDA DE PAUW and CONOVER HUNT, *Remember the Ladies*

Marie Rosalie Bonheur (1822–1899), famous for her extraordinary paintings of horses and animals, was the first woman artist to receive the coveted cross of the French Legion of Honor. Diligent about anatomical accuracy, Rosa dissected animal parts obtained from a butcher and went regularly to slaughterhouses on the outskirts of Paris. To avoid the taunts of attendants and observers while she worked, she donned men's clothes, obtaining official authorization from the prefect of police.

—ANN SUTHERLAND HARRIS and LINDA NOCHLIN, *Women Artists 1550–1950*

The Cassatt film cites the amazement of Degas that "a woman paints as well as that," and also displays a brief news item from the *Philadelphia*

Ledger, commenting on Miss Cassatt's return for a visit to her native city after triumphs in Europe. "She has been studying painting in France and owns the smallest Pekingese dog in the world," it states.
>   —PERRY MILLER ADATO, speaking of the film she made about Mary Cassatt

In 1886 the painter Thomas Eakins was asked to resign his professorship at the Pennsylvania Academy for having asked male models in his Ladies' Life Class to remove their loincloths, possibly creating the first female group in history to be institutionally exposed to a fully disrobed male.
>   —*NYT*

From the first moment I handled my lens with a tender ardor, and it has become to be a living thing, with voice and memory and creative vigor.... I longed to arrest all beauty that came before me, and at length the longing has been satisfied.
>   —JULIA CAMERON, photographer (1863), in *Annals of My Glass House*

Why are we all still afraid of being *other* than men? Women are still in hiding. This attitude pervades the art that is being made. The art contains the seeds of change, more or less invisible now—but growing, growing.
>   —LUCY R. LIPPARD, *From the Center*

Talk not of genius baffled. Genius is master of man. Genius does what it must, and Talent does what it can.
>   —OWEN MEREDITH, "Last Words of a Sensitive Second-rate Poet"

To tell the truth, one is not born a genius, one becomes a genius, and the feminine situation has, up to the present, rendered the becoming practically impossible.
>   —SIMONE DE BEAUVOIR, *The Second Sex*

Michelangelo was high on the scaffolding in the Sistine Chapel, putting his finishing touches on the ceiling. He called down to a monk below: "Well, how do you like it?" The monk responded, calling up: "I think it could use another coat."
>   —JOE URIS

Everyone knows Audubon's *Birds of America*. But who remembers that Audubon was black?
> —AN ANTICATALOG

An American art collector in Italy purchased a magnificent Titian that he wanted to take back to the States. But the Mussolini government wouldn't let him.

"Get some native artist to paint a portrait of Mussolini right over the Titian," counseled a friend, "and then they'll think it's just a picture of Il Duce and will gladly let you take it."

The American had a painter do just that, and had no trouble getting the picture home. Then an artist scraped off Mussolini, and the Titian emerged. "Halloo!" said the artist, as he worked. "There seems to be something under this Titian."

He stripped off the Titian, and there was a portrait of—Mussolini!

Cubism means to paint what you can't see.
> —GERTRUDE STEIN

An American artist was visiting the Picasso ceramic workshop in the south of France. To her delight, Picasso himself was there.

She approached him timidly, addressing him in her Vassar French. "Master, which of your paintings do you consider your masterpiece?"

He answered, "La prochaine [the next one]."

All the really good ideas I ever had came to me while I was milking a cow.
> —GRANT WOOD

I once had the nerve to ask Picasso the question "What is art?" He answered, "Art is a lie which makes us see the truth."
> —JAMES DICKEY, POET, ON *Dick Cavett Show,* PBS

To be first-rate at anything you have to stake your all. Nobody's an artist "on the side."
> —ELEANOR CLARK, *Eyes etc.*

I paint; I'm a woman but I don't paint china. The first time I got a canvas I felt free. Art is overreaction to life. I love these early drawings; they show my innocent beginnings in a small town. Life is a sentence—you live it out. Maybe these portraits jump out at you too much. People like things that conform.
> —ALICE NEAL (in her seventies, elected to the Academy of Arts and Sciences), *Originals in Art,* PBS-TV series

I was the sort of child that ate around the raisin on the cookie and ate around the hole in the doughnut. So probably—not having changed much

—when I started painting pelvic bones I was most interested in the hole in the bone.
    —GEORGIA O'KEEFE

Maxwell Parrish was idling in his studio, chatting and having tea with his model. Suddenly, he heard his wife approaching—she would scold if she found him not working.

"Hurry," he said to his model. "My wife is on her way. Take off your clothes."

The arts are like a great pyramid, and the broader the base, the higher the peak. Every garage in this country has a basketball hoop, and all the kids are shooting baskets. Do they lower the level of basketball?
    —JOAN MONDALE

I began to see forms in ready-made things. I love wood so much, I wouldn't leave it flat. I got this piece at the school across the street. It had been part of a banister. It builds itself like growing—my aesthetic labor pains, I call them.
    —LOUISE NEVELSON, *Originals in Art,* PBS-TV program
       produced by Perry Miller Adato

One hopes every picture will be a new birth, a fresh experience within a growing framework. . . . I wanted to make sculpture that looked like my painting, but in the round, in metal. I wanted to give my message, but I had to let the medium tell me how I could get that message across.
    —HELEN FRANKENTHALER, CHANNEL 13 *Bulletin*

What consortium of bankers and advertising agencies decide that ordinary is more welcoming than elegant? That bland is beautiful?

There is something reassuring about the dignity of banks that counted architecture above amiability. Once a bank robber had to have panache, not just a paper bag. Who would dare hold up the Parthenon? Or the Pantheon? These were banks to fear and respect, not to pal around with. They put their money where their art was, and their monuments on Main Street, and we will never see their equals again.
    —ADA LOUISE HUXTABLE' *NYT*

The value of statuary is owing to its difficulty. You would not value the finest head cut upon a carrot.
    —SAMUEL JOHNSON

BEAUTY

I see some women turn the color of their hair with saffron. They are ashamed even of their own nation, ashamed that their procreation did not assign them to Germany and to Gaul: Thus, as it is, they transfer their *hair* thither! Ill, aye, *most* ill, do they aught for themselves with their flame-colored head, and think that graceful which in fact they are polluting! Nay, moreover, the force of the cosmetics burns ruin into the hair.
—TERTULLIAN, *On Women's Dress* (C. A.D. 220)

I choose, my dear madam, a happy medium: I sanction rouging. Paint, dear daughter, paint, since you so wish; but only on one cheek!
—THE BISHOP OF AMIENS, mid-eighteenth century, when asked about the use of rouge

It is eleven years since I have seen my figure in a glass. The last reflection I saw there was so disagreeable, I resolved to spare myself such mortification for the future.
—LADY MARY WORTLEY MONTAGUE (1757)

What makes Clodio, who was always fond of new faces,
So notoriously constant to Fulvia's embraces?
Ask Fulvia the cause—she can tell you the true one,
Who makes her old face every morning a new one.
—ANON., MID-EIGHTEENTH CENTURY

Even nature herself abhors to see a woman shorn or polled, a woman with cut hair is a filthy spectacle, and much like a monster; and all repute it a very great absurdity for a woman to walk abroad with shorn hair; for this is all one as if she should take upon her the form or person of a man, to whom short cut hair is proper, it being natural and comely to women to nourish their hair, which even God and nature have given them for a covering, a token of subjection, and a natural badge to distinguish them from men.
—WILLIAM PRYNNE, *Histriomastix* (1632)

There were still high-ranking women who flaunted fashion and refused to paint. Marie-Thérèse of Spain, first wife of the Dauphin Louis (son of Louis XV and father of Louis XVI), objected to painting her face. But upon her arrival in France in 1745, the king made it clear that she would

be expected to follow the French fashion, which demanded a chalk-white face, black patches, and flaming red cheeks. And the more the natural charms faded, the more heavily the paint was applied. Madame de Pompadour's final act, after receiving the last rites from her priest, was to rouge her face. Then she closed her eyes and fell asleep, and presently she was dead.
—RICHARD CORSAN, *Fashion in Makeup*

Give me a look, give me a face,
That makes simplicity a grace.
Robes loosely flowing, hair as free,
Such sweet abandon more taketh me,
Than all the adulteries of art;
They strike mine eyes, but not my heart.

—BEN JONSON

At the Movieland Wax Museum and Palace of Living Art in Buena Park, California, the curators have put arms on the Venus de Milo, they have also fixed her broken nose, and given her eyes and teeth and real hair. If Venus is supposed to be a universal symbol of beauty, the least she can be is whole.
—SUSAN SUBTLE and RUTH REICHL, *MS*

Roman women used face packs, which often had a pestilential stink because they were made of sheep fat and bread crumbs soaked in milk (a Poppean recipe) which after a few hours became rancid. Ovid advised barley, vetch, hen eggs, powdered stag's antler, twelve narcissus bulbs, gum, and honey to give the complexion a shining whiteness, and lupins, broad beans, white lead paint, red nitrate, orrisroot, kingfisher guano, myrrh, tree sap, honey, dried rose petals, salts of ammonia, and barley to eliminate pimples.
—STELLA J. REICHMAN, *Great Big Beautiful Doll*

No woman can be handsome by the force of features alone, any more than she can be witty only by the help of speech.
—RICHARD STEELE, *The Spectator* (1711–1712)

I derive no pleasure from talking with a young woman half an hour simply because she has regular features.
—THOREAU

Seldom is a Gothic head more beautiful than when it is broken.
—ANDRÉ MALRAUX

VENUS TRANSIENS

Tell me,
Was Venus more beautiful
Than you are,
When she topped
The crinkled waves,
Drifting shoreward
On her plaited shell?
Was Botticelli's vision
Fairer than mine;
And were the painted rosebuds
He tossed his lady,
Of better worth
Than the words I blow about you
To cover your too great loveliness
As with a gauze
Of misted silver? . . .

       —AMY LOWELL

Holes are bored through the lower part of the left nostril for the nose ring, and all around the edge of the ear for jewels. This may appear barbarous to the foreign eye; to us it is a beauty. Everything changes with the clime.
       —ANADABAL JOSHEE (1880)

You can take no credit for beauty at sixteen. But if you are beautiful at sixty, it will be your own soul's doing.
       —MARIE STOPES

American Women: How they mortify the flesh in order to make it appetizing! Their beauty is a vast industry, their enduring allure a discipline which nuns or athletes might find excessive.
       —MALCOLM MUGGERIDGE, *The Most of Malcolm Muggeridge*

Some girls are professional beauty queens. They start as Miss Fetus and go all the way up to Miss Medicare. That banner separates you from the rest of the world for a year, but you've got to keep a foot on the ground. When they cut the rope and set you adrift, it's difficult for a lot of girls to come down. Miss USA is a product with a short shelf life and the sooner you realize that, the better off you are.
       —PUBLIC RELATIONS DIRECTOR, to Beauty Queen Contestants

They want to know everything, especially if I have had my face lifted. I tell them, "Do you think I would look like this if I had?"
—BETTE DAVIS

I haunted the art galleries of London to study the various shades of coloring in the portraits of all ages. I also went to France, Spain, and Italy and, finally, to India, Egypt, and other tropical countries.
I was forced to try out my creations on my own face.
—HELENA RUBINSTEIN, in Richard Corsan, *Fashion in Makeup*

International Flavors & Fragrance, Inc., maintains that there is no flavor or fragrance that cannot be duplicated. It admits, however, that it is not always completely satisfied with a creation—for instance, its attar rose scent.
"No, we're not happy," says Mr. Kmitis. "We've been working on it for years. If we can send people to the moon and go to the bottom of the ocean, we'll get that rose."
—N. R. KLEINFIELD, *NYT*

"Beauty" my mother would call me, and "Jewel-of-pure-gold"; then she would let me go, watching her creation—her masterpiece, as she said—grow smaller as I ran down the slope. I may have been pretty; my mother and the pictures of me at that period do not always agree. But what made me pretty at that moment was my youth and the dawn, my blue eyes deepened by the greenery all round me, my fair locks that would only be brushed smooth on my return.
—COLETTE, *My Mother's House and Sido*

We discovered the existence of a strong physical attractiveness stereotype: Attractive people are assumed to be kinder, more genuine, sincere, warm, sexually responsive, poised, modest, sociable, sensitive, interesting, strong, more exciting, more nurturant, and of better character than the less attractive.
—DR. ELLEN BERSCHEID, psychologist

My daughter and I boarded a jammed bus. . . .
In the corner seat, facing my daughter, sat a little, apple-cheeked old lady. As we clung to our straps, she gazed up admiringly at my daughter and said, "Darling, you have such beautiful, tiny, pearly white teeth."
My daughter acknowledged the compliment with a smile and a thank-you. After a moment's pause, the old lady turned to me and said:
"Yours are lovely, too, if they are your own!"
—"METROPOLITAN DIARY," *NYT*

""!!!**
...

CHILDREN

WHY THEMISTOCLES' CHILD RULED THE WORLD

The child of Themistocles governed his mother;
The mother governed her husband;
The husband governed Athens;
Athens governed Greece;
Greece governed the world.
Therefore, Themistocles' child governed the world.

> —RALPH L. WOODS, *A Third Treasury of the Familiar*

Childhood shows the man as morning shows the day.
> —JOHN MILTON

[They] Rank their children, in their earliest years,
Among their cats and dogs, their bulls and bears;
Mere animals whose gambols now and then
May raise a laugh, and turn the rising spleen
Ere reason dawn'd, or Cunning Learnt disguise.

> —POEM PRINTED IN ENGLAND IN 1775

Those people (Texas Indians) love their offspring the most of any in the world, and treat them with the greatest mildness.
> —JOURNAL (C. 1770)

Three turkeys fair their last have breathed,
And now this world forever leaved;
Their father, and their mother too,
They sigh and weep as well as you;
Indeed, the rats their bones have cranched,
Into eternity theire launched.
A direful death indeed they had,
As wad put any parent mad;
But she was more than usual calm,
She did not give a single dam.

> —MARJORIE FLEMING, age six (1809)

WHAT SHALL OUR YOUNG PEOPLE READ?

A good book or paper for a child is like a companion, and its influence is very similar. The child who reads nothing but romances and sensational literature weakens its intellect, depraves its morals, and is unfitted for the duties of a useful life.
—*Hill's Manual,* handbook of etiquette (1873)

THERE WAS A CHILD WENT FORTH

*. . . His own parents, he that had father'd him and she that had
conceiv'd him in her womb and birth'd him,*
They gave this child more of themselves than that,
They gave him afterward every day, they became part of him.
The mother at home quietly placing the dishes on the supper table,
*The mother with mild words, clean her cap and gown, a wholesome
odor falling off her person and clothes as she walks by.*
*. . . The family usages, the language, the company the furniture, the
yearning and the swelling heart, . . .*

  —WALT WHITMAN

Familiarity breeds contempt—and children.
  —MARK TWAIN, unpublished diaries

I have often thought what a melancholy world this would be without children, and what an inhuman world, without the aged.
  —SAMUEL TAYLOR COLERIDGE

In the man whose childhood has known caresses and kindness, there is always a fiber of memory that can be touched to gentle issues.
  —GEORGE ELIOT

The fault no child ever loses is the one he was most punished for.
  —CESARE BECCARIA, Eighteenth Century

Childhood sometimes does pay a second visit; youth never.
  —MRS. JAMESON

There exists a passion for comprehension, just as there exists a passion for music. That passion is rather common in children, but gets lost in most people later on. Without this passion there would be neither mathematics nor natural science.
  —ALBERT EINSTEIN

W. C. Fields had given a woman his autograph, and then politely inquired about her offspring. The woman said pridefully, "He's a tough little one."

"Madam, there's no such thing as a tough child—if you parboil them first for seven hours, they always come out tender."
—CARLOTTA MONTI, *W. C. Fields and Me*

The first idea that the child must acquire, in order to be actively disciplined, is that of the difference between good and evil; and the task of the educator lies in seeing that the child does not confound good with immobility, and evil with activity . . . our aim is to discipline for activity, for work, for good; not for immobility, not for passivity, not for obedience.
—MARIA MONTESSORI

Separating Negro children from others of similar age and qualifications because of their race generates a feeling of inferiority that may affect their hearts and minds in a way unlikely ever to be undone.
—CHIEF JUSTICE EARL WARREN

Children are unpredictable. You never know what inconsistency they're going to catch you in next.
—FRANKLIN P. JONES

There is no more brilliant hope on earth today than this new thought about the child . . . the recognition of the child, children as a class, children as citizens with rights to be guaranteed only by the state; instead of our previous attitude toward them of absolute personal ownership— the unchecked tyranny, or as unchecked indulgence, of the private home.
—CHARLOTTE PERKINS GILMAN, *The Home* (1903)

It is not easy to straighten in the oak the crook that grew in the sapling.
—GAELIC PROVERB

Although he seemed a happy and contented child, his parents worried about his being an only child, especially one morning at breakfast when he looked at them both and asked earnestly, "Couldn't I *at least* have a little sister?"

The best way to keep children home is to make the home atmosphere pleasant—and let the air out of the tires.
—DOROTHY PARKER

There are only two lasting bequests we can hope to give our children. One of these is roots; the other, wings.
—HODDING CARTER

"From the day your baby is born," counseled a famous scholar, "you must teach him to do without things. Children today love luxury too much. They have execrable manners, flaunt authority, have no respect for their elders. They no longer rise when their parents or teachers enter the room. What kind of awful creatures will they be when they grow up?"

The scholar who wrote these words, incidentally, was Socrates, shortly before his death in 399 B.C.
    —BENNETT CERF, *Stories to Make You Feel Better*

It was no wonder that people were so horrible when they started life as children.
    —KINGSLEY AMIS

An infant has all its sense channels open and is not a lump of stuff to be turned upside down and slapped.
    —R. D. LAING

Who of us is mature enough for offspring before the offspring themselves arrive? The value of marriage is not that adults produce children but that children produce adults.
    —PETER DE VRIES

Ninety-nine out of one hundred parents reply in one of the following ways [to their children's questions]:
• "You go find something to play with."
• "If you don't stop, I'll scream."
• "Don't ever interrupt a person when he's reading."
• "Why don't you go outside and play?"
• "You're a spoiled brat."
• "You just love to see how far you can go before I get mad."
• "Nice children don't do that."
    —DR. THOMAS GORDON, psychologist

God bless the child who's got his own,
Who's got his own. . . .
    —From a song sung by Billie Holliday

Once, in a lecture, a busybody in the audience asked me: "Professor, has science discovered any way to improve human intelligence?" "Yes, of course," I said, "feed kids better."
    —GEORGE WALD, Nobel Laureate, in "The Biological
        Imperatives"

Our children don't begin as persons, but as concepts. With certain far-reaching social rights—and resultant destinies. For we intend them never to suffer, physically or mentally. Or not until they become us.

Fearful of "child labor," we offer them—sport. So that by once more preconceiving the young, we may have found our own way of downgrad-

ing them. And all this we do under the banner of social justice, and the blanket of love.
— HORTENSE CALISHER

Children have more need of models than of critics.
— PETRUS JACOBUS JOUBERT

I do not teach children; I give them joy.
— ISADORA DUNCAN

Remember that no child is dumb anymore. . . . he is suffering a *developmental lag;* problems in the *cognitive* area. *Hyperactive* or *hyperkinetic* is the opposite, a hopped-up kid who can't concentrate, who when asked to recite does forty laps around the classroom.
— JOHN T. BEAUDOUIN and EVERETT MATTLIN, *The Phrase-Dropper's Handbook*

Never grow a wishbone, daughter, where your backbone ought to be.
— CLEMENTINE PADDLEFORD

Anybody who hates children and dogs can't be all bad.
— W. C. FIELDS

I believe children are handwrought.
— OSSIE DAVIS, actor

Once when famed British actor Beerbohm Tree's young daughter Viola in her anger broke a window, "My child," her father said to her, "this is wickedness." "No, Father," she answered, "this is heredity."

Every person needs recognition. It is expressed cogently by the child who says, "Mother, let's play darts. I'll throw the darts and you say 'wonderful.'"
— M. DALE BAUGHMAN

I went to her birthday party. It was very boring. The ice cream was horrible. The cake was horrible. So I took some of the presents.
— LILY TOMLIN, as "Edith Anne," her five-year-old character

I know a three-year-old girl named Susan who could invariably find middle C on the piano after her mother pointed it out to her only once. Her mother was impressed, naturally enough, by her small daughter's musical aptitude. But one day, after the piano keys had been cleaned, Susie couldn't find middle C any more. Middle C had been where the egg was.
— PEG BRACKEN, *The I Hate to Housekeep Book*

The child and his father, a wealthy grower, have frequent disagreements. In a drawing of migrants cutting celery, the boy shows the sun, enormously enlarged, glaring mercilessly down on the workers in the field. His father dislikes the picture. "The sun is exaggerated," he says.

    —ROBERT COLES, *Eskimos, Chicanos, Indians and The Privileged Ones*

Not long ago I was tucking my daughter into bed, and after gazing intensely at me from her pillow she said solemnly, "You know what, Mommy, I would risk my life for you."

I gave her a big hug, and while we were embracing I answered, "And you know what, Eliza, I would risk my life for you, too."

There was a moment of silence while we digested each other's pledges and then, from the plane of my shoulder, she said, "Mommy, I just have one question."

"Yes?" I encouraged.

"What does 'risk' mean?"

    —"METROPOLITAN DIARY," *NYT*

In California, you work out your aggressions on the freeways because you spend so much time staying cool in the living rooms. When my daughter was three years old, she got into the swing of it by leaning out the car window and yelling, "If you can't drive it, park it!"

    —CYRA MCFADDEN

Oh, what a tangled web do parents weave
When they think that their children are naïve.

    —OGDEN NASH

A little girl and her mother went to visit friends. The mother began fondling and cooing over the new baby in the family. The little girl watched her mother and quizzically asked, "Mom, why don't you get rid of those pills and have another baby?"

    —BEN ALGASE

I had just put my young son to bed for the umpteenth time and my patience was worn thin. When I heard him cry "Mama" again, I yelled to him, "If you call 'Mama' one more time, I'll spank you!" After that there was quiet. Then, just as I sat down, I heard a wee whisper, "Mrs. Green, may I have a drink?"

    —JEAN GREEN, in *Catholic Digest*

A gifted small girl has explained that pins are a great means of saving life, "by not swallowing them."

    —C. E. MONTAGUE

Dear Santa,
This is the last letter I can write to you. Next year I will be seven and I won't believe in Santa Claus anymore.

Love,
Michelle

—BILL ADLER, *Love Letters to Santa*

Setting out in this world, a child feels so indelible. He only comes to find out later that it's all the others along his way who are making themselves indelible to him.
—EUDORA WELTY

LITTLE GIRL: "I'm going to see the whole world—just as soon as I am allowed to cross the street."

Mother, watching her daughter shuffling across the front lawn: "Please dear—your posture—straighten your shoulders. Look up."
"But, Mother," answered the girl, "if I looked up, how would I ever find four-leaf clovers?"

In a game of chess between a father and his eight-year-old daughter, the little girl moved the pawn in the wrong direction.
"You can't do that, Sarah!" Father corrected, returning the pawn. "You have to move FORWARD."
Sarah thought for a moment, walked to the other side of the table—and moved the pawn FORWARD.
—BEN ALGASE

HOW TO EAT LIKE A CHILD

Spinach: Divide into little piles. Rearrange again into new piles. After five or six maneuvers, sit back and say you are full.

Ice-cream cone: Ask for a double scoop. Knock the top scoop off while walking out the door of the ice-cream parlor. Cry. Lick the remaining scoop slowly so that the ice cream melts down the outside of the cone and over your hand. Stop licking when the ice cream is even with the top of the cone. Be sure it is absolutely even. Eat a hole in the bottom of the cone and suck the rest of the ice cream out the bottom. When only the cone remains with ice cream coating the inside, leave on car dashboard.

Chocolate-chip cookies: Half-sit, half-lie on the bed, propped up by a pillow. Read a book. Place cookies next to you on the sheet so that crumbs get in the bed. As you eat the cookies, remove each chocolate chip and place it on your stomach. When all the cookies are consumed, eat the chips one by one, allowing two per page.
—DELIA EPHRON, *NYT*

""!!!**
CONVERSATION

HOW TO PLEASE IN CONVERSATION

Use clear, distinct words to express your ideas, although the tone of your voice should be subdued.

Be cool, collected, and self-possessed, using respectful, chaste, and appropriate language.

Always defend the absent person who is being spoken of, as far as truth and justice will permit.

Allow people that you are with to do their full share of the talking if they evince a willingness to converse.
  —*Hill's Manual,* handbook of etiquette (1873)

Speech is silver, silence golden; speech sows, silence reaps.
  —PERSIAN SAYING

Conversation is but carving!
Give no more to every guest
Than he's able to digest
Give him always of the prime
And but little at a time
Carve to all but just enough
Let them neither starve nor stuff,
And that you may have your due
Let your neighbor carve for you.
  —JONATHAN SWIFT

Sometimes the women are required to sit and "be a good listener" because they are not otherwise needed. At other times, they are required to fill silences and keep conversation moving, to talk a lot.
  —FROM A STUDY BY PAMELA FISHMAN, sociologist

Wit has truth in it; wisecracking is simply calisthenics with words.
  —DOROTHY PARKER, *Writers at Work*

Ideal conversation must be an exchange of thought, and not, as many of those who worry about their shortcomings believe, an eloquent exhibition of wit or oratory.
  —EMILY POST, *Etiquette*

Some old people require some effort on your part. . . . Ask their opinions of what is happening today in society and technologically. . . . Keep in mind you are talking to a living person, not a national shrine. Do not pile on the condescending praise and reverent attention.

—BARBARA WALTERS, *How to Talk to Practically Anybody About Practically Anything*

Dorothy Parker and a friend were once discussing a celebrity whose garrulousness was unrivaled.

"She's so outspoken," observed the friend.

"By whom?" inquired Miss Parker.

Seated at the Round Table [at the Hotel Algonquin] one afternoon, the puckish, uninhibited, and very bald [Marc] Connelly [playwright] felt a man run his hand from Connelly's forehead to the back of Connelly's head.

"That feels just like my wife's behind," the fellow said. Marc waited just a split second before he answered.

"So it does," came the reply.

—HOWARD TEICHMAN, *Smart Aleck*

He's the kind of bore who's here today and here tomorrow.

—BINNIE BARNES

"You've really got a Thing about language, haven't you?" said a man who sat next to me at a luncheon recently. "What's your hang-up? I think the whole new language trip is because people are really into being upfront about their feelings these days instead of intellectualizing, so we need a whole new way of describing all that stuff . . . the feelings. I mean, ten years ago we didn't even know they were there. And anyway, you can't say it doesn't communicate.

"Like right now we're having this discussion, for example, and I say, 'I know where you're coming from.' Are you going to tell me you don't know what I mean by that?" . . .

"Are you trying to say you understand why I feel the way I do about empty rubber-stamp language?" I asked, coming down hard on the consonants.

My luncheon partner smiled infuriatingly. "You see?" he said. "I *knew* you knew where I was coming from."

—CYRA MCFADDEN, on "Psychobabble" (West Coast)

A gossip talks about others, a bore talks about himself—and a brilliant conversationalist talks about you!

—*Redbook*

When someone disagrees with me, I do not have to immediately start revising what I just said.
—HUGH PRATHER, *Notes to Myself*

Silence is one great art of conversation.
—WILLIAM HAZLITT

Often when I speak enthusiastically of something in history or in poetry, I receive no response, and I feel that I must change the subject and return to the commonest topics, such as the weather, dressmaking, sports, sickness, "blues," and "worries."
—HELEN KELLER, *The Story of My Life*

Let's get out of these wet clothes and into a dry martini.
—ALEXANDER WOOLLCOTT

There can be no fairer ambition than to excel in talk; to be affable, gay, ready, clear, and welcome; to have a fact, a thought, or an illustration, pat to every subject; and not only to cheer the flight of time among our intimates. . . .
—ROBERT LOUIS STEVENSON, "Talk and Talkers," in *Memories and Portraits*

Never hold anyone by the button, or the hand, in order to be heard out; for if people are unwilling to hear you, you had better hold your tongue than them.
—EARL OF CHESTERFIELD

A woman, housebound with two small children, was urged by her husband to join him at a company dinner party. She spent time at the library catching up on current events and the latest books. At the dinner, she found herself next to a distinguished guest whom she charmed with her repartee. She was doing very well indeed, when she suddenly noticed that everyone at the table was silently staring at her. Why, she wondered, and then realized that she was cutting the meat on her dinner partner's plate into small pieces.

FIRST WOMAN: "Sorry I'm late, I simply could not get off the phone with that woman. Every time I tried to hang up, she had one more thing to say."
SECOND WOMAN: "Where did you meet her, anyway?"
FIRST WOMAN: "Oh, she's in my assertiveness training class."
—"METROPOLITAN DIARY," *NYT*

A good listener is not only popular everywhere, but after a while he knows something.
—WILSON MIZNER

The words of children clearly show that a "freer" language is more dynamic.

I have heard mine (ages three and four) say:

"Mommy's switching clothes to go tennising."

"She's in the living room milking the baby."

"This sure is a prickly road."

"Roman's not letting me unroll the skin from this pencil!"

    —DIANA MILESKO PYTEL, "Why Kids Say the Darndest Things," *The PTA Magazine*

Wit has a deadly aim and it is possible to prick a large pretense with a small pin.

    —MARYA MANNES, "Controverse," *But Will It Sell*

Humor . . . is rarely malicious; . . . but laughs its way into the heart. . . . Unlike the poisoned barb of satire and the killing point of wit, humor is healing . . . recreative, and rejuvenating.

    —LOUIS UNTERMEYER

You're not called on to like everything in this world. Nor to speak up about all you don't like.

    —JESSAMYN WEST

Even out of football season, men approach their homes in the evening with all the detachment of a census taker. He garages the car, feels the stove to see if there's anything going for him, changes his clothes, eats, and retires to the living room where he reads the newspaper and engages in his nightly practice of finer isometrics—turning the television dial. He remains in a state of inertia until the sound of his deep, labored breathing puts the cork on another confetti-filled evening.

    —ERMA BOMBECK, *At Wit's End*

Reading maketh a full woman, conference a ready woman, and writing an exact woman.

    —FRANCIS BACON (amended)

The other day my husband backed out of an unfamiliar parking lot and hit a tree. I behaved very well, sat quietly, and didn't say a word. He turned to me and said, "For heaven's sake, can't you look where I'm going?"

Saratoga, September 11, 1956

Dearest Mrs. White,

In a note to me dated August 10 you rashly placed a postscript saying, and I quote, Let me know how you are. So this is to let you know how I am, and maybe it will teach you a lesson never to ask people how they are because, you know, they almost always tell you. I never ask anybody

how he is. I follow FPA's [Franklin P. Adams, columnist] practice: I saw him encounter one of the club bores at The Players one time and Frank said, "Hello, Fred, howareyouthat'sfine."
—FRANK SULLIVAN, *The Letters*

A comedian once entertained at a party to which Dorothy Parker had been invited. The man seated next to her, full of scorn, cast a withering look at the laughing guests.

"I'm afraid I can't join in the merriment," he drawled. "I can't bear fools."

"That's strange," Miss Parker chuckled. "Your mother could."

We always deeply resent the person at a party who, while he speaks with us, keeps his eyes roving around the room as if in search of someone bigger and better to talk to.
—DOROTHY WALWORTH

In a small town, a man knocked at the door of a restaurant and asked the owner, a woman, for some butter. "This sandwich is so dry," he said, "I can hardly eat it."

"I'm sorry," she answered, "but I don't open until eleven."

"Please," said the man, "I'd be much obliged."

"Sorry, I do not open until eleven," she repeated.

"Madame, do you know who I am? I am the governor of the state."

"Sir, do you know who I am? I am the lady with the butter!"
—JOHN MOTLEY

Be dogmatic.

When pretending to a knowledge you do not have, you must sound totally sure.

If you mispronounce a French word, do it in such a way that the other person will wonder if *he* has been saying it incorrectly all these years. *Spotlight the obscure.*

Someone praises the current Wagnerian soprano's Brunnhilde; you say that Flagstad's was superior—which is probably true anyhow.

"Not since" is standard:

"Not since the fall of the Second Temple has there been such a debacle."

"Not since the Missouri Compromise."

Call upon the past.

"Jacqueline's [Onassis] style is much more Anne of Cleves than Maria Theresa," which brings most such conversations to a standstill—and should.

Authorities.

This rule is drawn from the master source of all bluffing, the college term paper. Whether you have something to say or not, have a famous name who agrees with you.

Make up the quote. "As Lucretius said, the child without discipline grows into the man without will."
>—JOHN T. BEAUDOIN and EVERETT MATTLIN, *The Phrase-Dropper's Handbook*

Talking is like playing the harp; there is as much in laying the hand on the strings to stop their vibrations as in twanging them to bring out their music.
>—OLIVER WENDELL HOLMES, *The Autocrat of the Breakfast Table*

Of words and feathers it takes many to make a pound.
>—GERMAN SAYING

*Then we talked—oh, how we talked; her voice so cadenced in the
>   talking,
Made another singing—of the soul! a music without bars. . . .*
>—ELIZABETH BARRETT BROWNING, *Poems of 1844*

There is no such thing as conversation. It is an illusion. There are intersecting monologues, that is all.
>—REBECCA WEST

In the view of at least one of his fellow Georgians, President Carter has lost some of his southern accent since he moved to Washington. One of a group of school children from Vienna, Ga., told Mr. Carter that he was "beginning to talk funny." The president replied, "Everyone talks funny in Washington."
>—ALBIN KREBS, *NYT*

I have sometimes said that flattery is all right—if you don't inhale.
>—ADLAI STEVENSON

Air your prejudices but don't get the reputation as the woman who "can't stand" things. It matters little that you "can't stand peonies," and least of all to the peony.
>—DOROTHY URIS, *A Woman's Voice*

Telling your troubles is swelling your troubles.
>—ANON.

Two in distress make sorrow less.
>—ANON.

Give sorrow words: the grief that does not speak,
Whispers the o'erfraught heart and bids it break.
      —SHAKESPEARE

It was not [the Israeli woman's] silence that startled me (God knows there's enough female silence and male holding-forth in America). It was the expression on her face. She was sitting with her arms crossed on her chest, her mouth in a fixed smile, watching both me and her husband, and in her eyes was an expression of slightly superior boredom; the smug indulgence of an adult watching children play at being adults.

It was the facial expression of all the women I had grown up among, the women who sat silently in the presence of adult conversation, looking smug and bored in precisely this way. It was the look of Mrs. Einstein, saying: "Yes, I know Albert's a genius, but he *still* forgets to put his galoshes on when it rains."

That look was the ultimate defense of the powerless—of those who create artificial authority where there is no actual authority.
      —VIVIAN GORNICK, "Hers," *NYT*

COOKING FOOD

NEW MILK!

"Meeleck, Come! Meeleck, Come!"
Here's New Milk from the Cow,
   Which is so nice and so fine.
That the doctors do say,
   It is much better than wine.

You who have money, (alas! I have none.)
Come buy my lilly white corn, and let me go home.

      —MAHLON DAY, *The New-York Cries, in Rhyme* (1825)

It may be received as an axiom that the social progress of a community is in direct proportion to the number of its dinner parties. Cheerfulness of mind is essential to a good digestion, as a good digestion is essential to cheerfulness of mind. Sterne said, "A man's body and his mind are like

a jerkin and a jerkin's lining; rumple the one, you rumple the other."
 The host who has compelled a guest to ask him for anything, is almost a dishonored man.
  —ABBY MERRILL ADAMS, *Sense in the Kitchen* (1884)

Never call it "Hominy Grits"
Or you will give Charlestonians fits!
When it comes from the mill, it's "grist";
After you cook it well, I wist,
You serve "hominy"! Do not skimp;
Serve butter with it and lots of shrimp.
  —JUNIOR LEAGUE OF CHARLESTON, *Charleston Receipts*

COUNTRY SYLLABUB

Mix half a pound of white sugar with a pint of fine cider, or of white wine, and grate a nutmeg. Prepare them in a large bowl, just before milking time. Then let it be taken to the cow, and have about three pints milked into it, stirring it occasionally with a spoon. Let it be eaten before the froth subsides. If you use cider, a little brandy will improve it.
  —MISS LESLIE, *Directions for Cookery in Its Various Branches* (1839)

Ratifia is a drink
That ought to make you pause and think.
The drink is thimble-sized, it's true,
But what that thimble does to you!!!
Remember, e'er you grow too bold,
That David knocked Goliath cold!
  —JUNIOR LEAGUE OF CHARLESTON, *Charleston Receipts*

MINT JULEP

Pluck the mint gently from its bed, just as the dew of evening is about to form upon it. Select the choicer sprigs only, but do not rinse them. Prepare the simple syrup and measure out a half-tumbler of whiskey. Pour the whiskey into a well-frosted cup and throw away the other ingredients and drink the whiskey.
  —HENRY WATERSON, Louisville editor

Chatted food is half digested.
  —OLD PROVERB

Dinners have become a means of government, and the fates of peoples are decided at a banquet. This is neither a paradox nor even a novelty, but a simple observation of facts. If we look at any historian, from the time of Herodotus to the present, it will seem that, without even except-

ing conspiracies, no great event ever took place that was not previously concocted, planned, and determined at a banquet.
—ANTHELME BRILLAT-SAVARIN

There is no such thing as a pretty good omelet.
—FRENCH PROVERB

The Pilgrims landed at Plymouth Rock because they ran out of beer. A statement from their ship's log: "For we could not now take time for further search or consideration; our victuals being much spent, especially beer."
—GEORGE L. HERTER and BERTHE E. HERTER, *Bull Cook and Authentic Historical Recipes and Practices*

It is amazing how serious kitchens are. In my experience, kitchens are much more serious than living rooms. In living rooms, we talk about money and weather. In kitchens, we talk about children and history. Maybe we are serious in kitchens because we are armed with tools for stabbing, and stirring. Anyway, a kitchen seems to be a sort of garage for the emotions, a repair shop. I have, in kitchens, permitted myself to pretend to be profound. It is in bedrooms that I am laughable.
—JOHN LEONARD, "Private Lives," *NYT*

Women have made Lyons' gastronomic reputation. We're part of a tradition. . . . You must be indefatigable and impassioned. Cooking and making love are the same. They both stem from the desire to give pleasure.
—MADAME LEA, famous cook of Lyons, France

One of the prime Roman boors, Lucullus, served dinners that would cost $7,000 a plate at the present rate of exchange, while the populace ate barley gruel. One of his menus included nightingales' (Luscinia megarhyncha) tongues (which, being constantly used, are too muscular to be palatable), peacocks' brains (which flake too small to be conveniently forked), and the livers of black-veiled mourning fish (whose restricted diet gives them a flavor inferior to the wayfaring North American smelt).
—PAUL and QUINTANILLE, *Intoxication Made Easy*

A professor of English, a stickler for grammar, ordered figs and cream at a coffee shoppe. Handed a bowl of figs swimming in fresh cream, he handed the dish back to the waitress.
"I ordered figs and cream," he said firmly.
"There they are," said the girl.
"This is figs *with* cream," insisted the professor.
The distinction not being apparent to her, the waitress began to protest. "But I don't see . . . ."
"Madam," he interrupted impatiently, "look at it this way. Would you say a woman and child were the same as a woman *with* child?"

She ate so many clams that her stomach rose and fell with the tide.
—LOUIS KRONENBERGER, *The Cutting Edge*

Three million frogs' legs are served in Paris—daily. Nobody knows what became of the rest of the frogs.
—FRED ALLEN

The old rule for salad dressing still stands: Four persons are wanted to make a salad. A spendthrift for oil, a miser for vinegar, a counselor for salt, and a madman to stir it all up.

RECIPE FOR A SALAD

To make this condiment, your poet begs
The pounded yellow of two hard-boiled eggs;
Two boiled potatoes, passed through kitchen sieve,
Smoothness and softness to the salad give;
Let onion atoms lurk within the bowl,
And, half-suspected, animate the whole.
Of mordant mustard add a single spoon,
Distrust the condiment that bites so soon;
But deem it not, thou man of herbs, a fault,
To add a double quantity of salt;
Four times the spoon with oil from Lucca drown,
And twice with vinegar procured from town;
And, lastly, o'er the flavored compound toss
A magic soupçon of anchovy sauce.
Oh, green and glorious! Oh, herbaceous treat!
'Twould tempt the dying anchorite to eat:
Back to the world he'd turn his fleeting soul,
And plunge his fingers in the salad-bowl!
Serenely full, the epicure would say,
Fate cannot harm me, I have dined today.

—SIDNEY SMITH (1771–1845)

What would have happened if, near Shehodet Monastery, the goats had never eaten of the fruit of the coffee-shrub? If the imam had never discovered the sleep-dispelling energy of this marvelous plant, had never extracted its divine and demoniacal powers? What if this Prometheus among plants had never become known to man?
—ERNEST R. VERLAG, *Coffee*

Strength is the capacity to break a chocolate bar into four pieces with your bare hands—and then eat just one of the pieces.
—JUDITH VIORST, *Redbook*

Grub first, then ethics.
—BERTHOLT BRECHT

Never underestimate the place of food in the life of the French; when a couple, whether married or not, no longer has any desire for each other, the table remains a far stronger bond than bed.
—PHILLIPPE JULLIAN, *Town & Country*

A chef who would dilute his béarnaise with cream sauce to save a few pennies ought to have his toque ripped off and tossed into the fire!
—AN INDIGNANT CHEF, in Craig Claiborne, "De Gustibus," *NYT*

The only real stumbling block is fear of failure. In cooking you've got to have a what-the-hell attitude.
—JULIA CHILD

A McDonald's hamburger patty is a piece of meat with character. Now consider the hamburger bun, it requires a certain type of mind to see beauty in a hamburger bun. Yet, is it any more unusual to find grace in the curved silhouette of a bun ... than in the arrangement of textures and colors in a butterfly's wing? Not if you view the bun as an essential material in the art of serving a great many meals fast. . . .
—RAY KROC, president of McDonald's, in *Grinding It Out*

Couples who cook together stay together. (Maybe because they can't decide who'll get the Cuisinart.)
—ERICA JONG

For its merit, I will knight it and make it "Sir—loin."
—CHARLES II, *The Family Circle Cook Book*

Vegetarianism is harmless enough, although it is apt to fill a man with wind and self-righteousness.
—R. M. HUTCHINSON

If you're a vegetarian it's a way of life. You're not going to deal with anything that's untruthful. You only want natural things for your body.
  When I was a meat eater, I had to have something sweet after every meal. Now that desire is totally absent. After about a month, the taste buds get sharp. I can wax ecstatic on the taste of the grape. It's the most heavenly thing. Natural sweets are fantastic; they're much sweeter than sugar. An apple or a raisin is so sweet it makes me delirious.
—THEODORE MANN, director

"Sugar!" she cried. "Ernie, so much sugar in your cereal!"

We came to an agreement. One night she'd cook, the next I would. The first night, I ate sesame-coated eggplant fried in peanut oil, apple juice, and steamed pecan pie. The next night, I did mozzarella cheese and pasta.

"Ernie, so many empty calories! We're not getting any value from this meal."

By the following months, love had been ravaged by my taste for salt and spice and her Nature's way, honey and eccentrically named teas.

—ERNEST NEILL, *Wisdom's Child*

My sister Dora tried in vain to fathom the mystique of instinct baking.
"How much flour do you use, Ma?"
"What do you mean, how much do I use?"
"I mean a cup, a half cup . . . ?"
"What do you need cups for? You use your head."
"OK. So how many eggs?"
"Not too many."
"How much sugar?"
"Not too much."
"How much salt?"
"Not too salty."
"How much water?"
"A mouthful."
"What! OK. So how long do I leave it in the oven?"
"It shouldn't burn."

—SAM LEVENSON, *In One Era & Out the Other*

In New Hampshire, providing your wife with green wood for cooking used to be grounds for divorce.

—SARAH D. HASKELL, *The Kitchen Almanac*

One wine writer once likened a champagne to "a young girl in a long white dress in a summer garden." Another, more succinct but just as imaginative, pondered a wine for a while then pronounced: "It has broad shoulders and very narrow hips." Still others resort to arcane flummery such as "It starts well and has a pleasant finish, but it dies on the middle palate." One of the more creative wine experts around once sipped a glass, raised his head, and said, "Marigolds." Then he took another sip and said, "I was wrong. Not marigolds. Dwarf marigolds."

—FRANK J. PRIAL, "The Literary Art of Wine Tasting," *NYT*

SIMPLICITY

Dear Lucy, you know what my wish is—
I hate all your Frenchified fuss;
Your silly entrées and made dishes
Were never intended for us.

No footman in lace and in ruffles
Need dangle behind my armchair;
And never mind seeking for truffles,
Although they be ever so rare.
But a plain leg of mutton, my Lucy,
I prithee get ready at three;
Have it smoking, and tender and juicy,
And what better meat can there be?
And when it has feasted the master,
'Twill amply suffice for the maid;
Meanwhile I will smoke my canaster,
And tipple my ale in the shade.

    —WILLIAM THACKERAY

Aunt Sophie was at home in the Bronx when her telephone rang.

"Hello, Mom?" said the voice on the other end.

"Yes, darling," said Aunt Sophie.

"Gosh, Mom, I hate to bother you, but I don't know what to do."

"What's the matter, darling?" asked Aunt Sophie.

"Well, the kids are sick; I've got a splitting headache myself; the maid didn't come; and I've got thirty women from Hadassah coming over for a luncheon meeting this afternoon. I know that you're not feeling well and I hate to bother you, but I just don't know what to do."

"Don't worry, darling," said Aunt Sophie. "I'll take care of everything. First, I'll cook plenty of food and pack up two shopping bags."

"Gee, Mom, you're a lifesaver. But with your bursitis, how will you carry two shopping bags?"

"Don't worry, darling," said Aunt Sophie. "What do you think a mother is for?"

"Oh, Mom, you're a real lifesaver. I don't know how to thank you."

"Don't thank me," said Aunt Sophie. "I'll take care of everything. But tell me one thing. Did Sam pick up any food before he went to work?"

"Sam? Who is Sam?"

"Don't joke," said Aunt Sophie. "I'm talking about your husband, Sam."

"But my husband's name isn't Sam. It's Gary." There was a pause before the woman continued, "Excuse me, is this TRemont 6-4673?"

"No, I'm sorry," said Aunt Sophie. "This is TRemont 6-4672."

"Oh," said the caller in a plaintive voice, "does that mean you're not coming?"

    —"METROPOLITAN DIARY," *NYT*

Tripe, like certain alluring vices, is enjoyed by society's two extremes, the topmost and the lowermost strata, while the multitudinous middle classes of the world look upon it with genteel disdain and noses tilted. Patricians relished tripe in Babylon's gardens, plebeians have always welcomed it as something good and cheap, and always the peasant cook has taught the prince how to eat it.

    —*Wise Encyclopedia of Cookery*

Desserts . . . remain for a moment or two in your mouth and for the rest of your life on your hips.
　　　　—PEG BRACKEN, *The I Hate to Cook Book*

Swallow your pride occasionally. It's nonfattening.
　　　　—FRANK TYGER, in *Quote*

Woman diner to friend: "I haven't lost weight since I've been counting calories and carbohydrates, but my arithmetic has improved."
　　　　—DORIS MATTHEWS, in *Family Circle*

Some women can keep a leftover going like an eight-day clock. Their Sunday's roast becomes Monday's hash, which becomes Tuesday's stuffed peppers, which eventually turn up as Tamale Pie, and so on, until it disappears or Daddy does.
　　　　—PEG BRACKEN, *The I Hate to Cook Book*

In Taiwan, Wun-Yu Chen, developer of a prize-winning watermelon, gives this rule for watermelon ripeness: Tap the watermelon on the center with your knuckle. If it sounds like you're tapping your forehead, it's underripe. If it sounds like your chest, it's ripe. If it sounds like your stomach, it's overripe.
　　　　—GEORGIA DULLES, *NYT*

Our toaster works on either AC or DC, but not on bread. It has two settings —too soon and too late.
　　　　—SAM LEVENSON, *In One Era and Out the Other*

DANCE

Dancing? Oh, dreadful! How it was ever adopted in a civilized country I cannot find out; 'tis certainly a barbarian exercise, and of savage origin.
　　　　—FANNY BURNEY, in *Cecilia* (1782)

[Isadora Duncan] dared take away the scenery to reveal the majesty of the gesture.
　　　　—*The Dance*, PBS-TV program

We see Isadora Duncan every time we look at dance, so fully have her movement and creation been absorbed. In her day, everything about Isadora's art was revolutionary: her filmy, loose-fitting costumes, her

flowing hair—in the midst of a society which had little sympathy for the dance. But the society changed, as did the dance.
—Lois Dragin, *Dance*

There is a family tree for modern dance upon which everyone can be placed. Duncan and Graham. These are two of the great figures of twentieth-century dance, but they are so totally different. It was Duncan who by her own efforts called forth the very concept of the modern dance. She showed first the world and then America that Americans could dance. Graham's achievement was different. She codified freedom and gave license the shaping hand of thought, the mind of drama.
—CLIVE BARNES

It was Robert Edmond Jones [famous stage designer] who said, "Doomed to be an artist." You hear the footsteps behind you, and if you don't, you had better look out.
—MARTHA GRAHAM

Martha Graham's first professional experience as a dancer was with the Dennishawn Dancers, a less controversial and publicly admired troupe than the one which Graham founded. After one of her own performances, a woman who remembered her from the former troupe came backstage to scold: "It's dreadful! Martha, how long do you expect to keep this up?" Martha answered, "As long as I have an audience." Over 150 dances and nearly half a century of performances later, she still has an audience.
—ADAPTED FROM DON MCDONAGH, *Martha Graham*

I said I would dance. Uncle Cecil [de Mille] thought this interesting. He'd seen some dancers he found attractive and provocative. Father had seen none and was appalled. Tennis, yes. Dancing, no. "You see," said Mother, "your father knows you will be accepted anywhere if you play fine tennis."
—AGNES DE MILLE, *Speak to Me, Dance with Me*

The situation [financial crisis in the arts] is chronic. I have come to the conclusion that it isn't going to improve because the performing arts are neither a necessity nor a service.
There's no Eleventh Commandment that says, Thou shalt have symphony orchestras.
Only a very small elite feel that art is a necessity. The rest treat it as a diversion.
—LINCOLN KIRSTEIN

New York's City Center of Music was launched by Mayor Fiorello La Guardia. But he never could be converted to enjoying the ballet there. He said, "I'm a guy who likes to keep score. With ballet I can't tell who's ahead."
—LEONARD LYONS

The arts budget in this country is equivalent to running the Pentagon for six hours. With a record like that, I'd say America has to look at its priorities. . . . We remember ancient Egypt for its art. What will future generations remember about us?
— JOHN O. CROSBY, impresario

Rudolf Nureyev's talent for brevity is at its peak with hostesses. Once, when he was dancing every night on a long U.S. tour, he explained a truth in four concise words: "Chicken lunch, chicken performance."

To the lady who gushed, "Mr. Nureyev, I just can't leave without speaking to you," he said simply. "Why?"

I love, too, his fund of Russian maxims, such as: "Ask wife three times and do opposite."

A mutual friend, who saw him with the Canadian ballet, asked, "Where is Margot now?" And Rudolf, putting on a mock tragic face, replied, "She is dancing with younger man."
— MARGOT FONTEYN, *Autobiography*

Some of the greatest musicians and connoisseurs of the dance were present at Balaswaraswati's debut at the age of seven at a South Indian temple. How could a seven-year-old child understand the subtleties and the nuances of the philosophical implications of the legends and convey their meaning so deeply? How did Mozart write works of symphonic dimensions at the same age? How did Yehudi Menuhin play the Beethoven violin concerto at the same age?
— NARAYANA MENON, in the book about Balasaraswati, India's greatest classical dancer

Spanish dancer José Molina's good looks speak for themselves. When they are combined with a pout, virtuoso footwork, and a calculated display of temperament, glower here and there, a bout of lapel-flinging, and a slinky entrance with pelvis thrust forward—the effect can be electric.
— ANNA KISSELGOFF, dance critic

Why are men impersonating women funny while women impersonating men are not? It is a matter of gravity. A heavy thing trying to become light is automatically funnier than a light thing trying to become heavy.
— ARLENE CROCE, dance critic

The Radio City Rockettes are the most famous chorus line ever. The sixty greatest legs in the world rise and fall in perfect time on the stage of the music hall.

RULES FOR ROCKETTES:

· Rockettes do not hold on to each other on line.
· Rockettes are not wild or wanton.
· Rockettes do not (usually) go on to star on Broadway.
· No suntan lines allowed.

- False eyelashes must be worn to work.
- Rockettes *must* kick in time.
  —SUSAN SUBTLE, *New Dawn*

The fad of today is disco, but there's always been a fox-trot. Each generation has its own fox-trot, and it's done to the generation's own music. A
slow fox-trot, or at least a very slow fox-trot, is long on mood, though short
on style, and it is pleasant to know that someone, especially the kids, is
doing it.
  —JOHN CORRY, *Daily News*

[The Roseland ballroom] was like looking into a completely different
world. But it lives for dancing; it lives by itself. . . . These people who go
to Roseland, it's what they've always done, since they were very young.
They live for the atmosphere there, for the act of dancing.
  —RUTH PRAWER JHABVALA, novelist

Wearing only ostrich feathers, Sally Rand performed her sensuously
slow fan dance to Debussy's *Clair de Lune.* Her act alone pulled in
enough money to guarantee the entire 1933 Chicago Fair's financial success.
  —*Woman's Almanac*

Alicia Alonso is asked, "What is the hardest part of dancing?" and she
answers "Dancing well."
  —ARLENE CROCE, dance critic

To enter the School of the Imperial Ballet is to enter a convent whence
frivolity is banned, and where merciless discipline reigns.
  —ANNA PAVLOVA

The human tragedy of artists must, at some time, bring itself to the
attention of all earnest thinkers and seekers after truth. That something
is terribly wrong with the whole round of artists' lives must be apparent
to anyone who takes the trouble to observe it.
  —RUTH ST. DENIS, *An Unfinished Life*

We made dancing look like the fun it was.
  —IRENE and VERNON CASTLE, ballroom dancers

We've been doing [the Twist] for years. Only we called it the Florida
Swamp Shimmy.
  —KATHERINE DUNHAM

Dancing is like bank robbery. It takes split-second timing.
  —TWYLA THARP

"""|||

DIVORCE

They eat, but they do not talk. They look, but not at each other. Their eyes and ears are turned toward a pair on the banquette opposite: a man and a woman locked in each other's gaze, speaking softly, inaudibly, sometimes laughing together. . . .

The older, speechless couple shrivels inside. Were they ever like that? . . . They are, of course, the sepulcher of a dead marriage, a man and woman who once thought they had it made.

—NORMAN SHERESKY and MARYA MANNES, *Uncoupling*

A favorite picture star, who married well—and often—found it expedient to get a divorce in a hurry a few months ago. Her lawyer suggested Mexico.

"But I don't speak Spanish," she protested.

"That's all right," said the lawyer. "Whenever there's a pause, all you have to do is say *si, si.*"

The star created a great sensation in the little Mexican village, and when she appeared in court, the whole town turned out to witness the event. There was a great deal of emoting and bowing, and the star said *"si, si"* very firmly on numerous occasions. Suddenly the crowd gave a great cheer.

"Well, I guess I'm divorced," she said complacently.

"Divorced, my eye," cried the perspiring attorney. "You've married the mayor!"

Not long ago, on TV I was discussing the family, and someone in the audience asked, "Since your three marriages were failures, what right do you have to comment on the family?" Well, I *don't* consider my marriages as failures! It's idiotic to assume that because a marriage ends, it's failed. . . . Adultery is *not* a reason for divorce! The only valid one is the death of a union. Today, it's ludicrous to expect that two people stay connected for their lifetimes.

—MARGARET MEAD, in *Cosmopolitan*

My wife divorced me because of illness. She got sick of me.
—*Encyclopedia of Jewish Humor*

Ironically, the [final] scene Lucy and Desi ever played together in *I Love Lucy* seemed to explain their marital problems in just a few lines:

LUCY: Honest, honey, I just wanted to help.
RICKY: From now on, you can help me by not trying to help me. But thanks, anyway.

As per the script, they embraced and kissed. But before the kiss, Lucy removed the moustache she was wearing to impersonate Kovac's chauffeur. The [studio] audience laughed appropriately . . . for the last time.

"I filed for divorce the day after," said Lucy.

— BART ANDREWS, *Lucy and Ricky and Fred and Ethel*

The alimonized wife bringing up the children without father is no more free than she ever was.

— GERMAINE GREER, *The Female Eunuch*

The trouble is that nothing can be a gift when the man holds legal and financial power over you. How can one love one's keeper? That's the question. You don't have a lover. You have a keeper. One of the things my ex-husband said when we split was, "The next time I get married, all the bankbooks will be in my name."

— ERICA JONG, in an interview with Ellen Frankfurt

Your ambition and her boredom—these were two of the main spears in the side of your marriage. Twist one and the other turned with it. Because you earned a lot of money, she didn't have to work. Because she didn't have to work, she nearly choked on her freedom. Your money made possible her boredom. . . .

She began to resent the time you spent at your desk; you, knowing her resentment, began to resent the time you spent away from it. Twist one spear and the other turned with it.

— JOSEPH EPSTEIN, *Divorced in America*

The inability to divorce, in Colonial America, often led to hatred and violence between wives and husbands. Bathsheba Spooner, of a prominent Massachusetts family, murdered her husband in 1778. Before her execution she explained "that her match with her husband was not agreeable to her. Domestic dissentions soon took place, and went on from step to step, till she conceived an utter aversion to him; at length she meditated his destruction, laid several plans, and never gave over till the fatal act was committed."

— ADAPTED FROM LINDA DE PAUW AND CONOVER HUNT, *Remember the Ladies*

Many [divorced men] complain of feeling like Bozo the clown, whose only function is to entertain the children.

— IRA VICTOR, president of the two hundred-member Fathers United for Equal Rights of New York

Somehow, full-custody fathers manage a full parenting load along with their careers, usually by hiring top-notch help and pitching in enthusiastically on nights and weekends. Some of them demand more flexible hours from their employers. Young widowers do the same. In fact, to watch some of the more popular television series of recent years, one would think a man alone raising children is uniquely blessed. And perhaps, by being concerned daily with details of feeling, he is.
—GAIL SHEEHY, *Passages*

Seen as a whole [divorce], has a distinct culture—or more accurately, a *subculture* of the American culture we all share. We often refer to that subculture as *the world of the formerly married,* or FMs.

The newly separated person has just stepped across the border from the familiar land—no matter how bad—of marriage, into the *terra incognita* of postmarital life.
—MORTON and BERNICE HUNT, *The Divorce Experience*

The worst reconciliation is preferable to the best divorce.
—CERVANTES

""!!!**
•••

EDUCATION

Greek mathematician Euclid was engaged to teach the science of geometry to a young boy who was the heir to the Egyptian throne. But the prince balked at learning a system of logic that required him to prove so many elementary theorems before he could move on.

"Is there no simpler way you can get to the point?" he demanded. "Surely, the crown prince need not be expected to concern himself with such minutiae."

"Sire," responded Euclid, giving teachers through the ages an unforgettable phrase, "there is no royal road to learning."

Better be unborn than untaught, for ignorance is the root of misfortune.
—PLATO

Learning is an ornament in prosperity, a refuge in adversity, and a provision in old age.
—ARISTOTLE

Be to her virtues very kind;
Be to her faults a little blind;
Let all her ways be unconfin'd;
And clap your padlock—on her mind.
> —MATTHEW PRIOR, "An English Padlock," seventeenth century

Is it reasonable that an intelligent being should at present be so degraded, as to be allowed no other ideas, than those which are suggested by the mechanism of a pudding, or the sewing of the seams of a garment?
> —JUDITH SARGENT MURRAY, in *Massachusetts Magazine* (c. 1800)

An official proclamation issued by Yale's president, Ezra Stiles, in 1783:
Let it be known unto you, that I have tested Miss Lucinda Foote, aged twelve, by way of examination, proving that she has made laudable progress in the languages of the learned, viz., the Latin and the Greek; to such an extent that I found her translating and expounding with [perfect] ease, both words and sentences in the whole of Vergil's Aeneid, in selected orations of Cicero, and in the Greek testament. I testify that were it not for her sex, she would be considered fit to be admitted as a student ... of Yale University.
> —LYNN SHERR and JURATE KAZICKAS, *American Women's Gazetteer*

Where any mental superiority exists, a woman is generally shunned and regarded as stepping out of her "appropriate sphere," which, in their view, is to dress, to dance, and ... to read the novels which inundate the press, and which do more to destroy her character as a rational creature, than any thing else.
> —SARAH M. GRIMKE, *Letters on the Equality of the Sexes and the Condition of Women* (1838)

Every morning I picked up a little pail of milk and bread, and walked five miles to school; every afternoon, five miles home. But I walked always on winged feet.
> —MARY MCLEOD BETHUNE (c. 1890)

Without undervaluing any other human agency it may be safely affirmed that the common school, improved and energized as it can easily be, may become the most effective and benignant of all the forces of civilization.
> —HORACE MANN

Chance favors the prepared mind.
> —JAMES BRYANT CONANT, former president Harvard University

The babies did not go toward the things which it was supposed would have pleased them, like for example, toys; neither were they interested in fairy stories. Above all they sought to render themselves independent of adults in all the actions which they could manage on their own: manifesting clearly the desire not to be helped, except in cases of absolute necessity. And they were seen to be tranquil, absorbed and concentrating on their work, acquiring a surprising calm and serenity.
 —MARIA MONTESSORI, *Il Bambino in Famiglia*

The *Little Red School Book,* a British semiunderground text aimed at educating children about sex has been seized by police to see if it merits prosecution, and also roundly condemned by various authorities. That's no way to keep it out of young hands—the only sure way of rendering it harmless is to make it a prescribed text immediately.
 —*Punch*

Parents never fully appreciate teachers unless it rains all weekend.

The founding fathers in their wisdom decided that children were an unnatural strain on parents. So they provided jails called schools, equipped with tortures called education. School is where you go between when your parents can't take you and industry can't take you.
 —JOHN UPDIKE

It's no longer smart, faddish, clever and chic to be crummy.
 —ROBERT HINSINGER, dean, Ridgewood, N.J. high school

My daughter's algebra teacher was giving out the homework assignment. "Do the first ten problems on page 116"—ballpoint pens jotted that down swiftly and silently—*"and* from one to fifteen on the next page"—more jotting, with some audible sighs—*"and..."* Here one young miss said, in a stage whisper, "My *poor* father!"

The major impact of intelligence tests is in education. In the 1920s, liberals looked upon IQ tests as a means of promoting "an aristocracy of talent" rather than one based on wealth and class. In practice it worked out rather differently. There is ample evidence that group IQ tests are culturally biased and that the net effect is to perpetuate rather than minimize socioeconomic and cultural differences.... "Look at the inner-city kids who score 60 or 70 on their tests and are shunted aside by the school system," said Dr. Kamin. "Then you see them outsmart the police and deal with pushers. They're hardly stupid."
 —*NYT Mag.*

A Texan was having dinner with friends in Houston when the conversation turned to children. "Someday when you're down our way," he said, "I'd like to have you see my son's ranch. He's only sixteen, but he's already got himself a magnificent spread—and he earned every bit of it."

One friend asked how a sixteen-year-old managed to earn a big ranch. The Texan replied, "By hustling. That boy got two A's and a B on his report card."

    —Woodmen of the World

I have a son in college, and when he's home there's no food in the refrigerator. And I can't get food for the refrigerator because there's no gas in the car. And I can't put gas in the car because there's no money in the sugar bowl. And I can't put money in the sugar bowl—because I have a son in college.

    —Reader's Digest

Wife to husband, at their candle-lit dinner table, "Who would have dreamed we'd be sitting here with a daughter at West Point and a son at Vassar!"

    —New Woman

A liberal education ought to encourage the development of a tough and disciplined mind. It ought to serve a genuinely "liberating" function—it should help to foster a critical independence and to free us from our own forms of slavery, from the parochialisms of our time and place and station.

    —WILLIAM G. BOWEN, president of Princeton University

Pay no heed to those stories of backbiting on Madison Avenue. They are a mild broth compared to the witches' brew that professors are capable of stirring up in the deceptively mild environment of the campus.

That's why I urge my former colleagues to stay put in their precarious, executive suites. The grass is not greener in academia, and the ivy can be very poisonous.

    —PROF. CHARLES S. STEINBERG, Hunter College, former
      vice-president CBS-TV

A student who parked her car on the University of Toronto campus found this note on it from the Great Communicator, Marshall McLuhan: "You are parking in my spot. Please find another for yourself elsewhere."

The following day she replied to his note, "Dear Professor: As you will realize, I moved. I am most grateful to you. Your note is the first of your writings I have fully understood."

Any personnel manager will tell you that yesterday's generation of non-student is today's generation of nonworker.... During an interview, they hardly listen to the duties of the job being explained to them. They are the ones who ask many questions about salary, vacations, sick days, and other benefits. They shop employers for benefits..., then a nonworker usually progresses into other nons. He is usually a nonreader, a nonvoter,

a nonjoiner, a noninvolver, nonbeliever, nonachiever. His world is himself. The playpen that limited his world as an infant is still there.
—SAM WITCHEL, *NYT*

Bennington College and I are most grateful for your coverage of my graduation address. However, you did refer to me as having "dropped out of Bennington."

This is just not true. I left Bennington College some thirty years ago on my nonresident term to get experience in the field in which I was majoring (drama dance). I auditioned at the William Morris Agency and got a job on Broadway.

Let it be known that as soon as I am through getting experience, I will return to Bennington College and get my degree.
—CAROL CHANNING, *Newsweek*

The professors at Harvard wanted to honor their president, Charles Eliot, who had had a revolutionizing effect on education there. So they held a dinner for Eliot at an elegant Cambridge club at which a speaker offered this toast: "Permit me to congratulate you on the miracles you have performed at the university. Since you became president, Harvard has become a storehouse of knowledge." The other professors cheered.

Then Eliot rose and said, "That is true. But I scarcely deserve the credit for that." He chuckled. "It is simply that the freshmen bring so much, and the seniors take away so little."

A famous teacher had long been married but had no child. Someone said to the wife, "Madam, your husband is an advanced mathematician."

"Yes," she replied, "but he doesn't know how to multiply."
—LOUIS UNTERMEYER, ed., *Great Humor*

COLLEGE REUNION

An eye-straining reunion
I discerned this from the start—
An eager getting together
To see who was falling apart.

—"METROPOLITAN DIARY," *NYT*

When I was eighteen I set out to educate myself. I saw somebody doing the *New York Times* crossword puzzle and that became my college education. One puzzle would take an entire week because it had to be completely researched. I'd look up all the words in the dictionary, then use the encyclopedia, *Bartlett's Quotations,* the world atlas, gazeteers, biographical dictionaries, every reference book I could find.

I did that for five years while I worked as a soda jerk, short-order cook, a sign painter in a department store, a model, and a fashion coordinator. People would invite me away for a weekend and I'd take my puzzles with me.

It took me a year before I could even do half of a puzzle. After five years, I could finally do them without reference books. And that is my whole education. That's how I learned to think.

I may be uneducated, but I've got a doctorate in crossword puzzles.
      —ELLEN BURSTYN to Rex Reed, *Book Digest*

All you need to teach is a blackboard, books and a pair of legs that will last through the day. If you gave me $20,000 worth of audiovisual equipment, I'd leave it out on the sidewalk.
      —MARVA COLLINS, teacher in an inner-city one-room
      schoolhouse

We have kept our children so busy with "useful" and "improving" activities that we are in danger of raising a generation of young people who are terrified of silence, of being alone with their own thoughts. . . .
      —EDA J. LESHAN, *The Conspiracy Against Childhood*

Professor Norbert Wiener, genius of twentieth-century linguistics and philosophy, was walking down a street near the Massachusetts Institute of Technology, where he taught. A fellow professor, approaching Wiener, detained him to ask a question, then excused himself and started off.

"Pardon me a moment, Smith," queried Wiener, "but when we stopped to talk, in which direction was I walking?"

"Why, that way, toward Massachusetts Avenue."

"Oh, good," Wiener responded, pleased. "In that case, I've already had lunch."

My education is dismal. I went to a series of schools for mentally retarded teachers.
      —WOODY ALLEN

Warren [a college teacher] (he is really a composite figure) may be at what magazines like to call a "midcareer crisis." He does not think he has had a bright idea in months. His head nods during faculty meetings, dogs snarl at him, the sandwiches from the vending machines taste like cardboards from the laundry, and the secretary in the dean's office ignores him.

Mostly it is the students. A few years ago, when he started teaching, he thought they would welcome him for his knowledge, offering him their upturned brains like cereal bowls, waiting to be filled.

Instead, he says, they sit there like patients in a dentist's waiting room, reading magazines, picking flotsam from their teeth, and drawing arrows in their notebooks.

Still, he tries to cope. He goes to the Faculty Club and sits before the fireplace drinking a diet beverage and practicing self-hypnosis to calm his spiritual indigestion.
      —RICHARD G. CASE, *NYT*

Mounted on the wall of a rest room at the University of Texas at Austin is one of those hot-air machines for drying one's hands. A sign taped next to the actuating button reads: "For a short lecture by the dean, push button."

The great physicist, Dr. Robert Millikan, overheard the maid at his home answering the telephone. "Yes," she said, "this is where Dr. Millikan lives, but he's not the kind of doctor that does anybody any good."
> —JAMES C. HUMES, *Speaker's Treasury of Anecdotes About the Famous*

A student arrived at a teacher's desk after class with an empty hand where the assignment was to be.

"You won't believe this," she said and he nodded. "I was riding home with a friend of mine in her boyfriend's car. It's got a lot of rust holes in the floor. When we turned a corner, my notebook—the one with my notes for the assignment—it fell down through one of the holes and dropped into a mud puddle. I couldn't do the assignment."

A student came up after class and said he was sorry but he couldn't hand in his paper that day. He said, "I left it in my other car."

"I had it in my suitcase but the airlines lost it. You know how they are."

"My room was robbed while I was home last weekend. They got everything, including my assignment for your class."

"Didn't you get it? I mailed it from home. It probably got lost in the mail. You know how they are."

"My grandmother died."

"My roommate spilled coffee on it."

"My mother washed my shirt. My paper was in the pocket."

"It was in my room a week ago but now I can't find it. I think someone in the class stole it. You know how they are."

A young woman protested to a teacher that she couldn't take the final exam he just handed out. "I'm allergic to the paper," she said.
> —ROBERT G. CASE, *NYT*

WHAT THE PARENT HEARS	WHAT THE TEACHER MEANS
George's social adjustment has not been quite what we hoped.	The kids all hate George.
Debby is overly interested in the work of other children.	Debby copies every chance she gets.
Bruce doesn't always respect the property of others in the class.	Bruce steals like crazy.
Jane is exceptionally mature socially	Jane is the only girl in fifth grade with pierced ears, eye shadow, and dates.

> —PEGGY BAINBRIDGE in Willard Espy, *Words at Play*

When a woman inclines to learning there is usually something wrong with her sex apparatus.
—FRIEDRICH NIETZSCHE

The pictures the language paints on [Helen's] memory appear to make an indelible impression; and many times, when an experience comes to her similar in character, the language starts forth with wonderful accuracy, like the reflection from a mirror. . . . One day in Alabama, as we were gathering wild flowers near the springs on the hillsides, she seemed to understand for the first time that the springs were surrounded by mountains, and she exclaimed: "The mountains are crowding around the springs to look at their own beautiful reflections!" I do not know where she obtained this language, yet it is evident that it must have come to her from without, as it would hardly be possible for a person deprived of the visual sense to originate such an idea.
—ANNE M. SULLIVAN, from Helen Keller's *The Story of My Life*

. . . I often wanted attention and I wanted it smartly. And I trained the children in a way that is new only, maybe, in degree. Most teachers have some simple way of calling a room to attention; some use a bell, some rap a ruler, and most, I should think, use their voices. But where the sounds of learning and living are allowed in a room, a voice would need to be lifted and sharpened and could be unrepresentative of a gentle teacher; so, predictably, I used the keyboard. No crashing chord, no alarming octave, but eight notes from a famous master: the first eight notes from Beethoven's Fifth Symphony. What was good enough for him was good enough for me, since, whereas he demanded attention for the rest of the symphony from several thousand people, I wanted it for only a sentence.
—SYLVIA ASHTON-WARNER, *Teacher*

If you educate a man you educate a person, but if you educate a woman you educate a family.
—RUBY MANIKAN, Indian church leader

In the CBS television play, *Tell Me Where It Hurts,* a husband is overheard complaining about an over-forty wife who is returning to college. "I told her she'd be fifty by the time she got her degree. 'I'll be fifty anyhow,' she told me!"
—CAROLE ROSENTHAL, in *Woman in the Year 2000*

I had them taken down and sent over to the library. There wasn't a role model among them.
—SISSY FARENTHOLD, new president of Wells College, on seeing a row of portraits of her twelve male predecessors

""!!!**

ENVIRONMENT: COUNTRY/CITY

When you get right down to it, who needs a tiger? What difference would it make to the future of mankind if all the big cats did end up in coats and boots and rugs? Perhaps we need not care all that much whether or not in Asian jungles there is grace and speed and strength and surge of life. Who needs a tiger?

But think for a moment about our own descendants, those generations that will follow us. Have we the right, the wisdom, to make such decisions for them—to say, "This you may see and know and experience, but not that"?

Let's see, how would it sound: "Auto! Auto! Burning bright . . ."

    —ROGER CARAS, naturalist

Remember when atmospheric contaminants were romantically called stardust?

    —LANE OLINGHOUSE

I think that . . . repeated blackouts point out again an obvious fact that too many forget: We ought not to operate our electric system on the bare edge of sufficiency, because then Jupiter sends a lightning bolt and we are in trouble.

    —DR. EDWARD TELLER

The black smoke billowing from the chemical plant is clearly in violation of environmental law. Who is to blame? The worker who failed to check a meter? The maintenance crew? The purchasing agent? The design engineer? Or was it the company president?

Carelessness, negligence, and incompetence are not defenses.

    —S. PROKASH SETHI

Social policy cannot wait for our scientists to give us the precision we would prefer in regulating hazardous chemicals. Until we have precise methods for determining chemical safety, prudence must prevail: We must regard suspect chemicals, indicted on the imperfect evidence of animal tests, guilty until proved innocent.

    —GUS SPETH, member of the Council on Environmental Quality

Not long ago a magazine aimed at a rural audience printed a picture of a deserted farmhouse in a desolate, sand-swept field, then offered a prize for the best hundred-word essay on the disastrous effect of land erosion. A bright Indian lad from Oklahoma bagged the trophy with this graphic contribution:

Picture show why white man crazy. Cut down trees. Make too big tepee. Wind blow soil. Grass gone. Door gone. Window gone. Squaw gone. Whole place gone to hell. No pig. No corn. No pony.

Indian no plow land. Keep grass. Buffalo eat grass. Indian eat buffalo. Hide make plenty big tepee. Make moccasin. All time eat. Indian no need hunt job. No hitchhike. No ask relief. No build dam. No give dam.

White man heap crazy.
    —BENNETT CERF, *Stories to Make You Feel Better*

You haven't lived until you've died in California.
    —MORT SAHL

Yet it would do Mother an injustice to portray her as a dippy metaphysician, even though just the other day an old unmarked envelope full of seeds she once gave me fell from a book I opened. She had forgotten to tell me in the accompanying letter what the seeds were, and when I checked back with her she said they were giant sequoias.
    —PHYLLIS THEROUX, "Hers," *NYT*

Children alive today may live to see the first man on Mars and the last elm tree in the United States.
    —*Buffalo News*

What's all this fuss about plutonium? How can something named after a Disney character be dangerous?

They say if there is a leak in a nuclear power plant the radiation can kill you. Nix! Radiation cannot kill you because it contains absolutely no cholesterol. They say atomic radi-i-ation can hurt your reproductive organs. My answer is, so can a hockey stick. But we don't stop building them.

I told my wife that there was a chance that radiation might hurt my reproductive organs but she said in her opinion it is a small price to pay.
    —JOHNNY CARSON, *The Tonight Show*

I would rather be a superb meteor, every atom of me in magnificent glow, than a sleepy and permanent planet.
    —JACK LONDON

After testing samples of snow from several Kansas City areas, Research Chemist David Roberts, a specialist in heavy-metal poisoning, discovered amounts of lead that measured six times the level specified in the Environmental Protection Agency's clean-water standards. Even water

from the polluted Kansas River proved less leaden than the snow. According to Roberts, car exhausts and factories are spewing into the environment one thousand times the natural level of lead, and snow acts as a "scrubber" that washes it away. The cliché can now be modernized to read "Dirty as the driven snow."
—*Time*

After making its way through the gray slush of the streets, the taxi drove through the pristine whiteness of the park. The passenger exclaimed, "Look at those trees—they're gorgeous!" The taxi driver nodded. "This is where it should snow," he said.

There may be issues more serious than one involving the future of the oceans of our planet and the life within them, but surely they are few.
—FEDERAL JUDGE LEVIN H. CAMPBELL

A maggot must be born in the rotten cheese to like it.
—GEORGE ELIOT

Talking to the suntanned New Mexican about the weather in the state, the tourist asked, "Doesn't it ever rain here?" The native replied, "Mister, do you remember the story of Noah and the Ark, and how it rained forty days and forty nights?"
"Sure I do," the man answered.
"Well," drawled the southwesterner, "we got half an inch that time."
—*Funny, Funny World*

A veteran coast watcher, Anne W. Simon pleads for an end to the steady destruction of the world's coastlines: "Sand meets water's force with its natural tendency to move. Its soft answer turns away the sea's wrath."
—PETER STOLER, in review of Anne W. Simon, *The Thin Edge*

Saving soap slivers is, when you think of it, next to recycling paper, buying non-aerosol sprays, conserving gas and patchwork quilting. These are things for fond offspring to exult in to tell to their kayaking group: "Mom's very with it. She's into organic kohlrabi, and she saves soap slivers."
—SANDRA CLARK, *NYT*

If you can't find a specific problem with your TV, radio, or other device, it may be that nothing is wrong with it. You have simply fallen victim to a jammed electronic environment.
—CHARLES MILLER, *U.S. News & World Report*

As the poet said, "Only God can make a tree"—probably because it's so hard to figure out how to get the bark on.
—WOODY ALLEN, *Without Feathers*

There haven't been civilizations without cities. But what about cities without civilizations?
—SAUL BELLOW, *The Adventures of Augie March*

THE FORECAST

... [W]Be have snapped our locks, pulled down our shades,
Taken all precautions. We shall not be disturbed.
If the earth shakes, it will be on a screen;
And if the prairie wind spills down our street
And covers us with leaves, the weatherman will tell us.

—DAN JAFFE

Aboard a bus during the evening rush hours a woman passenger struggled to make her way to the exit door, all the while crying in the immemorial way of passengers fearful of being hauled beyond their rightful destination: "I'm getting out, don't close the door. I'm getting out, don't close the door."
   To which the exasperated driver finally retorted: "If ya can't get off, ya shun't get on."
—"METROPOLITAN DIARY," *NYT*

One hears the hoarse notes of the great ships in the river, and one remembers suddenly the princely girdle of proud, potent tides that bind the city, and suddenly New York blazes like a magnificent jewel in its fit setting of sea, and earth, and stars.
—THOMAS WOLFE

At length the dead cities, Troy, Corinth, Sparta, will do a danse macabre with New York, Berlin, Paris.
—HENRY S. HASKINS

APARTMENT HOUSE

A filing-cabinet of human lives
Where people swarm like bees in tunneled hives,
Each to his own cell in the towered comb,
Identical and cramped—we call it home.

—GERALD RAFTERY

The city, half imagined (yet wholly real), begins and ends in us, lodged in our memory.
—LAWRENCE DURRELL

A city that is large for its time is always an impractical settlement because size greatly intensifies whatever serious practical problems exist in the economy at a given time.
—JANE JACOBS

The only people who really have their housing choice conditioned are people whose skins announce they are different.

It is only black people who we assume we can keep out because of the badge of our skin color.
　　—PATRICIA ROBERTS HARRIS, Secretary, Housing and Urban
　　　　Development

City: millions of people being lonesome together.
　　—HENRY DAVID THOREAU

He gave the impression that many cities had rubbed him smooth.
　　—GRAHAM GREENE

Los Angeles: seventeen suburbs in search of a city.
　　—ANON.

One thing I noticed right away when I came to live in the small town is they are always talking about something that used to be here but isn't anymore.
　　—RICHARD BISSELL

ETHICS
PHILOSOPHY

Slavery is wrong by whatever name it is called, or in whatever guise it lurks, and whenever it appears. But it is especially heinous, black, and cruel when it masquerades in the robes of law and justice and patriotism. So was American slavery clothed in 1859, and it had to die by revolution, not by milder means.
　　—W. E. B. DU BOIS

Adopted and proclaimed by the General Assembly
of the United Nations on December 10, 1948:

All human beings are born free and equal in dignity and rights. They are endowed with reason and conscience and should act toward one another in a spirit of brotherhood.

I have always held firmly to the thought that each one of us can do a little to bring some portion of misery to an end.
—ALBERT SCHWEITZER

Yes, we can doubtless gain your case for you; we can set a whole neighborhood at loggerheads; we can distress a widowed mother and her six fatherless children, and thereby get for you six hundred dollars to which you seem to have a legal claim, but which rightfully belongs, it appears to me, as much to the woman and her children as it does to you. You must remember, however, that some things legally right are not morally right. We shall not take your case, but we will give you a little advice for which we will charge you nothing. You seem to be a sprightly, energetic man. We would advise you to try your hand at making six hundred dollars in some other way.
—ABRAHAM LINCOLN

There are a thousand hacking at the branches of evil to one who is striking at the root.
—HENRY DAVID THOREAU

From the poetry of Lord Byron, they drew a system of ethics compounded of misanthropy and voluptuousness—a system in which the two great commandments were to hate your neighbor and to love your neighbor's wife.
—THOMAS MACAULAY, "On Moore's *Life of Lord Byron*"

The only rule that can be safe from internal contradiction must embrace all mankind.
There is such a rule, often stated and very well stated too. For example, "Do unto others. . . ." But, for myself, I prefer the more rigorous Kantian version: "Treat everyone, yourself included, as an end; never treat anyone merely as a means."
—BARROWS DUNHAM, *Ethics Dead and Alive*

Ever since Nixon, nobody has asked me why I am teaching a course like Policy Choice as Value Conflict.
—PROF. BRUCE PAYNE, Duke University, on public policy

Risk! Risk anything! Care no more for the opinions of others, for those voices. Do the hardest thing on earth for you. Act for yourself. Face the truth.
—KATHERINE MANSFIELD, *Journals*

He that will not reason is a bigot; he that cannot reason is a fool; and he that dares not reason is a slave.
—WILLIAM DRUMMOND

By trying we can easily learn to endure adversity. Another man's that is.
  —MARK TWAIN, *Pudd'nhead Wilson's Calendar*

If I care for myself alone,
What can I effect?
If not now, when then?
  —HILLEL

Prejudice is an unwillingness to be confused with facts.
  —H. L. MENCKEN

Where, after all, do universal human rights begin? In small places, close
to home—so close and so small that it cannot be seen on any map of the
world. Yet they are the world of the individual person: the neighborhood,
the school or college, the factory, farm, or office. Such are the places
where every man, woman, and child seeks equal justice equal dignity
without discrimination. Unless these rights have meaning there, they
have little meaning anywhere.
  —ELEANOR ROOSEVELT

If some great Power would agree to make me always think what is true
and do what is right, on condition of being turned into a sort of clock and
wound up every morning before I got out of bed, I should instantly close
with the offer.
  —THOMAS HENRY HUXLEY

General notions are generally wrong.
  —LADY MARY WORTLEY MONTAGU

WHICH PROVERB?

When in Rome, do as the Romans do.
Above all, to thine own self be true.

The bigger, the better.
Good things come in small packages.

The more, the merrier.
Two is company, three's a crowd.

Better safe than sorry.
Nothing ventured, nothing gained.

Too many cooks spoil the broth.
Many hands make light work.

The pen is mightier than the sword.
Actions speak louder than words.

Clothes make the woman.
Never judge a book by its cover.

> —ADAPTED FROM M. H. GREENBLATT, in Willard R. Espy, *Words at Play*

My mother-in-law used to say hunger embarrassed her, especially in children, more especially in her own children. Some people, she said, believed in Christianity or Judaism or Capitalism. She believed in Not Starving.

> —MADELINE GILFORD, *170 Years of Show Business*

Philosophy deals with the larger generalizations and therefore seems remote and even terrible. If you say to yourself, "I shall have whole-wheat bread for dinner," . . . you and everyone will find the business understandable. Now, if you further say, "I shall have whole-wheat bread for dinner because it is nourishing," you remain perfectly understandable, though you have passed into dietetics. If, next, you detail the reasons why whole-wheat bread is nourishing, you enter a number of sciences like chemistry and physiology. . . . Pausing a little at this point, you will say perhaps, "Well, anyhow, the more nourishing my diet, the healthier I shall be." Here you add medicine to the sciences you have already skimmed, and your generalization has, accordingly, a yet wider range. . . . But now suppose it occurs to you or to someone else to ask, "How is it possible that a collection of plant seeds, winnowed and milled and baked and eaten and digested, can transform themselves into bone and tissue?" . . .

How can it indeed? Evidence, as gathered by the sciences, seems to show that it does. But how does it? The answer lies beyond the sciences in philosophy.

> —BARROWS DUNHAM, *Man Against Myth*

A little work, a little sleep, a little love and it is all over.

> —MARY ROBERTS RINEHART

You can't put the facts of experience in order while you are getting them, especially if you are getting them in the neck.

> —LINCOLN STEFFENS

It was evening. I was walking homeward on Pennsylvania Avenue near the Treasury, and as I looked beyond Sherman's statue to the west the sky was aflame with scarlet and crimson from the setting sun. But, like the note of downfall in Wagner's opera, below the skyline there came from little globes the pallid discord of the electric lights. And I thought to myself the Götterdämmerung will end, and from those globes clustered like evil eggs will come the new masters of the sky. It is like the time in which we live. But then I remembered the faith that I partly have ex-

pressed, faith in a universe not measured by our fears, a universe that has thought and more than thought inside of it, and as I gazed, after the sunset and above the electric lights there shone the stars.
—OLIVER WENDELL HOLMES

Some days confidence shrinks to the size of a pea, and the backbone feels like a feather. We want to be somewhere else, and don't know where— want to be someone else and don't know who.
—JEAN HERSEY, *The Shape of a Year*

Once on a Time there were Two Brothers who Set Out to make their Way in The World.

One was of a Roving Disposition, and no sooner had he settled Down to Live in One Place than he would Gather Up all his Goods and Chattles and Move to another Place. From here again he would Depart and make him a Fresh Home, and so on until he Became an Old Man and had gained neither Fortune nor Friends.

The Other, being Disinclined to Change or Diversity of Scene, remained all his Life in One Place. He therefore Became Narrow-Minded and Provincial, and gained None of the Culture and Liberality of Nature which comes from Contact with various Scenes of Life.

MORALS:

This Fable teaches that a Rolling Stone Gathers No Moss, and a Setting Hen Never Grows Fat.
—CAROLYN WELLS, "The Two Brothers" (c. 1900)

We must constantly build dikes of courage to hold back the flood of fear.
—MARTIN LUTHER KING, JR.

I have accepted fear as a part of life—specifically the fear of change, the fear of the unknown; and I have gone ahead despite the pounding in the heart that says: turn back, turn back, you'll die if you venture too far.
—ERICA JONG

It is undesirable to believe a proposition when there is no ground for supposing it true.
—BERTRAND RUSSELL

A MAN TO THE UNIVERSE

A man said to the universe:
"Sir, I exist!"
"However," replied the universe,
"The fact has not created in me
A sense of obligation."

—STEPHEN CRANE

When I hear somebody sigh, "Life is hard," I am always tempted to ask, "Compared to what?"
—SYDNEY J. HARRIS, *Majority of One*

As a lifelong working reporter and working woman, I have found little time for reflection, and little inclination. I *knew* my life was a doodle; no need to examine it. I was also aware that Socrates would not have approved of this attitude (I didn't much approve of it myself), but I had followed another philosopher, Satchel Paige: "Don't look back. . . . it may be gaining on you."
—SHANA ALEXANDER, *Talking Woman*

I do not want the peace which passeth understanding. I want the understanding which bringeth peace.
—HELEN KELLER

Albert Einstein was at a scientific meeting when a noted astronomer said, "To an astronomer, man is nothing more than an insignificant dot in an infinite universe."
"I have often felt that," Einstein replied. "But then I realize that the insignificant dot who is man is also the astronomer."

The scholar must from time to time return to the people and learn their life, that he may continue to live himself.
—ALVIN JOHNSON

Life is too short to be little.
—BENJAMIN DISRAELI

As a man tramps the woods to the lake he knows he will find pines and lilies, blue heron and golden shiners, shadows on the rocks and the glint of light on wavelets, just as they were in the summer of 1354, as they will be in 2054 and beyond. He can stand on a rock by the shore and be in a past he could not have known, in a future he will never see. He can be part of time that was and time yet to come.
—WILLIAM CHAPMAN WHITE, *Adirondack Country*

Some people are always grumbling that roses have thorns; I am thankful that thorns have roses.
—ALPHONSE KARR

I don't believe in the generation gap. I believe in *re*generation gaps. Each day you regenerate—or else you're not living.
—DUKE ELLINGTON

Nothing in life is to be feared. It is only to be understood.
    —MARIE CURIE

What is the use of a house if you haven't got a tolerable planet to put it on?
    —HENRY DAVID THOREAU

If you live in the street called Now, *in a house named* Here—
If you live at number Here North Now Street, *let us say,*
Then immediate things, discomfort, sorrow, it is clear,
Are of first importance; you could feel no other way.
But if you pitch your tent each evening nearer the town
Of your true desire, and glimpse its gates less far,
Then you lay you down on nettles, you lay you down
With vipers, and you scarcely notice where you are. . . .
    —EDNA ST. VINCENT MILLAY, *Conversation at Midnight*

The question is not where civilization began, but when will it.
    —ANON.

An ounce of application is worth a ton of abstraction.
    —BOOKER T. WASHINGTON

Murphy's Law—If anything can go wrong, it will.
O'Toole's Commentary on Murphy's Law—Murphy was an optimist.
Law of Selective Gravity—An object will fall so as to do
    the most damage.
Jenning's Corollary—The chance of bread falling with the
    buttered side up is directly proportional to the cost
    of the carpet.
Maier's Law—If the facts do not conform to the theory,
    they must be disposed of.
Boren's Law—When in doubt, mumble.
    —ARTHUR BLOCK, *Murphy's Law and Other Reasons Why
        Things Go Wrong*

After thirty years in Husserliana and Ingardiana, I am just beginning to understand it.
    —DR. ANNA-TERESA TYMIENIECKA, The World Institute for
        Advanced Phenomenological Research and Learning

What is clear is this: Philosophy, in the current Anglo-American vein, has largely relinquished—indeed it has scorned—those central areas of metaphysics, of ethics, of aesthetics, of political thought, that constituted the mainstream and splendor of the philosophic tradition. It has left reality, the obstinate, messy sovereignty of the everyday world, to witch

doctors on the one hand, and to intellectual terrorists on the other. What it offers instead is dry tack for teeth on edge.
—GEORGE STEINER

I have tried too in my time to be a philosopher; but, I don't know how, cheerfulness was always breaking in.
—OLIVER EDWARDS

Although the founding fathers never intended that slaves, servants, Indians—or women—would share in the freedoms they demanded for themselves, the libertarian ideals they conceived remain a vital legacy. Virtually every American reform movement in the past two hundred years has gone to the Declaration of Independence for its principles.
—LINDA DE PAUW and CONOVER HUNT, *Remember the Ladies*

Serenity of spirit and turbulence of action should make up the sum of man's life.
—VITA SACKVILLE WEST, "Heritage"

FAMILY HOME

The trees in the streets are old trees
  used to living with people,
Family-trees that remember your
  grandfather's name.
    —STEPHEN VINCENT BENÉT, "John Brown's Body"

I cannot tell you . . . how much I enjoy *home* after having been deprived of one for so long, for our dwelling in New York and Philadelphia was not *home,* only a sojourning. The General and I feel like children just released from school or from a hard taskmaster, and we believe that nothing can tempt us to leave the sacred roof tree again, except on private business or pleasure. We are so penurious with our enjoyment that we are loath to share it with anyone but dear friends, yet almost every day some stranger claims a portion of it, and we cannot refuse. I am again settled down to the pleasant duties of an old-fashioned Virginia housekeeper, steady as a clock, busy as a bee, and cheerful as a cricket.
—MARTHA WASHINGTON, in a letter to a friend (1797)

My machines sportingly grant me a head start, confident that they will beat me in the end. Either I get up a half hour early in the morning to start plugging in or I stay up a half hour later to turn the dial that sets the clock that starts the coffee that triggers the thermostat that flips the switch that starts the oil burner that blows the fuse that shuts off the alarm and everything else that lives in the house that Sam built. We eat by candlelight quite often. It's so romantic.
    —SAM LEVENSON, *In One Era & Out the Other*

I want a house that has got over all its troubles; I don't want to spend the rest of my life bringing up a young and inexperienced house.
    —JEROME K. JEROME

The American front lawn is a sacred temple. It is meant to be looked at and worshiped. It must be kept neatly mowed at all times and free of all objects. No child may leave a doll or a baseball glove on it. A member of the family may step on the lawn long enough to perform the manicuring rites, or may hire some other priest to do the job. But it would be unthinkable for a husband, his mowing labors done, to sprawl on the newly mown grass and read the Sunday paper.
    Quite often I see a husband and wife sitting in their garage on camp chairs, side by side, looking at their front lawn. They sit amid their tools and power mowers and children's bicycles and old washing machines— the overflow and detritus of daily life—staring reverently at the holy grass. What strange power keeps them from bringing their chairs out onto the grass, to delight in its greenness and grassiness? I think they're afraid that their neighbors will swarm down on them, with axes, for profaning the neighborhood.
    —WILLIAM ZINSSER, "Letter from Home," *NYT*

When I was at home I was in a better place.
    —SHAKESPEARE, *As You Like It*

A House is not a Home.
    —POLLY ADLER

Many a man who thinks to found a home discovers that he has merely opened a tavern for his friends.
    —NORMAN DOUGLAS

Nobody shoulders a rifle in defense of a boardinghouse.
    —BRET HARTE

There is the housekeeper who is, for want of a better word, a bureaucrat. Her head is a compendium of useful information pertaining to stain eradication, laundry shortcuts, wood preservation, and fluffiness agents.

Her puppy is either trained in a week or drowned, and where she has the jump on the rest of us is in her ability to understand where dirt can hide; over doorjambs, underneath high-chair seats, behind the dryer—places the rest of us didn't even know existed. And it doesn't help to find out that she has just finished *War and Peace* either.

—PHYLLIS THEROUX, "Hers," *NYT*

The easiest way to find something lost around the house is to buy a replacement.

—JACK ROSENBAUM, in San Francisco *Examiner & Chronicle*

Why does the washing machine take two socks and give back only one? Various theories have been advanced over the years, as, for example, that the washing machine eats one of the socks. Arlberg's brilliant monograph, "The Dynamics of Laundry," demolished this theory with laboratory evidence.

Postmortems on more than 1,200 washing machines which had expired suddenly during the rinse cycle showed no trace of socks in their digestive systems. Arlberg's investigations showed that the washing machine thrives almost entirely on the diet of crushed buttons, navel lint, and small turtles left in the pants pockets of young boys.

—RUSSELL BAKER, *NYT*

Every night the cottage rung,
As they sung:
"Oh Dulce, dulce domum!"

—"HOME SWEET HOME," seventeenth-century song

A lady once called at 1 Merrion Square and found it in the possession of bailiffs [as a result of financial reversals in the Wilde family]:

There were two strange men sitting in the hall, and I heard from the weeping servant that they were "men in possession." I felt so sorry for poor Lady Wilde and hurried upstairs to the drawing room where I knew I should find her. Speranza was there indeed, but seemed not in the least troubled by the state of affairs in the house. I found her lying on the sofa reading *Prometheus Vinctus* of Aeschylus, from which she began to declaim passages to me, with exalted enthusiasm. She would not let me slip in a word of condolence, but seemed very anxious that I should share her entire admiration for the beauties of the Greek tragedian which she was reciting. . . .

—TERENCE DE VERE WHITE, "The Parents of Oscar Wilde"

All happy families resemble one another; every unhappy family is unhappy in its own fashion.

—TOLSTOI, *Anna Karenina*

Family jokes, though rightly cursed by strangers, are the bond that keeps most families alive.
  —STELLA BENSON, *Pipers and a Dancer*

[It was] a family enjoying the unspeakable peace and freedom of being orphans.
  —GEORGE BERNARD SHAW, *You Never Can Tell*

Parents wonder why the streams are bitter, when they themselves have poisoned the fountain.
  —JOHN LOCKE

The first thing to recognize is that—despite all the talk about equality—men are different from women. The most important difference (after the anatomical and obvious) is that men can't do anything alone. This is basic. It's been like that since they went off together in packs to hunt, while women stayed alone and swept the cave. It's been reinforced by the Industrial Age: One man turns the bolt while the other man holds the nut. It's in the union contract.

You've probably noticed this already in the traditional man's jobs around the house. Whenever your husband fixes anything, he wants you to hand him the screwdriver. He's three whole steps up a ladder, the screwdriver is on the floor, and he'll yell for you to come from another room rather than step down and get it.
  —BARBARA HOLLAND, *Woman's Day*

The simple fact of being a mother does not, by itself, indicate a capacity or willingness to render a quality of care different from that which the father can provide.
  —JUDGE SYBIL HART KOOPER, N.Y. County Family Court

When we speak of which parent can more satisfactorily raise the child, gender is irrelevant. It is not enough to speak of custody in terms of men's rights, paternal or maternal deprivation. The real issue is *parental* deprivation.
  —DR. LEE SALK

A farm is an irregular patch of nettles bounded by short-term notes, containing a fool and his wife who didn't know enough to stay in the city.
  —S. J. PERELMAN

Several days before Christmas [in Florida], I began to notice that my wife was suffering from crying spells, all of them of short duration. I would find her weeping quietly in what seemed like elegant if uncomfortable surroundings. . . .

On the twenty-second, a large package arrived from the North and I noted the familiar handwriting of our daughter-in-law. I carried the package into the living room, dumped it on the sofa, slit its throat with my jackknife, and left it for my wife to dissect. (She is methodical at Christmas and keeps a record of gifts and donors.) Soon I heard a sharp cry, "Come here! Look!" I found her standing on the hearth with her nose buried in a branch from a balsam fir, which she had hung over the fireplace. With it hung a harness strap of sleigh bells. The branch had unquestionably been whacked from a tree in the woods behind our son's house in Maine and had made the long trip south. It wore the look and carried the smell of authenticity. "There!" said my wife, as though she had just delivered a baby.

—*Essays of E. B. White*

Birds in their little nests agree;
*   And 'tis a shameful sight*
When children of one family
*   Fall out, and chide, and fight.*

—ISAAC WATTS, *Divine Songs,* eighteenth century

Living well is not so much the realization of a dream as it is a blend of hard economic reality and relentless resolve. The real prizes—the rent-controlled penthouse, the parlor floor with thirteen-foot ceilings and wood-burning fireplaces—go to the swift, the canny, the ruthless, and the rich. The rest of us just compromise.

—ADA LOUISE HUXTABLE, *NYT*

The newly hung door and window frames [were] painted dark green. . . . Sheets of white cedar veneer were secured over the rafters, making a warm-toned, rustic ceiling. A Mexican guitar and Colorado coyote pelt decorated one log wall. On the front porch, a Brazilian hammock swayed back and forth in the wind. . . .

I remembered the pioneers again. They had slept up in lofts warmed by heat rising from their fireplaces and safe from prowling wild animals. A sleeping loft was the answer. . . . It was snug, and at night I slept practically in the branches of balsam firs. Their fragrance continually filled the air. . . .

—ANNE LA BASTILLE, *Woodswoman*

Our family is not yet so good as to be degenerating.

—KURT EWALD

Dear Son,

Now that you have reached the magic age fourteen, the time has come to tell you about the bees and flowers. There is a male bee and a female bee, although I haven't the slightest idea which is which. As for the flowers—we get ours from the Plaza Florists, Inc. Well, that takes care of *that.* Write soon.

> Affectionately,
> Father

—DONALD OGDEN STEWART, in a letter to his son away at prep school

Accidents will occur in the best-regulated families.
—CHARLES DICKENS, *David Copperfield*

No matter how many communes anybody invents, the family always creeps back.
—MARGARET MEAD

The quickest way for a parent to get a child's attention is to sit down and look comfortable.
—LANE OLINGHOUSE, in *The Wall Street Journal*

There are three ways to get something done: do it yourself, hire someone, or forbid your kids to do it.
—MONTA CRANE, in *Sunshine Magazine*

As a sort of joke, when people asked me what a humanistic architect was, I'd tell them it was an architect who designs toilets lower to the ground to reassume the original position for natural functions.

What we live in is no longer determined by us. We have given over that right to architects, contractors, decorators, and magazines which impose someone else's fantasy, someone else's taste on us. We're so insecure we need to buy someone else's idea.
—FRITZ PERLS, architect

Changes in our society are occurring so rapidly that the experts can't gather information on the family fast enough, put it on computer tape and analyze it before things change again and the information is out of date.

And of all these variations, it is the working mother who has had the most impact of all.
—KRISTIN A. MOORE, social scientist

Woman gardener feeding scrawny sapling: "Don't you want to grow up like other trees? Don't you *want* a nest of robins in your hair?"
—LICHTY, Publishers-Hall Syndicate

As long as the family and the myth of the family . . . have not been destroyed, women will still be oppressed.
—SIMONE DE BEAUVOIR

There are no illegitimate children—only illegitimate parents.
>   —JUDGE LEON R. YANKWICH

Dearest Mary,
  There has been quite a bit of excitement here. Harvey W., he used to own the gasoline station, shot his wife Sunday. I'm enclosing the clipping from the newspaper. Sally S., Eleanor's fifteen-year-old sister, is pregnant and she won't say who the father is. There has been some teenage violence at the high school. Three people were sent to the hospital. (I'm also enclosing a clipping.)
  . . . Once again, dear, please think about coming home. Paris is no place for a young girl to be alone.

>   Love,
>   Mother
>   —ART BUCHWALD, *Down the Seine and Up the Potomac*

. . . In my heart, Truman will go down in history for his attitude toward his undergarments—he washed his own.
>   —LILLIAN ROGERS PARKS

The men seem to be able to make it, despite all the uprooting, while the women tend to fall apart. They lose their identity because they can't keep transferring their credentials— or status they've achieved—to each new city. Their husbands, automatically, have status, through their jobs.
>   —ROBERT SEIDENBERG, *Corporate Wives—Corporate Casualties?*

A family's private life is as immoderate and insensate, compared to its public life, as our thoughts are, compared to our speech.
>   —RANDALL JARRELL, in the Introduction to Christina Stead, *The Man Who Loved Children*

TO A BROWNSTONE FRONT

Away back in the golden age
When you housed folks of quality;
Then, little did you realize
Your end would be this poverty.

Men, like houses, have broken dreams,
For my ambition was, you see,
When but a lad, to become rich
And buy the house you used to be.

>   —FRED W. KOKE, "Metropolitan Diary," *NYT*

FASHION

... Because the daughters of Zion are haughty, and walk with stretched forth necks and wanton eyes, walking and mincing as they go, and making a tinkling with their feet ... the Lord will take away the bravery of their tinkling ornaments about their feet ... the chains, and the bracelets ... the bonnets, and the ornaments of the legs, and the headbands ... and the earrings, the rings, and nose jewels ... And it shall come to pass, that instead of sweet smell there shall be stink; and instead of a girdle a rent; and instead of well-set hair baldness; and instead of a stomacher a girding of sackcloth; and burning instead of beauty.
—ISAIAH

If she have good eares, show them; good haire, lay it out; good legs, weare short cloathes; a good hand, discover it often, practice any art, to mend breath, clense teeth, repaire eyebrows, paint and professe it.
—BEN JONSON

Ceaselessly spinning in its silk, the stupid silkworm.
—T'CHEN, tenth century

The barge she sat in like a burnished throne,
Burned on the water. The poop was gold;
... For her own person, it beggared all description.
She did lie in her pavilion, cloth-of-gold of tissue,
O'erpicturing that Venus where we see
The fancy outwork nature. ... From the barge
A strange invisible perfume hits the sense
of the adjacent wharfs.
—SHAKESPEARE, *Antony and Cleopatra*

Born into an old-fashioned family at Ping-hsi, I was inflicted with the pain of foot-binding when I was seven years old. I was an active child who liked to jump about, but from then on my free and optimistic nature vanished. ... Binding started in the second lunar month: Mother consulted references in order to select an auspicious day for it. I wept and hid in a neighbor's home, but Mother found me, scolded me, and dragged me home. She shut the door, boiled water, and from a box withdrew binding, shoes, knife, needle, and thread. I begged for a one-day postponement, but she washed and placed alum on my feet and cut the toenails. She then bent my toes toward the planter with a long binding cloth. She ordered me to walk. The pain proved unbearable.

Beatings and curses were my lot for covertly loosening the wrappings. . . . After several months, all toes but the big one were pressed against the inner surface. Mother would remove the bandage and wipe the blood and pus which dripped from my feet.

Every two weeks, I changed to new shoes. Each shoe was one to two tenths of an inch smaller than the previous one. . . . After changing more than ten pairs of shoes, my feet were reduced to a little over four inches.

Four of the toes were curled in like so many dead caterpillars. It took two years to achieve the three-inch model. My feet became humped and odiferous. How I envied the natural-footed!

    —HOWARD S. LEVY, *Chinese Footbinding*

Spartan women's dress was appropriate to their life-style. They wore the Dorian *peplos,* with slit skirts which bared their thighs and permitted a freedom of movement impossible to women dressed in the voluminous Ionian *chiton.* Ancient opinions varied on whether their scanty costume encouraged chastity or licentiousness. Herodotus states that at one time all Greek women wore the Dorian dress, which was fastened at the shoulders with broochpins. However, the Athenian women once used these pins as weapons on a man who brought them news of their husbands' deaths, and were then punished by the men and forced to dress in the Ionian *chiton,* which, being stitched, did not require pins.

    —SARAH B. POMEROY, *Goddesses, Whores, Wives & Slaves*

The barbers and wigmakers have come armed with their dummy heads, and have been bold enough to pretend that it is their function to dress the hair of ladies. . . . They hold their razors to our throats, and it is against this tyranny that we are obliged to implore the help of Justice. . . .

The profession of wigmaker belongs to the mechanic arts, and that of the ladies' hairdresser to the liberal arts. . . . the coiffeur must be a painter, familiar with *nuances,* with the use of *chiaroscuro,* and with the distribution of light and shade . . . the whiteness of the skin will be relieved by the dark tint of the hair, and the too vivid brilliancy of the blonde will be attenuated by the ashen color that we apply to the hair.
. . .

    —THEODORE CHILD, *Wimples and Crisping Pins,* eighteenth
      century

Fond pride of dress is, sure,
          a very curse;
Ere fancy you consult,
          consult your purse.

    —BENJAMIN FRANKLIN, *Poor Richard's Almanac*

All women, of whatever age, rank, profession, or degree who shall, after this Act, impose upon, seduce, and betray into marriage any of His Majesty's subjects by virtue of scents, paints, cosmetic washes, artificial teeth or false hair, iron stays, bolstered hips, or high-heeled shoes, shall incur the penalty of the law now in force against witchcraft and like misdemeanors.
> —ACT OF PARLIAMENT (1779)

To the lady . . . who shall so arrange her few garments as to appear nearest to naked.
> —A GEORGIA NEWSPAPER (1801) sarcastically offering a prize to the young ladies wearing the Empire style—no corsets and very little underclothing.

Plump and rose was my face
And graceful was my form.
Till fashion deemed it a disgrace
To keep my body warm.

> —*Connecticut Courant* (1801)

. . . [W]omen's hair was frizzed and stretched over a cushion or rolls . . . which were stuffed with a variety of unsavory materials, including cow tails, straw, hay, horsehair, wool, and old hair removed from wigs. . . . These heads took hours to complete, so women left them intact for long periods. Naturally, they attracted an even wider variety of vermin and insect life than the simple hairstyles of the poor and middle-class women, which could be brushed fairly clean.
> —LINDA DE PAUW and CONOVER HUNT, *Remember the Ladies*

I have seen [a headdress] rise and fall above thirty degrees. About ten years ago it shot up to a very great height, insomuch that the female part of our species were much taller than the men. The women were of such enormous stature that we appeared as grasshoppers before them.
> —JOSEPH ADDISON, *Spectator* (1711)

Flamboyant dress, immense hat—a flowerstand of roses or a veritable aviary of birdwings. . . . Mouth crimson with rouge, eyes rimmed with kohl. . . .
> —DESCRIPTION OF AN EIGHTEENTH-CENTURY COURTESAN, in Cornelia Otis Skinner, *Elegant Wits and Grand Horizontals*

That courtier was in the right, who dated the commencement of the French Revolution from the day when a nobleman appeared at Versailles without buckles on his shoes.
> —*The Complete Hand-Book of Etiquette for Ladies and Gentlemen* (nineteenth century)

Heigh! ho! in rain and snow,
The bloomer now is all the go.
Twenty tailors take the stitches,
Twenty women wear the breeches.
Heigh! ho! rain or snow,
The bloomer now is all the go.

    —DOGGEREL, mid-nineteenth century

Even protected by pantalettes, skirts, and long stockings, fashionable female bathers were not considered beach-worthy without a male companion. Resisting the pressure to pair off with just anyone, many of the wealthy women chose to pay for their beach partners, creating a lucrative business (with hourly, daily, or seasonal rates) for some otherwise unemployed young men. The gigolo enterprise continued until the late 1890s, when it suddenly occurred to the taste makers that a single woman on the beach was acceptable after all.
    —*American Woman's Gazetteer*

The first really excellent cheap hoopskirt
The most elegant most comfortable corsets
Imperial dress elevator (to raise long skirts above muddy sidewalks)
    —MAIL-ORDER ITEMS, in *Mme. Demorest's Mirror of Fashion*
      (1860)

A fully-equipped Santal belle . . . carries two anklets and perhaps twelve bracelets, and a necklace weighing a pound, the total weight of ornaments on her person amounting to thirty-four pounds of bell metal—a greater weight . . . than one of our drawing room belles could well lift. . . .
    —QUENTIN BELL, *On Human Finery*

Fashion is that by which the fantastic becomes for the moment universal.
    —OSCAR WILDE

Under an early *Vogue* drawing of two young ladies in animated conversation is the following caption:
PENELOPE: I'm in awful luck.
PERDITA: What's the matter?
PENELOPE: I'm engaged, and I have still eight new dresses of which I will never have a chance to try the effect.

Under a drawing of a sporting young couple with bicycles:
VAN WITTER: If you will excuse me, Miss Lovely, I will go make myself more presentable for dinner.
MISS LOVELY: Impossible, Mr. Van Witter.
    —*Vogue* (c. 1898), in Edna and Ilka Chase, *Always in Vogue*

HOW TO CLEAN CORSETS

First take out the steels, then scour thoroughly with warm lather of white castile soap, using a small scrubbing brush; never dip in water; when clean, let cold water run off them freely so as to rinse thoroughly. Dry without ironing, after pulling lengthwise to make shapely.

> —CHARLES SIMMONS, *Aunt Sue's Standard Cyclopoedia of Recipes* (1901)

In 1914, Mary Jacob, a New York debutante, who hated the restrictive corseting of the time, one evening before a dance, helped by her French maid, constructed a brassiere out of two handkerchiefs and some pink ribbon. This she patented as [the first] "Backless Brassiere." She made a few hundred samples, and sold the patent for $15,000. Later estimates put her patent's value at $15,000,000.

> —JOAN and KENNETH MACKSEY, *The Book of Women's Achievements*

In background and temperament Clare Booth and Marya Mannes were poles apart. It was the time of repeal [of Prohibition] when the first potable beer was reappearing in the markets and restaurants. The *Vogue* editorial staff was in conference, discussing whether it mightn't be fun to do an article about a beer party and who should write it. Clare drifted in from *Vanity Fair* magazine and listened.

"I don't think that's *Vogue* material," she said loftily; "I doubt that Mrs. Harrison Williams, for example, would serve beer."

Our earthy Miss Mannes snorted, "Why not, for God's sake? Has her money affected her palate?"

> —EDNA and ILKA CHASE, *Always in Vogue*

The American woman has been laboring under an excess of fashion. Eventually she will look inside Fashion's bright cellophane wrapper before she buys the contents. She will seriously consider the quality and the usefulness of the very newest thing, the epitome of all chic, the height of all glamour. She will settle comfortably back in an old sweater and skirt and idly remark to 90 percent of what she sees: I SAY TO HELL WITH IT.

> —ELIZABETH HAWES, *Fashion Is Spinach*

Obviously, if the waist is immediately under the breasts or down around the hips, you can't be tight-laced. And if the female body can't be tight-laced, female conduct can't be tight-laced either.

> —JAMES LAVER, British authority on costume

Why don't you . . .

Rinse your blond child's hair in dead champagne to keep its gold, as they do in France?

> —DIANA VREELAND, *Harper's Bazaar* (1936)

. . . because I prefer to let my child go to hell in her own way, as they do in America.
— S. J. PERELMAN, *MS*

We received half a dozen wires from Hollywood frantically describing how Marlene had taken to wearing pants. At this time slacks were still a novelty in the United States and their use was deemed almost as shocking to the female public as the wearing of bloomers had been fifty years previously. . . .
We pleaded with Marlene to give them up but she was adamant. . . .
Fortunately for us, business in cloaks and suits was bad and the manufacturers welcomed the appearance of a new garment for women. We rode on the crest of a wave of slacks which swept the entire country.
— ARTHUR MAYER, *Merely Colossal*

Especially designed gas protection costume at a reasonable price of 40/—. This outfit is made of pure oiled silk and is available in dawn, apricot, rose, amethyst, Eau de Nil green, and pastel pink. The wearer can cover a distance of two hundred yards through mustard gas and the suit can be slipped over ordinary clothes in thirty-five seconds.
— AD OF HARVEY NICHOLS AND CO. OF LONDON (World War II)

Combination levity and bloodshed. In one street flag waving and kissing; next street duel; sniper versus partisan. . . . Flowing Veronica Lake style hair very prevalent.
(Cable sent to *Vogue* from Paris, June, 1944, at the end of the German occupation.)
— EDNA WOOLMAN CHASE and ILKA CHASE, *Always in Vogue*

. . . These pseudo-active (though really infantile) attitudes toward woman's dress explain what anthropologists have observed without being able to explain: "Concealment affords a greater stimulus than revelation."
— EDMUND BERGLER, psychiatrist, *Fashion and the Unconscious*

Italian women: They've [just] gone from basic black to blue jeans and marching, from the Middle Ages to future shock.
— CANDICE BERGEN, actress, making a film in Italy

The duchess of Windsor, confined to her bedroom in her beautiful house in the Bois de Boulogne in Paris, is just as chic, lying there, as she was when she was the toast of the international set.
The duchess' hair is kept coiffed perfectly and its reddish-brown shade maintained. Although she does have great difficulty speaking, she still sees a few close friends when she can, receiving them beautifully

groomed in a pale blue dressing gown and pale blue beads and earrings under a pale blue coverlet.
—"SUZY SEZ," *Daily News*

A lady who rules Fort Montgomery
Says the wearing of clothes is mere mummery;
   She has frequently tea'd in
   The costume of Eden,
Appearing delightfully summery.
—EDMUND LEAR

Saint Laurent has excellent taste. The more he copies me, the better taste he displays.
—"COCO" CHANEL (1971)

The museum visitor spotted a picture of a group of men sitting around a table. All wore long hair, stretch pants, boots, and fancy jackets.
   They were signing the Declaration of Independence.
—*New Woman*

No longer does society say that to be serious one must dress seriously; or to compete in a man's world one must appear competent in no-nonsense clothes; . . . or that youthfulness is a look to be attained at all costs. The woman knows that to be in fashion is to look like an extension of her own mind, self, and body. The women's movement dealt the final blow to the old fashion law and order.
—CARRIE DONOVAN, *NYT Mag.*

I began wearing hats as a young lawyer because it helped me to establish my professional identity. Before that, whenever I was at a meeting, someone would ask me to get coffee—they assumed I was a secretary. Nothing wrong with being a secretary, but I had other plans.
—BELLA ABZUG

I mean, Santa—after all darling, *always* dressed the same? If you call *that* dressing, when only a touch of. . . . Oh, well, almost *anything* would be better. Like some sort of a glazed chintz print. Now that could be—well, *too too* divine really!
—HALSTON

Woman is the mold into which the spirit of the age pours itself.
—JAMES LAVER, British authority on costume

I'm not a driven businessman but a driven artist. I never think about money. Beautiful things make money.
—GEOFFRY BEANE, designer

GOING TO PIECES

No "layered" look for the likes of me!
I have to dress too hurriedly;
So when this dumb style disappears,
This gal won't grieve—she'll just
Shed tiers.

—PHYLLIS JAFFE, "Metropolitan Diary," *NYT*

Heels are at highest heights ever—supposedly the most "feminine" type of footwear: Health authorities rail, yet women go mincing along, feeling uncomfortable—yet looking and feeling in fashion. Extremely high heels continue to be accepted usage, an integral part of sex appeal.

The resiliency of the human body, particularly the female, is great indeed.

—EVE MERRIAM, *Figleaf*

The last time high heels were at the peak of popularity, I saw two to three women a week with sprained ankles. If you multiply that number by the 800 practicing podiatrists in the New York metropolitan area, you've got a lot of sprained ankles in any given week.

—DR. NORMAN KLOMBERS

It's easy to tell the women in style—they've either been to Paris or to the attic.

—FORT WORTH *Star-Telegram*

[Diana Vreeland] walked into that cellar [the Metropolitan Art Museum Costume Institute] that didn't have three visitors a day and look what she's done. . . . It's interesting that someone who created fashion is now a curator of fashion. She's now the keeper of the flame when she ignited it before.

—RICHARD AVEDON

You know, don't you, that the bikini is only the most important invention since the atom bomb?

—DIANA VREELAND

FEMINISM

Are dogs divided into hes and shes, or do they both share equally in hunting and in keeping watch and in the other duties of dogs? or do we entrust to the males the entire and exclusive care of the flocks, while we leave the females at home, under the idea that the bearing and suckling their puppies is labor enough for them?

No, he said, they share alike; the only difference between them is that the males are stronger and the females weaker.

But can you use different animals for the same purpose, unless they are bred and fed in the same way?

You cannot.

  —PLATO

WOMEN'S CHORUS

They're always abusing the women,
as a terrible plague to men;
They say we're the root of all evil,
and repeat it again and again;
Of war and quarrels and bloodshed,
all mischief, be what it may;
And pray then, why do you marry us,
if we're all the plagues you say?
And why do you take such care of us,
and keep us so safe at home,
And are never easy a moment if ever we chance to roam?
When you ought to be thanking heaven
that your plague is out of the way,
You all keep fussing and fretting,
"Where is my plague today?"
If a Plague peeps out of the window, up go the eyes of men;
If she hides,
then they all keep staring until she looks out again.

  —ARISTOPHANES (c. 400 B.C.)

Recollect all the institutions respecting the sex, by which our forefathers restrained their undue freedom, and by which they subjected them to their husbands; and yet, even with the help of all these restrictions, you can scarcely keep them within bounds. If, then, you suffer them to throw these off one by one, to tear them all asunder, and, at last, to be set on an equal footing with yourselves, can you imagine that they will be any longer tolerable to you? The moment they have arrived at an equality with you, they will have become your superiors.

  —CATO (215 B.C.)

Woman is woman's natural ally.

  —EURIPIDES

If men should be praised whenever they perform great deeds . . . how much more should women be extolled.

  —GIOVANNI BOCCACCIO

We would have every arbitrary barrier thrown down. We would have every path laid open to woman as freely as to man.... If you ask me what offices they may fill, I reply—any. I do not care what case you put; let them be sea captains, if you will.

—MARGARET FULLER (1845)

What, sir, would the people of the earth be without woman? They would be scarce, sir, almighty scarce.

—MARK TWAIN

For my part I distrust all generalizations about women, favorable and unfavorable, masculine and feminine, ancient and modern.

—BERTRAND RUSSELL

When Grandma was a girl she didn't do the things the girls do today. But then the Grandmas didn't do the things the Grandmas do today.

—FROM L. and F. COPELAND, eds., *10,000 Jokes & Stories*

If Eve, the first woman God ever made, was strong enough to turn the world upside down all alone, these women together ought to be able to turn it back and get it right side again. And now they are asking to do it, the men better let them.

—SOJOURNER TRUTH at a suffrage meeting in Akron, Ohio, in 1851

I cannot say that I think you are very generous to the ladies, for whilst you are proclaiming peace and good will to men, you insist upon retaining an absolute power over wives.

—ABIGAIL ADAMS, to her husband, John Adams

His answer:
In Practice you know We are the subjects. We have only the Name of Masters, and rather than give up this, which would completely subject Us to the Despotism of the Peticoat, I hope General Washington, and all our brave Heroes would fight....

I, Sarah Smith, School-mistress, the wife of William Smith, take this method to inform the public not to trust or credit the said Smith on my account, for I shall never pay any of his contractions.... I nine years have been his wife, tho' he for a widower doth pass, when he meets a suitable lass; for his wicked doings I never more can him abide, nor he never more shall lie by my side.

—AN EIGHTEENTH-CENTURY AMERICAN NEWSPAPER

For my arguments, Sir, are debated by a disinterested Spirit—I plead for my sex, not for myself. Independence I have long considered the grand blessing of life. The basis of every virtue—and independence I will ever

secure by contracting my wants, though I were to live on a barren heath.
> —MARY WOLLSTONECRAFT, *A Vindication of the Rights of Women*

I ask no favors for my sex. . . . All I ask of our brethren is that they will take their feet from off our necks, and permit us to stand upright on that ground which God designed us to occupy.
> —ANGELINA GRIMKE (1828)

The night before Lucy Stone was born [in 1818], a sudden shower sent the men of the family rushing to the hayfield to save the hay. The pregnant woman was left alone, and that night had to milk the Stones' eight cows. It is not surprising then when she was told her new baby was a daughter, Lucy's mother said, "Oh dear! I am sorry it is a girl. A woman's life is so hard."
> —ELINOR RICE HAYES, *Morning Star*

Do not consider me as an elegant female, but as a rational creature.
> —ELIZABETH BENNET, in Jane Austen, *Pride and Prejudice*

It is really a stillborn thought to send women into the struggle for existence exactly as men. If, for instance, I imagined my sweet, gentle girl as a competitor, it would only end in my telling her, as I did seventeen months ago, that I am fond of her and that I implore her to withdraw from the strife into the calm uncompetitive activity of my home.
> —SIGMUND FREUD

Alfred Howard, a parks director in Miami, barred breast-feeding women from his parks because "breast-feeding is . . . an act for the home, not a public park where kids play."
> —MS

We have lived through the era when happiness was a warm puppy, and the era when happiness was a dry martini, and now we have come to the era when happiness is "knowing what your uterus looks like."
> —NORA EPHRON, *Crazy Salad*

I suppose that in a low birthrate world, the goals of women's liberation will be automatically won, because a women without a baby had better be treated like a human being or she'll have a baby.
> —ISAAC ASIMOV

Equal rights for the sexes will be achieved when mediocre women occupy high positions.
> —FRANÇOISE GIROUD, France's first Secretary of State for Women's Affairs

If these women's libbers were nice to their husbands, their husbands would let them do what they want to do, too. They just don't want to be nice. They want to be ugly.
—PHYLLIS SCHLAFLY

RIGHTS OF WOMAN

(Tune: My Country, 'Tis of Thee)

God save each Female's right,
Show to her ravish'd sight
   Woman is free;
Let Freedom's voice prevail.
And draw aside the veil,
Supreme Effulgence hail,
   Sweet Liberty. . . .

Let snarling cynics frown,
Their maxims I disown,
   Their ways detest;
By man, your tyrant lord,
Females no more be aw'd,
Let Freedom's sacred word,
   Inspire your breast.

   —ANON. in Vera Lawrence, *Anthology of Song*
      (Eighteenth Century)

A feminist is a man or a woman who already knows for a fact that men and women are equal, and who wants society to wake up to that fact, so the world can stop operating at half-strength. So that half the brains, half the inspiration, half the joy and beauty, half the human resources in the world will no longer be wasted.
—MARLO THOMAS, actress

If you scratch a homemaker, you'll find a feminist one eighth of an inch from the surface.
—LETTY COTTIN POGREBIN, writer

RONA BARRETT to Cher: "Would you ever sell your body to survive?"
CHER: "No, man, I'd edit *Vogue* first."
—*MS*

Feminism means finally that we renounce our obedience to the fathers and recognize that the world they have described is not the whole world. Masculine ideologies are the creation of masculine subjectivity; they are neither objective, nor value-free, nor inclusively "human."
—ADRIENNE RICH

I was my own person. Not theirs. They (the promoters) expect you to kiss the flag and talk about how much you like Nixon. I talked about what a terrible thing the war was. They were upset when I referred to myself as Ms. and spoke out in favor of abortion on demand and ERA. It's tough being a beauty queen nowadays.

—AMANDA JONES, former Miss U.S.A. (of 1973), *Daily News*

One time Cheryl decided to play nurse and we put napkins on our heads. Leroy was the patient and we painted him with iodine so he'd look wounded. A nurse, I wasn't gonna be no nurse. If I was gonna be something I was gonna be the doctor and give orders. I tore off my napkin, and told Cheryl I was the new doctor in town. Her face corroded. "You can't be a doctor. Only boys can be doctors. Leroy's got to be the doctor."

"You're full of shit, Spiegelglass. Leroy's dumber than I am. I got to be the doctor because I'm the smart one and being a girl don't matter."

"You'll see. You think you can do what boys do but you're going to be a nurse, no two ways about it. It doesn't matter about brains, brains don't count. What counts is whether you're a boy or a girl."

—RITA MAE BROWN, *Rubyfruit Jungle*

In that last Suffrage Parade in 1919, Arthur [her husband] and I led the section for young married couples, and that big white horse with blond Inez Mulholland [Women's Rights leader] proudly astride was just ahead of us and believe me, we kept our distance. But there were those behind us who didn't always get the message in time. . . .

—LILLIE MAYER (in her late eighties)

Nowadays, a husband is more likely to comment dryly on his wife's peerless way with frozen vegetables or her deft handling of the dishwasher—hardly enough to make up for her potential market value. Men notoriously underrate the onerousness of such scrubbing and dusting as remain to be done. But a full-time maid is an unjustified expense now, whether you call her a wife or not, and a full-time mother is less fun than a full-time TV set.

—WILFRED SHEED, *Now That Men Can Cry*

If only we could raise women to the level of the Panama Canal.

—GLORIA STEINEM, on Congress's neglect of women's issues

If men could get pregnant, abortion would be a sacrament.

—POSTCARD, printed by the Center for Constitutional Rights

I think that one function of the women's movement is to try to keep humanizing society. Not because women are innately nurturing, but simply because they haven't been part of the establishment, and they don't think in those static terms.

This is the power of the powerful to define, to structure, to say: "This is the way the world works." It's enormous power. Among the powers of the weak, I think the first one is the power not to believe the powerful.
—ELIZABETH JANEWAY, in *Civil Liberties Preview*

My husband is fond of reminding me of the story of Moses, who kept the Israelites in the desert for forty years because he knew a slave generation could not found a new free society. The comparison with the women's movement is extremely apt, I think; I doubt that it will ever be possible for the women of my generation to escape from our own particular slave mentality. For the next generation, life may indeed be freer.
—NORA EPHRON, *Crazy Salad*

Speaking at a Salute to the Congress dinner sponsored by the Washington Press Club, freshman Rep. Millicent H. Fenwick, sixty-five, related: "When I was a member of the New Jersey State Assembly, making a speech proposing an Equal Rights Amendment, one of my male colleagues rose and, with real anguish, said, 'I just don't like this amendment; I've always thought of women as kissable and cuddly and smelling good.'
"The only answer, of course," Mrs. Fenwick continued, "was, 'That's the way I've always felt about men, and I hope, for your sake, that you haven't been disappointed as often as I have.' "
—*Reader's Digest*

The truly free woman is she who knows how to decline a dinner invitation without giving an excuse.

A woman reporter asked Bella S. Abzug, the [Houston] conference's presiding officer, if it was true that the conference was dominated by "lesbian-abortionists."
Lucy Komisar, a feminist writer from Manhattan who was standing in the audience, smiled wryly and without a moment's pause, said: "Well, they can't be both, can they?"
—JUDY KLEMESRUD, *NYT*

Yes, let us heal all the wounds at once. . . . This conference started out so starchy, but even with all that ritual, the authenticity came through. It makes you believe in women a lot.
—KATE MILLETT, as Betty Friedan got up to speak at the
Houston Conference (1977)

Scratch almost any man, and you'll find wistful memories of his mother darning socks and cooking Sunday lunch and sending his father off in the morning with swept lapels.
Women are still doing most of those things, but they are leaving the

problem of lapel lint to the suit-wearers and racing for the front door themselves.

"Linda," my mother worried me when I told her I'd been promoted at *Newsweek,* "you've got to learn to be more dependent."
—LINDA BIRD FRANCKE, "Hers," *NYT*

After hearing that women were to be accepted as members of the once-sacrosanct, all-male University Club, one old-timer shook his head and stared from his library chair. "What beats me," he said with a sigh, "are all those years I wasted worrying about communism."
—NEIL MORGAN

I would not want a woman flying on my wing. I want them back where they belong. I have always said I have nothing against a woman doing anything a man can do as long as she gets home in time to cook dinner.
—SEN. BARRY GOLDWATER

Women who insist upon having the same options as men would do well to consider the option of being the strong, silent type.
—FRAN LEBOWITZ, *Metropolitan Life*

GOVERNMENT

A leader is best
when people barely know he
exists.
Not so good
when people obey and acclaim
him.
Worse when they despise him.
But of a good leader
who talks little
when his work is done
his aim fulfilled
they will say:
"We did it ourselves."
—LAO-TSE (565 B.C.)

Govern a great nation as you would fry small fish.
—LAO-TSE

When we are planning for posterity, we ought to remember that virtue is not hereditary.
—THOMAS PAINE

A dialogue between a southern delegate and his spouse on his return from the Grand Continental Congress (1774):
HUSBAND: ... Consider, my Dear, you're a Woman of Fashion,
'Tis really indecent to be in such passion;
Mind thy Household-Affairs, teach thy Children to read,
And never, Dear, with Politics, trouble thy Head.

WIFE: Dost thou think that wise Nature meant thy shallow Pate,
To digest the important Affairs of a State?
Thou born! thou! the Machine of an Empire to wield?
Art thou wise in Debate? Should'st feel bold in the Field?
If thou'st Wisdom to manage Tobacco, and Slave,
It's as much as God ever design'd thee to have:
Because Men are Males, are they all Politicians?
Why then I presume they're Divines and Physicians,
And born all with Talents every Station to fill,
Noble Proofs you've given! no doubt, of your Skill.
—N.Y. HISTORICAL MUSEUM

... I doubt, too, whether any other Convention we can obtain may be able to make a better Constitution. For, when you assemble a number of men to have the advantage of their joint wisdom, you inevitably assemble with those men all their prejudices, their passions, their errors of opinion, their local interests, and their selfish views. From such an assembly can a perfect production ever be expected? It therefore astonishes me, sir, to find this system approaching so near to perfection as it does. ... Thus I consent, sir, to this Constitution because I expect no better, and because I am not sure that it is not the best.
—BENJAMIN FRANKLIN (September 17, 1787)

If the present Congress errs in too much talking, how can it be otherwise in a body to which the people send 150 lawyers?
—THOMAS JEFFERSON, *Autobiography*

Nearly all men can stand adversity, but if you want to test a man's character, give him power.
—ABRAHAM LINCOLN

I don't make jokes—I just watch the government and report the facts.
—WILL ROGERS

When I was a boy I was told that anybody could become president; I'm beginning to believe it.
— CLARENCE DARROW

All the ills of democracy can be cured by more democracy.
— ALFRED E. SMITH

I am against government by crony.
— HAROLD L. ICKES

I am ready and willing to testify before the representatives of our government as to my own opinions and my own actions, regardless of any risks or consequences to myself. . . . But to hurt innocent people whom I knew many years ago in order to save myself is, to me, inhuman and indecent and dishonorable. I cannot and will not cut my conscience to fit this year's fashions.
— LILLIAN HELLMAN, testimony before House Un-American Activities Committee (1952)

Thanks . . .
For giving us liberty's deathless chime
And a holiday in the summertime.
— PHYLLIS MCGINLEY, "Poem in Praise of the Continental Congress (A Fourth of July Hymn)"

When nations mature, they grow tolerant of evil. They accept as a simple fact of life the irresponsibility of public officials who condone corruption and who play favorites as they administer the nation's laws. It was so in the brightest and rottenest days of the Roman Empire, and it has been so ever since. By this standard of maturity, the United States has grown up.
— BLAIR BOLLES, *How to Get Rich in Washington*

Ronald Reagan [is] "simplistic" and "rash," but not unfit to be president.
— GERALD FORD

We should keep [the Panama Canal]. After all, we stole it fair and square.
— SEN. S. I. HAYAKAWA

A country that can put men on the moon can put women in the Constitution.
— REP. MARGARET HECKLER (Massachusetts)

As Juanita Kreps, the first economist to serve as secretary of commerce, sits at her desk, she looks directly across at a slightly off-center picture of Herbert Hoover, the only secretary of commerce to have become president of the United States.

"As many times as I've tried to fix it," said Mrs. Kreps, "Herbert Hoover always tilts to the right."
—LEONARD SILK, *NYT*

Congresswoman Pat Schroeder has the best answer. When asked how she could be both a congressperson and a mother she said: "I have a brain and a uterus, and I use both."
—LETTY COTTIN POGREBIN

Women outnumber men. They are more durable. They outlive us. They have better physiques, and generally speaking, better minds. It'll happen as soon as they put forward a candidate.
—SEN. J. WILLIAM FULBRIGHT on being asked what he thought of a woman president

People say nice things to me—like that I ought to run for president—which tells me that they like me. But I have my own deadline for how long I should be in Washington. I think you can get accustomed to red tape and many unfair things that go on in government. Once you stop getting angry about inefficiencies, waste, and injustice, you ought to get out. That's my time limit.
—REP. ELIZABETH HOLTZMAN, *Newsday*

You walk into a meeting in one of the departments and now there's another woman there. You see each other, maybe you wink, and you know you're both glad to see each other there. We've arrived—and we're looking for each other.
—REP. BARBARA MIKULSKI

Those who make peaceful revolution impossible will make violent revolution inevitable.
—JOHN F. KENNEDY

People are hanging on for dear life to the diminishing sphere of autonomy that they have.
They don't want to give the government a license to enter every nook and cranny of their personal lives.
—DANIEL YANKELOVICH, polltaker

They think they're real [the wax figures]. They beat up on Nixon. Worse. Smashed him to bits. Too bad—he was one of the best we ever made.
—TOM TIBERGHIEN, curator of the San Francisco Wax Museum

Not a single president has offered me a Cabinet post, despite the fact that I may be the only person of Cabinet stature in the country who has never yielded to a corrupt impulse.
All through school, I never cheated once, and whenever I saw people

who were cheating, I turned them in to the teacher. Afterward, they would beat me up in the schoolyard and throw dead cats through our living-room window, which annoyed my family.
—RUSSELL BAKER, *NYT*

""!!!**
HEALTH EXERCISE

DIALOGUE BETWEEN BENJAMIN FRANKLIN AND THE GOUT

Midnight, October 22, 1780

FRANKLIN: Eh! Oh! Eh! What have I done to merit these cruel sufferings?
GOUT: Many things; you have ate and drank too freely, and too much indulged those legs of yours in their indolence. . . . What is your practice after dinner? Walking in the beautiful garden of those friends, with whom you have dined, would be the choice of men of sense; yours is to be fixed down to chess. This is your perpetual recreation. . . . What can be expected from such a course of living? . . . Fie, then Mr. Franklin! I had almost forgotten to administer my corrections; so take that twinge,—and that.
FRANKLIN: Oh! Eh! Oh! Ohhh! As much instructions as you please, Madame Gout, and as many reproaches; but pray, Madame, a truce with your corrections!
—LOUIS UNTERMEYER, *Great Humor*

Light beer. Suddenly it's everywhere.
The future belongs to a pale and delicate brew that rinses the innards like gentle spring rain, that impacts on the metabolism like chicken bouillon. The perfect complement to a hearty dish of Melba toast and cottage cheese. A beer for joggers. A beer for weight watchers. If beer got any lighter, you could raise goldfish in it.
—JERRY ADLER, *Daily News*

Wouldn't it be simpler just to isolate and label the few things that are *not* injurious to health?
—OWEN ARNOLD, in *The Kiwanis Magazine*

At an exercise class: A seventy-year-old woman said, "I am too old *not* to exercise."

The preservation of health is a duty. Few seem conscious that there is such a thing as physical morality.
—HERBERT SPENCER

Some psychiatrists say asthma and other allergic reactions can surface in children who are constantly told not to cry.
—*Glamour*

Affliction—any loss of faculties or what gave life sense—is abominable; admit it; wail, rail, shake your fist. That's what I call healthy.
—ELEANOR CLARK, *Eyes etc.*

In the sauna one must behave as one would in church and no noise, shouting, or swearing is permitted.
—OLD FINNISH SAYING

On a flight from New Orleans to New York a few years ago the pilot heard a rhythmic thump, thump, thump at the rate of 140 thumps a minute. The pilot and copilot checked and rechecked their instruments, but were unable to find the cause. They considered turning back to New Orleans, but after about twenty minutes the thumps stopped as mysteriously as they had begun. After landing in New York a stewardess told the pilot, "What a weird passenger we had on this flight. A guy locked himself in the forward lavatory and jogged for twenty minutes."
—*Daily News*

"Pure, white, and deadly." That's what Dr. John Yudkin, internationally recognized nutritionist at Queen Elizabeth College in London, calls sugar.
—*New Woman*

Inside every emaciated woman lives a healthy woman waiting to be fed.
—STELLA J. REICHMAN, *Great Big Beautiful Doll*

Man is an intelligence in servitude to his organs.
—ALDOUS HUXLEY

When I feel like exercising, I just lie down until the feeling goes away.
—ROBERT M. HUTCHINS

We have always been taught to look good not feel good. For men, athletics was important to build character—what about women building character in the same way? When you exercise, it's between you and your muscles.
—BILLIE JEAN KING, on PBS

HOURS OF SLEEP

Nature requires five; custom gives seven;
Laziness takes nine, and wickedness eleven.
>—ANON.

Of all illnesses, the common cold, or as they call it now, a viral infection, is the most stupid. It's messy, it isn't dramatic, the sufferer gets no credit for being big and brave about it. You just can't make anything of it. Even a broken leg gets a little sympathy. Try to get anything at all out of a cold and you run into frustration.
>—*Vineyard Gazette*

Physical health is as much dependent on environmental and emotional factors as on measurements of blood pressure or temperature.
>—RENÉ DUBOS

Loneliness is not only pushing our culture to the breaking point, it is pushing our physical health to the breaking point. There is a biological basis for our need to form human relationships. If we fail to fulfill that need, our health is in peril.
>—JAMES LYNCH, *The Broken Heart*

We must love one another or die.
>—W. H. AUDEN

I've been on a constant diet for the last two decades. I've lost a total of 789 pounds. By all accounts, I should be hanging from a charm bracelet.
>—ERMA BOMBECK

TO PREVENT HAIR FALLING OFF

Take one-half pint French brandy, one tablespoonful fine salt, and one teaspoonful powdered alum. Let these be mixed and well shaken until they are dissolved; then filter, and it is ready for use. If used every day, it may be diluted with soft water.
>—AUNT SUE'S *Standard Cyclopoedia of Recipes* (1901)

Avoid fried meats, which angry the blood.
If your stomach disputes you, lie down and pacify it with cool
    thoughts.
Keep the juices flowing by jangling around gently as you move.
Go very light on the vices, such as carrying on in society.
The social ramble ain't restful.
Avoid running at all times.
>—SATCHEL PAIGE'S rules of life, quoted by Frank Sullivan

Most colonial Americans looked on bathing as a dangerous and unhealthy practice. Although colonists washed in spots with lye soap, few except Indians and African slaves were inclined to plunge entirely into water.
—LINDA DE PAUW and CONOVER HUNT, *Remember the Ladies*

If ye just about half-live, ye just the same as half-die; and if ye spend yer time half-dyin', some day ye turn in and die all over, without rightly meanin' to at all—just a kind o' bad habit ye've got yerself inter.
—DOROTHY CANFIELD FISHER

LANGUAGE WORDS

The English language is not weighted down with restrictions or, as Fowler called it, grammatical grundyism. On the contrary, it is rich with options. There are millions of words to choose from, some with the most subtle variations in meanings. And there are millions of combinations we can use to persuade, impress, inform, entertain, share experiences, write a scientific paper, accept a Nobel Prize, compose a romantic novel, or leave a funny note for the paperboy.
—JACK THOMAS, *Boston Globe*

There should be three days a week when no one is allowed to say: "What's your sign?" Violators would have their copies of Kahlil Gibran confiscated.
—DICK CAVETT

From the essays of high school students of American History:
During his term of office Woodrow Wilson had many foreign affairs.
During the first twenty years of the century there was much suffrage from women.
Under President Adams there were the Allen and Sedation Acts.
The collection also includes a couple of exceptional definitions:
Bigotry—being married to two or more people.
Social Darwinism—survival of the fetus.
—PAULINE LEVINE, *NYT*

Perhaps American English will have an equivalent for the lovely Japanese expression for a girl's first menstruation, "the year of the cleavage of the melon," or for the ancient Indian, "flower growing in the house of the god of love."

       —JANICE DELANEY et al., *The Curse*

In keeping with the new de-sexist thinking, a woman in Menlo Park, Calif., asked one of her children to "go out to the person box and see if the person person has brought us any person."

       —MRS. STANLEY SCOTT, quoted by Herb Caen in San Francisco *Chronicle*

On a visit to Grandpa's farm in Vermont, we were treated to a lesson in Yankee speech when we came upon Grandpa helping our young daughter write a letter to a friend. "Yes," we heard him say. "The word 'idear' is pronounced with an 'r'—but when you write it, the 'r' is silent."

       —GENEVIEVE EAGLE

Various words as they are used by Texans:

   Watt is the lightest of colors: "Yew look watt as a sheet." *Pour* is having little or no means of support: "Them folks is downriot pour." *Ward* is a unit of language: "Pardon me, could ah have a ward with yawl?" *Owe* is an overwhelming feeling of reverence: "There's one thang I stand in owe of."

   And *thank:* "Ah hope yawl enjoyed raidin' this book. But jes thank of what yew must sound làck to a Texan."

       —JIM EVERHART, *The Illustrated Texas Dictionary*

PLAINS ENGLISH—OR HOW TO UNDERSTAND THE CARTER ADMINISTRATION

Binniss: As in, "What I do at the awfiss, that's binniss—what I do on mah own time—that's my binniss."

Code (low temperature): "It wuz so code the worlves wuz eatin' sheep just for the wool."

The Southern gennamin complained to the doctor in Plains: "Ah got some problems with mah sleepin'." The Doc said, "That's a common complaint these days—how many hours do you lose in the average night?" He said, "Oh, no—ah sleep good nights and purty good mornings —but afternoons ah just toss and turn."

       —*Washington Star*

I try not to make what I am called a big matter, but people kept calling me and asking, "How do you want to be addressed?" Well I decided if a title counts so much in Washington, I want to be "Chair." Chairwoman is sexist, chairman is too sexist, and chairperson is a title men refuse to use.

       —ELEANOR HOLMES NORTON

Although the North American Indians had no written alphabet before they met the white man, their language was anything but primitive. The vocabulary of many Indian nations was as large as that of their French and English exploiters, and often far more eloquent. Compare the coldness of "friend" with "one-who-carries-my-sorrows-on-his-back."
> —JAMES E. MILORD, *United Church Observer*

In language, gender is particularly confusing.

Why, please, should a table be male in German, female in French, and castrated in English?

Even more startling is the fact that the French give the feminine gender to the components of the male anatomy that make him male, and the male gender to the components of the female anatomy that make her a female.
> —MARLENE DIETRICH, *ABC's*

What those who use *ize* overlook is that it is usually unnecessary, and always dull.

To *ize* a word is one thing. To *wise* it is another. Senator Birch Bayh of Indiana, campaigning said, "*energywise, economywise,* and *environmentalwise,* we have become obsessed with the problems."

The Wall Street Journal reporter spoke of the Democrats as a *factionalized* party.

A television news broadcaster announced that a deputy sheriff, killed in the line of duty, would be *funeralized* the following day.

The Reverend Allison Cheek, ordained in the Episcopal church: "I will not let the church inferiorize me again."

Sometimes I seem to hear thousands of voices raised in song:
I fell in love with you
First time I looked into
Them there *ize.*
> —EDWIN NEWMAN, *A Civil Tongue*

Neither can his mind be thought to be in tune, whose words do jarre; nor his reason in frame, whose sentence is preposterous.
> —BEN JONSON

Several years ago, Louis Sukofsky explained: "If you want me to understand, you'd better speak in a different anguish."

... We concoct books that all speak the same anguish. It is lumpensincere.

I quote George Orwell—"The great enemy of clear language is insincerity."

We wear sincerity now instead of combat boots; it tramps like a defeated army in one ear and out the other, across a shallow brain-pan: confessional gush.

There is (from Spain) a proverb: "Spanish is the language for lovers,

Italian for singers, French for diplomats, German for horses, and English for geese." I hear a lot of honking in the vicinity of the best-seller list.
        —JOHN LEONARD, "The Literary View," *NYT*

As the founder of New York's highly successful newspaper, the *Tribune,* Horace Greeley, a dedicated journalist, had one peculiarity: He was convinced that the word *news* was plural. Though his staff disagreed, he was adamant.
        Once, while traveling, Greeley sent a telegram to the home office which asked, "ARE THERE ANY NEWS?"
        A reporter responded, "NOT A NEW."

My equation is sufficiently complex to admit of various outcomes.
        —EDMUND BROWN, governor of California, when asked if he
            was a presidential candidate

It helps to develop a distinctive style, and the worse your handwriting is and the more cryptic your style, the better, since it will then be necessary for your subordinates to decipher what you've written, and ponder about what you really mean.
        —MICHAEL KORDA, *Success*

It's always seemed to me that black people's grace has been with what they do with language. In Lorrain, Ohio, when I was a child, I went to school with and heard the stories of Mexicans, Italians, and Greeks, and I listened. I remember their language, and a lot of it is marvelous. But when I think of things my mother or father or aunts used to say, it seems the most absolutely striking thing in the world.
        —TONI MORRISON, author

The English are a great people for clipping their words, for making one syllable do the work of two or three. For instance, if an American were dining with a British lady of quality and he wanted the Worcestershire sauce, he would say, "Lady Ursula, could I trouble you for the Worcestershire sauce?" but an Englishman would say, "Lady Ursula, pass the Woosh."
        —FRANK SULLIVAN, *A Visit to London*

The *man* in manager, management, manuscript, manufacture, and manifest comes from the Latin *manus,* meaning hand. The *man* in mandate derives from the Latin *mandare,* in command. *Manhattan* comes from a proto-Algonquin word *Menahanwi,* meaning island, and *human* comes from the Latin *humanus,* which goes back to an Indo-European root meaning earthling. I'd be glad to concede maniacal to males, but it happens that the Greek *mania* means madness, which is found in members of both sexes. That leaves us only man-of-war, a warship or a jellyfish capable of inflicting severe injury. That *man* undenia-

bly comes from the word meaning adult male human being—and I'd be content to leave it that way.
—ALMA GRAHAM, editor, author

It is no accident that the -ette form used to mean female in majorette is also used to mean small or diminutive in kitchenette and to mean imitation in leatherette.
—ALMA GRAHAM

Joe (Cigar) Jacobs (also Yussel the Muscle) in 1935 came up with his greatest line. He had gotten up out of a sickbed to attend what all good Ring Lardner characters called "The World Serious" in Detroit, betting heavily on the Chicagos. The Detroits won, and on his return the disgruntled Yussel qualified for the Losers' Hall of Fame with: "I should of stood in bed."
—TOM MCMORROW, *Daily News*

Man does not live by words alone, despite the fact that sometimes he has to eat them.
—ADLAI STEVENSON

She was not a woman of many words; for, unlike people in general, she proportioned them to the number of her ideas.
—JANE AUSTEN

The word *lady* is used correctly only as follows:
a. To refer to certain members of the English aristocracy.
b. In reference to girls who stand behind lingerie counters in department stores, but only when preceded by the word *sales.*
c. To alert a member of the gentle sex to the fact that she is no longer playing with a full deck. As in, "Lady, what are you—nuts or something?"
d. To differentiate between girls who put out and girls who don't. Girls who put out are tramps. Girls who don't are ladies. This is, however, a rather archaic usage of the word. Should one of you boys happen upon a girl who doesn't put out, do not jump to the conclusion that you have found a lady. What you have probably found is a lesbian.
—FRAN LEBOWITZ, *Metropolitan Life*

James A. H. Murray thought of the English language as something celestial—swirling, nebulous, with a bright density of words at the center and others flying off toward the margins of space and time. He came at last to regard the *Oxford English Dictionary* as "a great abyss that will never cry 'Enough.'" Out of that chaos he fashioned one of the monuments of English-speaking civilization.
—LANCE MORROW, *Time*

I never write *Metropolis* for seven cents because I can get the same price for *city.* I never write *policeman* because I can get the same money for *cop.*
　　　—MARK TWAIN

Rhoda Jenkins, an alumna of the University of Pennsylvania and a great-great granddaughter of Elizabeth Cady Stanton, has been sparring with representatives of her alma mater for a number of years. Taking strong exception to fund-raising letters that address her as "Dear Alumnus," she finally began to return them to the male president with a note beginning "Dear Madam."
　　　—CASEY MILLER and KATE SWIFT, *Words and Women*

We must use words as they are used or stand aside from life.
　　　—IVY COMPTON-BURNETT, novelist

American English came of age long ago as a written and spoken language. Its intrinsic sounds are as beautiful and effective as any English anywhere and, like a rich mother lode, it is ours for the digging.
　　　—DOROTHY URIS, *A Woman's Voice*

1856—"She has canceled all her social engagements."
1880—"She is in an interesting condition."
1895—"She is in a delicate condition."
1910—"She is knitting little booties."
1920—"She is in a family way."
1935—"She is expecting."
1956—"She's pregnant."
[1970—"None of your business."]
　　　—HARRY GOLDEN, *For 2¢ Plain*

The Democratic Speaker [of the House of Representatives] Tip O'Neill's forthright and fearless decision to change the name of the time Congress goes out of session from the lackadaisical "recess" to the dynamic "district work period" deserves the approbation of euphemists around the world.
　　　—WILLIAM SAFIRE, *NYT*

INCIDENT

Once riding in old Baltimore,
　Heart-filled, head-filled with glee,
I saw a Baltimorean
　Keep looking straight at me.

Now I was eight and very small,
  And he was no whit bigger,
And so I smiled, but he poked out
  His tongue and called me, "Nigger."

I saw the whole of Baltimore
  From May until December:
Of all the things that happened there
  That's all that I remember.

  —COUNTEE CULLEN

One last four-letter word for Lenny [Bruce].
Dead.
At forty.
That's obscene.
  —DICK SCHAAP

Brand a slang word or phrase as a fashion, and it is doomed to rapid extinction; call attention to its usefulness, and it will incorporate itself among the linguistic evergreens within a year.
  —ERIC PARTRIDGE

How about *copout,* that most useful slang term that can stand in for: *shirking one's duty, circumventing obligation, untrustworthiness, irresponsibility,* but *copout* says it shorter and possibly sweeter.
  —DOROTHY URIS, *A Woman's Voice*

We all know that the preferred term is *correctional facility* instead of *prison.* But did you know that now it's *behavior adjustment unit* (BAU for short) instead of *solitary confinement?*
  —KYW-TV

At Rutgers University the faculty does not file a grievance, it "institutes a problem-solving procedure."
  —FACULTY MEMO, Rutgers University

The people at Hahnemann Hospital [Philadelphia] wearing the insignia of the "Vertical Transportation Corps" are the elevator operators.
  —*Philadelphia Inquirer*

In Denmark it gets cold, so we don't stick our tongues out unless we're certain we can get them back in again.
  —VICTOR BORGE, explaining why his countrymen have trouble
   pronouncing the English *th*

Now why did you name your baby John? Every Tom, Dick, and Harry is named John.
> —SAM GOLDWYN

Man uses his brainpower at only about one-fourth capacity. I believe that people similarly use their power to communicate at no more than about one-fifth capacity: We often just stand there, face expressionless, arms hanging slack, eyes stationary, voice droning out language noises, getting neither at nor into each other the message to be communicated. We are disembodied voices; our bodies are only somnolent casings of skin, hair, flesh, and bone.
> —CARL CRONEBERG

When existing phrases didn't suffice, Diana Vreeland invented her own, as in "the beautiful people." When an existing word didn't say "it" she made one up. One word she invented, now defined in Webster's as "the quality of being exciting . . ." is credited to "origin unknown." But Webster's didn't check well enough. Vreeland herself made up the word that's quintessentially Vreeland: *pizzazz.*
> —*MS*

To the degree that people's names are a part of themselves, giving them up, no matter how willingly, is tantamount to giving up some part of personal, legal, and social autonomy. And through the transience and fragmentation that have characterized women's names, some part of the human female self-image has been sacrificed.
> —CASEY MILLER and KATE SWIFT, *Words and Women*

My humble spelling volume, like a star, casts its beams equally upon the peasant and the monarch.
> —NOAH WEBSTER, on his spelling book which sold 70 million
>   copies

A moth is not a moth in mother
Nor both in bother, broth in brother;
And here is not a match for there
Nor dear and fear for bear and pear;
And then there's dose and rose and lose
Just look them up and goose and choose,
And cork and work and card and ward
And front and font and word and sword,
And do and go and thwart and cart.

Come, come I've hardly made a start:
A dreadful language? Man alive,
I'd mastered it when I was five!

> —"A Rhyming Word" in *Manchester Guardian*

LAW

The Wicked Life and Woeful Death of the Beautiful Miss Rebecca Kannady who most inhumanly murdered her husband, John Cotton, Esq., in 1803.

... As the same luxuriant soil often sustains the vital cauliflower and the deadly henbane [it] nursed also Rebecca Kannady. . . .

After having played off all her light artillery aforesaid such as *new gowns* and *ribbons* etc., until she had gotten on the shady side of twenty, she was courted by Mr. Cotton. . . .

... Oh young men! Young women, draw nigh! . . . learn the lesson which pulpits so often have preached in vain. Oh! Learn the madness of those who prefer the Creature's to the Creator's love. . . .

... In short Mrs. Cotton came off clear; nay, more than clear, she came off conqueror . . . she stood at the bar in tears, with cheeks like rosebuds wet with morning dew, and rolling her eyes of living sapphires pleading for pity. . . .

Quoth one of the jury . . . "A murderer, sir! 'Tis false. Such an angel could never have been a murderer."

For which horrid act God permitted her, in the prime of life and bloom of beauty, to be cut off [with a rock] by her brother Stephan Kannady May 5, 1807.

    —PARSON M. L. WEEMS (1823)

Sir, the law is as I say it is . . . we have several set forms which are held as law, and so held and used for good reason, though we cannot at present remember that reason.

    —JOHN FORTESCUE, chief justice of the King's Bench (1458)

And some of the old language of law is beautiful, like the sonorous, majestic King James translation of the Bible.

For example, my favorite legalese is "anything herein to the contrary notwithstanding." Such phrasing excites delectation, its lilt evoking an ancient minuet, its rhythm comparable to e. e. cummings's "with up so floating many bells down."

    —WILLIAM SAFIRE, *NYT*

[Lawyers and judges have] a peculiar cant and jargon of their own, that no other mortal can understand.

    —JONATHAN SWIFT, *Gulliver's Travels*

At the pens of judges, "all the more" becomes "a fortiori," "above" is stretched to "heretofore" and a routine landlord-tenant dispute is elevated into a controversy between the "petitioner-landlord-appellant" and "the respondent-tenant-respondent."
—*N.Y. Law Journal*

Perhaps I could never succeed in intelligibly defining it [obscenity], but I know it when I see it.
—JUSTICE POTTER STEWART

One high-ranking judge tells of the time that he arrived late to a funeral. The first man he saw was Hugo Black, controversial Supreme Court Judge. Black was only present because he was expected to be; in fact, he'd always felt a dislike for the dead man.

The tardy guest tiptoed over to Black and asked him, "How far has the service gone?"

Black muttered to the other judge, "They just opened the defense."

At a trial for assault, a woman witness, who happened to be a carpenter, was being browbeaten by a lawyer.

"What distance were you from the parties when you saw the defendant strike the plaintiff?" she was asked.

"Exactly four feet and one inch," she replied.

"How is it possible," sneered the lawyer, "of you to be so very exact as to the distance?"

"To tell the truth," said the carpenter, "I thought perhaps some fool would ask me, and so I measured the distance."
—ADAPTED FROM LOUIS UNTERMEYER, ed., *Great Humor*

The motorist had always been law-abiding, but she tangled with a traffic officer. She claimed the policeman was wrong, one word led to another, and the motorist called the officer a jackass.

That landed her before a judge, who admonished, "You just can't go around calling police officers jackasses."

"Very well, Your Honor," said the motorist. "But would it be all right if I called a jackass a policeman?"

The judge said he didn't see how that would violate the law.

As the motorist was leaving the courtroom, she turned to the arresting officer. "Good-bye, policeman," she said cheerily.
—RALPH WOODS, *Third Treasury of the Familiar*

A witness kept answering questions with, "Well, I think . . ."

"Don't think, Madam," interrupted the lawyer. "Tell us what you know, not what you think."

"Well, I'm not a lawyer," she shot back. "I can't talk without thinking."

The makers of our Constitution undertook to secure conditions favorable to the pursuit of happiness. . . . They conferred, as against the government, the right to be let alone—the most comprehensive of rights and the right most valued by civilized men. To protect that right, every unjustifiable intrusion by the government upon the privacy of the individual, whatever the means employed, must be deemed a violation of the Fourth Amendment.
—JUSTICE LOUIS D. BRANDEIS

The law professor was lecturing on courtroom strategy. "In arguing a case, if you have the facts on your side, hammer on those facts. If you have the law on your side, hammer on that."
"What if you have neither?" asked a student.
"In that event," advised the professor, "hammer on the table."

Colonel Compromise is the best and cheapest lawyer.
—*The Viking Book of Aphorisms*

The law and the stage—both are a form of exhibitionism.
—ORSON WELLES

Let the fact be accepted that there is nothing to be ashamed of in a woman's organization, and let her whole education and life be guided by the divine requirements of her system.
—SUPREME COURT (1908)

To the five women impaneled on a jury in Wyoming:
You shall not be driven by the sneers, jeers, and insults of a laughing crowd from the temple of justice as your sisters have from medical colleges of the land. The strong hand of the law will protect you.
—JUDGE JOHN HOWE (1870)

Lawyers, I suppose, were children once.
—CHARLES LAMB

On a questionnaire from a federal agency, the last question was to "state the names and addresses of all professional employees broken down by sex."
The office manager replied, "None—our principal problem is alcoholism."
—NEW YORK CITY BAR ASSOCIATION

Words importing the masculine gender shall always include women, except where otherwise stated.
—THE ENGLISH LAW KNOWN AS LORD BROUGHAM'S ACT (1850)

The fervor and human feelings of Sacco and Vanzetti gave the glow of life to the weary stock phrases of those writing about them, and we do know now, all of us, that the most appalling cruelties are committed by apparently virtuous governments in expectation of a great good to come, never learning that the evil done now is the sure destroyer of the expected good. Yet no matter what, it was a terrible miscarriage of justice; it was a most reprehensible abuse of legal power.

—KATHERINE ANNE PORTER, *The Never-Ending Wrong*

I had rather take my chance that some traitors will escape detection than spread abroad a spirit of general suspicion and distrust, which accepts rumor and gossip in place of undismayed and unintimidated inquiry.

—JUDGE LEARNED HAND (1952)

"These," said [the lawyer] Pleydell, showing his fine collection of classical authors, "are my tools of trade. A lawyer without history or literature is a mechanic, a mere working mason; if he possesses some knowledge of these he may venture to call himself an architect."

—W. H. DAVENPORT, ed., *Voices in Court*

A lawsuit is not a scientific investigation for the discovery of truth, but a proceeding to determine the basis for, and to arrive at a settlement of, a dispute between litigants.

Truth, that is, the true facts, is only an ingredient of justice, which is something larger than truth and far more difficult to attain.

—PROF. EDMUND M. MORGAN

Where would Christianity be if Jesus got eight to ten years with time off for good behavior?

—N.Y. STATE SEN. JAMES H. DONOVAN, arguing for capital
    punishment

In the new code of laws which I suppose it will be necessary for you to make I desire you would remember the ladies and be more generous and favorable to them than your ancestors.

—ABIGAIL ADAMS, in a letter to her husband (1776)

In the Matter of the Motion to Admit Miss Levina Goodall to the Bar (1875):

Discussions are habitually necessary in courts of justice, which are unfit for female ears. The habitual presence of women at these would tend to relax the public sense of decency and propriety. If, as counsel threatened, these things are to come, we will take no voluntary part in bringing them about.

By the Court—The motion is denied.

—A. L. SAINER, *The Judge Chuckles*

One of the best jobs in the world for a pregnant woman would be a position on the Supreme Court. The work is sedentary and the clothing is loose-fitting.
—REP. PATRICIA SCHROEDER

LIFE AND DEATH

How often [writing] takes the ache away, takes time away,—I think in the end, there is no end, the thread frays rather than being cut.
—ROBERT LOWELL, in a letter to a fellow poet

Voltaire, forced to pay condolatory tribute to someone he hated, said: "I have just been informed that M.——— is dead. He was a staunch patriot, a talented writer, a loyal friend, a devoted husband and father—provided he is really dead."
—LOUIS KRONENBERGER, *The Cutting Edge*

We can plant wheat every year, but people who are starving die only once.
—FIORELLO H. LA GUARDIA

Our very hopes belied our fears,
  Our fears our hopes belied;
  We thought her dying when she slept,
  And sleeping when she died.
—THOMAS HOOD, "The Death-Bed"

The chief problem about death, incidentally, is the fear that there may be no afterlife—a depressing thought, particularly for those who have bothered to shave. Also, there is the fear that there is an afterlife but no one will know where it's being held. On the plus side, death is one of the few things that can be done as easily lying down.
—WOODY ALLEN, *Without Feathers*

Six feet of earth make us all of one size.
—ITALIAN PROVERB

LEAR: Why should a dog, a horse, a rat, have life,
And thou no breath at all. Thou'lt come no more,
Never, never, never, never, never.
—SHAKESPEARE, *King Lear,* to his dead daughter Cordelia

I remember emptying the room at one party at which, having listened to a great deal of monkey talk about old people, I delivered myself of an epigram. "Well," I said, rubbing my hands, "I have one consolation. You are all going to die."
—GILBERT MILLSTEIN, *Grey Power Blues*

I received an invitation from her that read like a command: "Madame Sarah Bernhardt expects you, on such and such a day, for lunch."
. . . I record here, with respect, one of the last poses of this great tragic actress, then about to reach her eightieth year: the delicate and withered hand offering the brimming cup, the flowery azure of the eyes, so young still in their network of fine lines, the questioning and mocking coquetry of the tilted head, and that indestructible desire to charm, to charm still, to charm right up to the gates of death itself.
—COLETTE, *Earthly Paradise*

Senator Chauncey Depew was a likable man and had many admirers. His friends once arranged a dinner party for him, at which his praises were sung all evening long. Then Depew was asked to say a few words himself.
The senator was not one to mince words. He rose and said with a smile, "It's pleasant to hear these nice words while I'm still alive. I'd rather have the taffy than the epitaphy."

Who must die must die in the dark, even though he sells candles.
—COLOMBIAN PROVERB

A man called on his minister, "Dr. Clark, I should like to inform you that it is my wish to be cremated when I die."
"Son," replied the reverend doctor, "if that's your desire, it shall be done. Where would you like your ashes to be placed?"
"If you please, sir," replied the man, "in Bloomingdale's."
"In Bloomingdale's!" exclaimed Dr. Clark, "but why?"
"Well, sir, if you deposit my ashes in the cemetery, my wife will never get out there, but in Bloomingdale's. . . ."

When I kissed her, it was like kissing cold iron. Whenever I touch cold iron the feeling comes back to me—the feeling of my mother's face, iron cold, and granulated.
—VIRGINIA WOOLF, *Moments of Being*

The last words of Gertrude Stein:
What is the question? . . . What is the question? . . .
If there is no question, there is no answer.
The last words of Elinor Wylie:
Is that all it is?
    —From the *Dictionary of Last Words*

Happy birthday. PS—If you keep having birthdays, you'll eventually die.
Love, Groucho.
    —GROUCHO MARX to a good friend

After the game the king and pawn go into the same box.
    —ITALIAN PROVERB

Be,
Beget
Begone.
    —JACK BENNY

His tongue is now a stringless instrument.
    —SHAKESPEARE, *Richard II*

We usually meet all our relatives only at funerals where someone always
observes, "Too bad we can't get together more often."
    —SAM LEVENSON

MOTHER'S FUNERAL

We took our seats in the black motorhearse. Poupette sat [with] the driver,
and I, at the back, next to a kind of metal locker.
    "Is she there?" asked my sister. "Yes." She gave a short sob: "The only
comfort I have," she said, "is that it will happen to me too. Otherwise it
would be too unfair."
    Yes. We were taking part in the dress rehearsal for our own bur-
ial.
    —SIMONE DE BEAUVOIR, *A Very Easy Death*

. . . I know now and knew then, that no dog is fond of dying, but I never
had a dog that showed a human fear of death, either. Death to a dog is
the final unavoidable compulsion, the least ineluctable scent on a fear-
some trail, but they like to face it alone, going out into the woods, among
the leaves, if there are any leaves when their time comes, enduring
without sentimental human distraction the Last Loneliness, which they
are wise enough to know cannot be shared by anyone.
    —JAMES THURBER, in Burton Bernstein, *Thurber, A Biography*

Sometime in her last year, Martha Washington burned all of the letters George had written to her over the past forty years. She would not allow his intimacies and secrets to be subjected to public scrutiny.

On May 22, 1802, on the seventeenth day of a severe fever, Martha requested the last sacraments from her minister. Calling for the white gown she had laid aside for the occasion, she spoke in a strong voice to her assembled grandchildren and other relatives concerning the great value of religion, the need for attention to practical duties, and the absolute importance of doing well for others. Her sermon finished and her bedclothes neatly arranged, she lay back on her pillow and closed her eyes. A few hours later, at noon, she died quietly in her sleep.

    —PAUL ENGLE, *Women in the American Revolution*

Make sure to send a lazy man for the Angel of Death.

    —YIDDISH PROVERB

LITTLE ELEGY

Without you
No rose can grow;
No leaf be green
If never seen
Your sweetest face;
No bird have grace
Or power to sing;
Or anything
Be kind, or fair,
And you nowhere.

      —ELINOR WYLIE

You can't weep for people who have left more in life than they have taken out.

. . .—*I love thee with the breath,*
Smiles, tears, of all my life!—and, if God choose,
I shall but love thee better after death.
    —ELIZABETH BARRET BROWNING, "How Do I Love Thee?"

She told me smilingly, "This *is* exaggerating the case!"—when I was warming her feet a few minutes before she died. . . .

    —ROBERT BROWNING

I leave you love. I leave you hope . . . I leave you racial dignity. . . .

    —MARY MCLEOD BETHUNE

. . . The smallest sprout shows there is really no death,
And if ever there was it led forward life, and does not wait
*   at the end to arrest it,*
And ceased the moment life appeared.
All goes onward and outward, nothing collapses,
And to die is different from what any one supposed, and
*   luckier.*

    —WALT WHITMAN, "Grass"

To weep overmuch for the dead is to affront the living.
    —ANON.

Tonight, France is a widow.
    —GEORGES POMPIDOU, on the death of Charles de Gaulle

    The body of
  Benjamin Franklin, printer,
  Like the cover of an old book,
    Its contents worn out
And stript of its lettering and gilding,
  Lies here food for the worms,
Yet the work itself shall not be lost,
    For it shall, as he believes,
      Appear once more,
        In a new
  And more beautiful edition,
  Corrected and amended
      By the Author.

Here lies I and my three daughters,
Killed by drinking Cheltenham
waters;
If we had stuck to epsom salts,
We'd not been a-lying in these here
vaults.

    —ANON., in Ralph L. Woods, *Third Treasury*
      of the Familiar

Thirteen years I was a virgin
* Two years I was a wife*
* One year I was a mother*
The next year took my life.
    —ANONYMOUS TOMBSTONE in Indiana

He lies below, correct in cypress wood,
And entertains the most exclusive worms.
 —DOROTHY PARKER, "The Very Rich Man"

GRAVESTONE EPITAPHS THAT NEVER WERE

"This is all over my head" (Robert Benchley); "This is just my lot" (Fredric March); "Here in nature's arms I nestle, Free at last from Georgie Jessel" (Eddie Cantor); "Pardon me for not getting up" (Ernest Hemingway).
 —*Working Woman*

A hypochondriac all her complaining adult life, Aunt Sue died. Inscribed on her tombstone were the words, *Now Will You Believe I Was Ill?*

Life is a jest
 and all things show it
I thought so once
 and now I know it.
 —JOHN GAY's epitaph
 (he wrote it for his own tomb)

ON A MUSIC TEACHER

Stephen and time
Are now both even:
Stephen beat time
Now time's beat Stephen
 —WILLARD ESPY,
 An Almanac of Words at Play

LOVE AND LOVING

An accomplished man before going out used to tie his wife's garter upon his breast, and could not bear to be absent from her a quarter of an hour; and this pair would never take a drink unless husband and wife alternately put their lips to the cup; and they did other things just as absurd in the extravagant outbursts of their warm but blind affection. Their love was of honorable birth, but it grew out of all proportion. . . . It is disgraceful to love another man's wife at all, or one's own too much. A wise man ought to love his wife with judgment, not with passion. There is nothing blacker than to love a wife as if she were an adulteress.

—SENECA

Love cannot be a duty because it is not subject to the will.

—BERTRAND RUSSELL

Him that I love, I wish to be free—even from me.

—ANNE MORROW LINDBERGH, *The Unicorn and Other Poems*

George Gershwin, pleased with himself, was once rhapsodizing about his latest musical score to some of his friends, among them dry-humored Oscar Levant.

Levant said nothing while Gershwin spoke. Then he asked, "George, if you had it to do over, would you fall in love with yourself again?"

ON SALT SPRINKLING

The Bird of Love, which lit
*   at our command,*
*   Too briefly halted.*
The moral? Keep the Shaker
*   close at hand,*
The Tail well salted.

—WILLARD R. ESPY, *Words at Play*

To a small layer of people it seems to be inconceivable that there should be a relationship between two women with love and comradeship and affection and care, which doesn't have any sexual basis. This is apparently considered rather suspect, as if this isn't possible. But it is.

—VANESSA REDGRAVE

But nothing came of anything. Oh there were cuddles in the backs of cars. And long drunken kisses in roachy New York kitchens over pitchers of warm martinis. And there were flirtations over fattening expense-account lunches. And pinches in the stacks of Butler Library. And embraces after poetry readings. And hand squeezes at gallery openings. . . . There were even some frank and open propositions (usually from men who didn't attract me at all). But nothing came of anything. I would go

home instead, and write poems to the man I really loved (whoever *he* might be).
—ERICA JONG, *Fear of Flying*

LILAC TIME

The lilacs are flowering, sweet and
  sublime
with a perfume that goes to the
  head;
and lovers meander, in prose and
  rhyme
trying to say—
  for the thousandth time—
what's easier done than said.

  —PIET HEIN

To be loved, certainly, is different from being admired, as one can be admired from afar, but to really love someone it is essential to be in the same room with the person, crouching behind the drapes.
—WOODY ALLEN, *Without Feathers*

Once the realization is accepted that even between the closest human beings infinite distances continue to exist, a wonderful living side by side can grow up, if they succeed in loving the distance between them which makes it possible for each to see the other whole against the sky.
—RAINER MARIA RILKE, *Letters: 1910–1926*

Platonic love is love from the neck up.
—THYRA SAMTER WINSLOW

WHY SO PALE AND WAN?

Why so pale and wan, fond lover?
  Prithee why so pale?
Will, when looking well can't move her,
  Looking ill prevail?
  Prithee why so pale?

Why so dull and mute, young sinner?
  Prithee why so mute?
Will, when speaking well can't win her,
  Saying nothing do't?
  Prithee why so mute?

Quit, quit, for shame; this will not move,
  This cannot take her;
If of herself she will not love,

Nothing can make her:
The devil take her!

    —SIR JOHN SUCKLING

"Mockery murders love," they say—and she
  Laughed in my face last night and slammed the door
I swore to go and stay away. But see,
  That was last night. And here I am once more.

    —ANON.

Love is a smoke raised with the fume of sighs;
Being purged, a fire sparkling in lovers' eyes;
Being vex'd, a sea nourish'd with lovers' tears:
What is it else? a madness most discreet,
A choking gall and persevering sweet.

    —SHAKESPEARE, *Romeo and Juliet*, II, 1

Frederic Chopin worried that his love for Delphine Potocka was bad for
his music. "Who knows what ballades, polonaises, perhaps an entire
concerto, have been forever engulfed in your little D-flat major?" (D-flat
major was "their code for the female organ, possibly because D-flat is the
black key between two white keys C and D.")

    —ANTONIA FRASER, *Love Letters*

ECHO

I asked of Echo, t'other day
  (Whose words are often few and funny),
What to a novice she could say
  Of courtship, love, and matrimony.
  Quoth Echo plainly,—"Matter-o'-money!"

    —JOHN G. SAXE

OUT OF SIGHT, OUT OF MIND

The oft'ner seen, the more I lust,
  The more I lust, the more I smart,
  The more I smart, the more I trust,
  The more I trust, the heavier heart,
The heavy heart breeds mine unrest,
Thy absence therefore I like best.

    —BARNABY GOOGE

He gave her a look you could have poured on a waffle.

    —RING LARDNER

... [E]very man has reserved a special place in his mind for the one woman he will elevate above the rest by virtue of association with himself.

Love between two equals would be an enrichment, each enlarging [one]self through the other. ... This accounts for the bliss that successful lovers experience: Lovers are temporarily freed from the burden of isolation that every individual bears.
—SHULAMITH FIRESTONE, *The Dialectic of Sex*

How do you know that love is gone? If you said you would be there by seven, you get there by nine, and he or she has not called the police yet —it's gone.
—MARLENE DIETRICH, *ABC's*

It was hard to tell whether the papas and mamas of that era were happily married. The subject was not open for discussion, certainly not with their children.

"Are you happy, Ma?"

"I got nothing else to think about?"

"Love, shmove!" Papa used to say. "I love blintzes; did I marry one?" The word *love* embarrassed them. It was an unmentionable, like *brassiere, hernia,* and *miscarriage.*

"Love," said Mama after many years of marriage, "is what you have been through with someone." ...

Papa wouldn't spend a penny on himself unless Mama spent on herself. Share and share alike. So the day Mama had all her teeth pulled, Papa bought a suit.
—SAM LEVENSON, *In One Era & Out the Other*

Men have died from time to time and worms have eaten them, but not for love.
—ROSALIND IN SHAKESPEARE, *As You Like It,* IV, 1

Love for too many men in our time, consists of sleeping with a seductive woman, one who is properly endowed with the right distribution of curves and conveniences, and one upon whom a permanent lien has been acquired through the institution of marriage.
—ASHLEY MONTAGU, *The Natural Superiority of Women*

QUESTION: How do you distinguish love from like?

ANSWER: Love is the same as like except you feel sexier. And more romantic. And also more annoyed when he talks with his mouth full. And you also resent it more when he interrupts you. And you also respect him less when he shows any weakness. And furthermore, when you ask him to pick you up at the airport and he tells you that he can't do it because he's busy, it's only when you love him that you hate him.

QUESTION: What is the difference between an infatuation and love?

ANSWER: Infatuation is when you think that he's as sexy as Robert Redford, as smart as Henry Kissinger, as noble as Ralph Nader, as funny as Woody Allen, and as athletic as Jimmy Connors. Love is when you realize that he's as sexy as Woody Allen, as smart as Jimmy Connors, as funny as Ralph Nader, as athletic as Henry Kissinger, and nothing like Robert Redford—but you'll take him anyway.

> —JUDITH VIORST, *Redbook*

Our own little room, our own furniture, a library of our own, quiet and regular work, walks together, an opera from time to time, a small—very small—circle of intimate friends who can sometimes be asked to dinner, every year a summer departure to the country for a month but definitely free from work! . . . And perhaps even a little, a very little, baby?

> —ROSA LUXEMBURG, to her socialist comrade and lover, Leo Jogiches (1898)

In nine cases out of ten, a woman had better show more affection than she feels.

> —JANE AUSTEN

. . . [A]ssuredly, woman's autonomy, if it spares men many troubles, will also deny them many conveniences; assuredly there are certain forms of the sexual adventure which will be lost in the world of tomorrow. But this does not mean that love, happiness, poetry, dreams, will be banished from it.

> —SIMONE DE BEAUVOIR, *The Second Sex*

If the felicity of last night has had the same effect on your health as on my countenance, you have no cause to lament your failure of resolution; for I have seldom seen so much live fire running about my features as this morning when recollections—very dear, called forth the blush of pleasure, as I adjusted my hair.

> —MARY WOLLSTONECRAFT, in a letter to philosopher William Godwin (1796)

Absence is love's foe, far from the eyes, far from the heart.

> —SPANISH PROVERB

[I am opposed to] *any legal intervention* or *constraint* to prevent people from adjusting their love relations precisely as they do their religious affairs in this country, in complete personal freedom; changing and improving them from time to time, and according to circumstances.

> —VICTORIA WOODHULL (1872)

If an individual is able to love productively, he loves himself too; if he can love only others, he cannot love at all.

> —ERICH FROMM

There was once a maiden of Siam
Who said to her lover, young Kiam
If you kiss me, of course,
You will have to use force,
But God knows you are
Stronger than I am.
　　　—ANON.

What they call "heart" is located far lower than the fourth waistcoat button.
　　　—G. C. LICHTENBERG

Better by far you should forget and smile,
Than that you should remember and be sad.
　　　—CHRISTINA ROSSETTI, "A Birthday"

It is as absurd to say that man can't love one woman all the time as it is to say that a violinist needs several violins to play the same piece of music.
　　　—HONORÉ DE BALZAC

Love which is only an episode in the life of men, is the entire history of the life of women.
　　　—MADAME DE STAEL

It's not love's going hurts my days
But that it went in little ways.
　　　—EDNA ST. VINCENT MILLAY

Young Europeans used to turn to older women because any sexual contact with contemporaries was taboo. Young Americans are now said to be turning to older women just as access to their contemporaries has reached an unprecedented level of permissiveness. Could it be that the sheltering warmth of a (still partially taboo) Mrs. Robinson can be more mysterious and reassuring to some recent Graduates than the jovially available classmates in striped pajamas whom they encountered in the shared dorms of Yale, Wisconsin and Penn State? The vagaries of sexual liberation are indeed difficult to forecast.
　　　—FRANCINE DU PLESSIS GREY, *NYT*

Oh, what a dear ravishing thing is the beginning of an amour.
　　　—APHRA BEHN

Sure we hate. Sure there's hostility, open and buried everywhere. But that's not the whole story, and I doubt it's as much as half of it. That's the point. I think people love each other a little, more than they hate each

other, and that's why we can go on. In pairs and in families and in multitudes. Love has a slim hold on the human corporation, like 51 percent, but it's enough.
> —PETER DE VRIES, quoted by Peg Bracken, in *I Didn't Come Here to Argue*

Love is the greatest refreshment in life.
> —PABLO PICASSO, quoted by Janet Flanner, PBS

""!!!
•••

MARRIAGE

As I ever hope to drink wine or ale, I'll tell you the truth of the husbands that I have married, three were good and two were bad. The three good ones were rich and old; they could scarcely hold to the contract by which they were bound to me. You know very well what I mean by this, by God! So help me God, I laugh when I think how pitifully I made them work at night! And, by my faith, I gave them no credit for it. . . . But I managed them so well by my own rules that each of them was blissfully happy and glad to bring me gay things from the fair.
> —GEOFFREY CHAUCER, Wife of Bath's Prologue, *Canterbury Tales*

Suffolk Court Session of 28 January, 1672–1673

MERCY VEERING'S SENTANCE

Mercy Veering convict of uncivill carriage with Sammuel Smith, & bad language & carriage towards her husband, John Veering. The Court Sentanceth her to bee whip't with twenty Stripes & to pay Fees of Court standing committed while the Sentance bee performed. Upon her peticion the Court respites the Execucion of her Sentance till after her next delivery of Childe.

SAMM SMITH'S SENTANCE

Samuell Smith, convict of uncivill carriages to & too great familiarity with Mercy the wife of John Veering. The Court Sentanceth him to bee whip't with thirty Strip.
> —COLONIAL SOCIETY OF MASSACHUSETTS

By marriage, the husband and wife are one person in law; that is, the very being or legal existence of the woman is suspended during the marriage.
> —SIR WILLIAM BLACKSTONE, *Commentaries on the Law of England* (1765–1769)

His *Unseasonable Weakness,* may no doubt sometimes grieve you, but then set against this, that it giveth you the *Dominion.* You must be very dextrous, if when your *Husband* shall resolve to be an *Ass,* you do not take care he may be *your Ass.*
> —GEORGE SAVILE, Marquis of Halifax, The Lady's New Year's Gift, or, *Advice to a Daughter* (1688)

Where there's marriage without love, there will be love without marriage.
> —BENJAMIN FRANKLIN, *Poor Richard's Almanac* (1734)

You may believe me, my dear Patsy, when I assure you, in the most solemn manner that, so far from seeking this appointment, I have used every endeavor in my power to avoid it, not only from my unwillingness to part with you and the family, but from consciousness of its being a trust too great for my capacity, and that I should enjoy more real happiness in one month with you at home, than I have the most distant prospect of finding abroad, if my stay were to be seven times seven years.
> —GEORGE WASHINGTON to his wife, Martha, upon his appointment as commander in chief of the colonial armies (1775)

All are good maids, but whence come the bad wives?
> —ENGLISH PROVERB

The subordination of your sex to ours is enforced by nature, by reason, and by revelation. Of course it must produce the most happiness to both parties. Mr. B. [the intended husband], if he is like others of his sex, will often require unreasonable sacrifices of your will to his. If this should be the case, still honor and obey him. . . . The happiest marriages I have known have been those when the subordination I have recommended has been most complete.
> —DR. BENJAMIN RUSH, letters to a young woman about to be married (c. 1800)

Marriage is:
- A friendship recognized by the police.
  > —ROBERT L. STEVENSON

- Like buying something new you've been admiring for a long time in a shop window. You may love it when you get it home, but it doesn't always go with everything else in the house.
  > —ANON.

- A world-without-end bargain.
  > —SHAKESPEARE

- The most expensive way to get your laundry done.
  > —CHARLES JAMES

• Alas! another instance of the triumph of hope over experience.
—DR. SAMUEL JOHNSON

In America the independence of woman is irrecoverably lost in the bonds of matrimony: If an unmarried woman is less constrained there than elsewhere, a wife is subjected to stricter obligations. The former makes her father's house an abode of freedom and of pleasure; the latter lives in the home of her husband as if it were a cloister.

The women of America, who often exhibit a masculine strength of understanding and manly energy, generally preserve great delicacy of personal appearance and always retain the manners of women. . . . I do not hesitate to avow that, if I were asked, to what the singular prosperity and growing strength of this people ought mainly to be attributed, I should reply—to the superiority of their women.
—ALEXIS DE TOCQUEVILLE, *On American Woman and American Wives* (1830)

A rich bride goes young to the church.
—GERMAN PROVERB

Our fond lovers are now united; and, as the honeymoon is over, it becomes necessary for them to come down from their romance, and enter upon the sober duties of a married life.

It was not long, therefore, before her husband began to experience little annoyances, in consequence of her want of domestic knowledge. The wife still imagines that all the power and peculiar influence which she possessed over him in the sweetheart-state, must of right continue. From this false view, induced by the self-sacrificing devotion of the lover, much unhappiness flows when the sweetheart becomes the wife.

The sweeping and dusting were carelessly done, and the furniture, from want of attention, began to look a little dingy, much to the annoyance of Mrs. Fairfield. Still, it did not occur to her that she was wrong in leaving everything to her servants.

Too frequently he was kept from his store in the morning, half an hour later than business required him to be there, in consequence of breakfast not being ready. Whenever this happened, he usually hurried away without the parting kiss.

"I fear he does not love me!" the young wife would often say, bursting into tears, as she closed her chamber door after her, and sat down to weep in abandonment of feelings.
—T. S. ARTHUR, "Sweethearts and Wives," in *Godey's Lady's Book* (1841)

It is always incomprehensible to a man that a woman should ever refuse an offer of marriage.
—JANE AUSTEN

Mr. Collins proposes to Elizabeth Bennet:

"My reasons for marrying are, first, that I think it a right thing for every clergyman in easy circumstances (like myself) to set the example of matrimony in his parish; secondly, that I am convinced it will add very greatly to my happiness; and thirdly, . . . it is the particular advice and recommendation of the very noble lady whom I have the honour of calling patroness. Twice has she condescended to give me her opinion (unasked too!) on this subject. . . .

She said, 'Mr. Collins, you must marry. A clergyman like you must marry. Chuse properly, chuse a gentlewoman for *my* sake; and for your *own*, let her be an active, useful sort of person, not brought up high, but able to make a small income go a good way. This is my advice. Find such a woman as soon as you can, bring her to Hunsford, and I will visit her. . . .' "

Mrs. Bennet, Elizabeth's mother, in a dialogue with Mr. Collins, the minister, whom Elizabeth has refused.

"But depend upon it, Mr. Collins," she added, "that Lizzie shall be brought to reason. I will speak to her about it myself directly. She is a very headstrong, foolish girl, and does not know her own interest; but I will *make* her know it."

"Pardon me for interrupting you, madam," cried Mr. Collins: "but if she is really headstrong and foolish, I know not whether she would altogether be a very desirable wife to a man in my situation. . . . Perhaps it were better not to force her into accepting me, because if liable to such defects of temper, she could not contribute much to my felicity. . . ."

—JANE AUSTEN, *Pride and Prejudice*

I believe that the marriage institution, like slavery and monarchy, and many other things which have been good or necessary in their day, is now *effete,* and in a general sense injurious, instead of being beneficial to the community, although of course it must continue to linger until better institutions can be formed. I mean by marriage in this connection, any forced or obligatory tie.

—VICTORIA WOODHULL (1872)

Marriage has teeth, and him bite very hot.

—JAMAICAN PROVERB

Many a man lives by the sweat of his frau.

—ANON.

Wedlock: The deep, deep peace of the double bed after the hurly-burly of the chaise longue.

—MRS. PATRICK CAMPBELL

Masters believed, with some cause, that married slaves would make less trouble, would work harder, and were less likely to run away. They were also glad to see slave children born to add to their property.

Since slave marriages could always be dissolved by the sale of one of the parties, the words spoken never included the phrase "till death us do part," nor was any reference made to the inappropriate command that no man should put asunder whom God had joined together.

—LINDA DE PAUW and CONOVER HUNT, *Remember the Ladies*

Ah gentle dames! it gars me greet,
To think how mony counsels sweet,
How mony lengthened, sage advices,
The husband frae the wife despises!

—ROBERT BURNS, "Tam o'Shanter"

Doant thou marry for munny, but goa wheer munny is!

—ALFRED, LORD TENNYSON, "Northern Farmer, New Style"

You can't change a man, no-ways. By the time his mammy turns him loose and he takes up with some innocent woman and marries her, he's what he is. If it's his nature to set by the hearthfire and scratch hisself, you just as good to let him set and scratch. If it's his nature, like Will Dover, my man, to go to the garage in his Sunday clothes and lay down under some backwoods Cracker's old greasy Ford and tinker with it, you just as good to let him lay and tinker. And if it's his nature, like Uncle Benny, to prowl; if it's his nature to cut the fool; why, it's interfering in the ways of Providence even to stop to quarrel with him about it.

—MARJORIE KINNAN RAWLINGS, "Benny and the Bird Dogs," in
E.B. and Katherine S. White, eds., *Subtreasury of American Humor*

In the film of Hemingway's *For Whom the Bell Tolls,* Gary Cooper and Ingrid Bergman launch their brief but beautiful love affair with some tender writhings in a sleeping bag high in the Spanish pine forests.

"I feel as though I want to die when I am loving thee."

"Oh," she says, "I die each time. Do you not die?"

"No. Almost . . . but did thee feel the earth move?"

"Yes. As I died. . . ."

Pretty heady stuff. It is no wonder "the earth moved" became a kind of turn-on for Hemingway fans.

A couple of honeymooners in the South Pacific were in a queen-sized bed on the seventh floor of an expensive resort hotel. They were making the most of the unfamiliar novelty of waking up beside each other, when . . . THE EARTH MOVED!

Trouble was, it kept on moving for about half a minute, with windows rattling and the whole seventh floor waving to and fro on the air. It was the first earth tremor New Caledonia had experienced since around 1920. Not a big one, not at all high on the Richter scale, but still a moving little gesture toward the newlyweds.

—HELEN GORDON, *New Woman*

Let there be spaces in your togetherness.
> —KAHLIL GIBRAN, *The Prophet*

When Sartre, on the brink of old age, fell in love with a much younger woman and wanted to marry her, de Beauvoir, like any legal spouse, considered it a violation of their [nonmarriage] contract. Sartre kept this last, particular triangle whole by legally adopting his young mistress; he would make her his daughter and heiress—an arrangement that seemed to suit everyone concerned.
> —MAVIS GALLANT, review of *The Common Journey of Simone de Beauvoir and Jean-Paul Sartre*

He prepared for months—running six miles daily. Finally he entered the twenty-six-mile contest and made it to the finish line. He limped to the telephone to call his wife. "Honey," she said, "would you pick up a loaf of bread and some milk on your way home?"
> —JOE URIS

Ilo Wallace told me that on the day of their marriage, Henry's father, who had been secretary of agriculture under both Harding and Coolidge, had given them a wedding present of a new Ford. She and Henry came out of the church after the ceremony, and Henry was so pleased with the sight of the Ford that he ignored the kissers and congratulators, went immediately to the car, and drove off. It was thought odd, but people said he was testing it for her comfort until a half hour passed, and then another. Toward late afternoon he returned, and called out from the driver's seat, "Get in, Ilo, I'd forgotten you."
> —LILLIAN HELLMAN, *Scoundrel Time*

When I first met my wife, she was a schoolteacher. I used to write her passionate love letters—and she'd send them back corrected. I must be the only man in the world who returned from his honeymoon and received a report card. It said: "Dick is neat and friendly and shows a keen interest in fun and games."
> —DICK LORD, comedian

One college president boasted that before hiring a new faculty or administrative staff member, he insisted on having breakfast with the candidate's family. It was his judgment that if the wife "didn't fix her husband a good breakfast," the man "wasn't a good risk."
> —ROBERT SEIDENBERG, *Corporate Wives—Corporate Casualties*

So you are with the army now! . . . Although no serviceman's career was ever *made* by his wife, many have been hindered or helped by the social skills of their wives, their flexibility, and their loyalty toward the army and its customs. . . . As an army wife, never forget that you are the "silent" member of the team, but a key "man." You belong to a strong team that has never lost a war (if you think we lost in Vietnam, ask some West Pointers), so take pride in the aims and ideals of the U.S. Army. . . . Marriage is the most important legal agreement you will ever make.

—*The Army Wife,* a book given by the U.S. Army to brides before their military weddings

I can't believe more relationships wouldn't survive if bedroom sharing were an elective rather than the required course. As children we dreamed of gaining the life stage of having our own rooms and our own things and we all wrote angry cardboard signs which read "PRIVAT—KEPE OUT AND THIS MEANS U!" So where is it written that having successfully attained adulthood, we no longer have that same need for privacy?

—LINDA BIRD FRANCKE, "Hers,"

If your changing your name proved your love for your partner, then American women love their husbands, while American men don't love their wives. On the other hand, it would mean that Egyptian, Chinese, and Icelandic couples do not love each other at all since their tradition is for the women to keep their own names. Russian women are given a choice, so the returns would be mixed. And Spanish-speaking women keep their own names but add the husband's name at the end. Changing the name is only a matter of tradition, not an act of love.

—*New Woman*

When a lady returned from Big Moose,
Her husband exclaimed, "What the deuce!
  I am quite reconciled
  To the call of the wild,
But where did you get the papoose?"

A ghoulish old fellow in Kent
Encrusted his wife in cement;
  He said, with a sneer,
  "I was careful, my dear,
To follow your natural bent."

—E.B. and KATHERINE S. WHITE, eds., *Subtreasury of American Humor*

Apparently men rarely dream about getting married. Well, that figures. Women have a magazine called *Bride,* but there's no magazine for men called *Groom.*

—MARY REINHOLZ

Some pray to marry the man they love,
  My prayer will somewhat vary:
I humbly pray to Heaven above
  That I love the man I marry.
  —ROSE PASTOR STOKES, "My Prayer"

It is true that I never should have married, but I didn't want to live without a man. Brought up to respect the conventions, love had to end in marriage. I'm afraid it did.
  —BETTE DAVIS, *The Lonely Life*

Rodney Dangerfield claims that he and his wife are trying a new approach: "We sleep in separate rooms, we have dinner apart, we take separate vacations—we're doing everything we can to keep our marriage together."
  —EARL WILSON, Field Newspaper Syndicate

A bachelor fed his requirements for the perfect partner into the dating computer. "I want a companion who is small and attractive, loves water sports, is fond of seafood, and enjoys group activities." Back came the answer: "Marry a penguin."
  —*New Woman*

Her father plays to a serviceable 18 handicap. Her mother has a lovely compact back swing and plays a rock-steady game. She once hit into the rough in 1936, found it a bad place to be and has never been back. . . . I had, in view of her family, made certain assumptions. I had pictured the two of us setting sail down the fairway of our marriage, so to speak.
  The morning after we were married, I got up early and called to her as I was shaving. "Got to get up, darling. We have a 9 o'clock tee time."
  She looked at me coolly and said, "There are a lot of dumb things in the world, dear. But lashing away at a golf ball is the dumbest of them all. You can go out and play if you want to. I'm going to stay here in bed."
  I left our first marital chamber with hot cheeks and stumbled to an erratic 97.
  —PETER ANDREWS, "A Golfer's Lament," *NYT*

The amount of women who flirt with their own husbands is scandalous. It is simply washing one's clean linen in public.
  —OSCAR WILDE

The wife had suffered mosquito bites on fishing trips, become exhausted on hunting trips, frozen through football games, and sweltered through baseball games.
  "Why can't you be like other husbands," she pleaded with her spouse, "and refuse to take me any place?"
  —LEO AIKMAN, *Atlanta Constitution*

A newly married couple went to the doctor and asked him to prescribe a method of birth control with *no possibility* of failure.

He turned to them and said, "I have just the thing. Eat an apple."

The two were surprised and delighted. "As simple as that?" they asked. "Do we eat the apple before, or after?"

"Instead," said the doctor.

—JEANNETTE BRANIN, San Diego *Union*

Marriage resembles a pair of shears, so joined that they cannot be separated; often moving in opposite directions, yet always punishing anyone who comes between them.

—SYDNEY SMITH, in Ralph L. Woods, *Third Treasury of the Familiar*

An executive's wife should watch her figure and don't nag.

—A FORD MOTOR COMPANY EXECUTIVE

QUESTIONS FOR AMERICANS (FEMALE)

How many wives does your husband have?
My husband, he has three:
One at the office, one in dreams
And me.

How many wives does your husband have?
My husband, he has two:
The imagined woman he married and
The true.

How many wives does your husband have?
My husband, he has none:
He's wed to money. That makes less
Than one.

—MARYA MANNES, *Subverse*

To quote Yeats, *How else but in custom and ceremony are innocence and beauty born?* You marry to be worthy of a gift, and want to say so out loud, but without shouting. One doesn't shout a prayer. Marriage is one of the few ceremonies left to us about which it is impossible—or at least self-demeaning—to be cynical. Then, in secret, be joyful.

—JOHN LEONARD, *MS*

""!!!
...

MEDICINE

When people's ill, they come to I,
I physics, bleeds, and sweats 'em;
Sometimes they live, sometimes they die.
What's that to I? I lets 'em.
      —JOHN C. LETTSOM, "The Candid Physician"

She should be young, and vigorous, learned in her art, able to take all-night vigils, strong of arms and hands for difficult cases of turning and extraction.... She must have slender hands, long fingers, tender feelings, sympathy, be hopeful, and above all, silent.
      —AN EARLY EIGHTEENTH-CENTURY MANUAL for midwives
        describing the ideal midwife

I see now why all I have suffered in body and mind from my physician is worse than useless. I see now that I have never had the disease for which I have been treated. Is it not shocking that I should have suffered what was so needless, when my physician did or ought to have known better?
      —Catharine Beecher, *Letters to the People on Health and*
        Happiness (1855)

My whole life is devoted unreservedly to the service of my sex. The study and practice of medicine is but one means to that great end.... It was to my mind a moral crusade to break the sex barrier in medicine.
      —DR. ELIZABETH BLACKWELL, *Autobiographical Sketches* (1848)

Elizabeth Blackwell's New York Infirmary for Women and Children was dedicated on May 12, 1857—a historic first—a hospital for women staffed by women.

One of the first patients at the hospital, a woman in labor, subsequently died of puerperal fever. Within an hour a large crowd had gathered on Bleecker Street. The leaders pounded on the hospital door with their fists and demanded that the lady doctors stop killing innocent women.

The men were armed with pickaxes and shovels. The instant Elizabeth appeared on the front steps, the mob let out a howl of rage.

Suddenly, a brawny man in overalls pushed his way to the front, demanded silence—and called out, "They took good care of my wife and children," he told them. "They're fine ladies and they do the best they can."

Amazingly, the clamor subsided, and the crowd drifted back to their homes.

Dr. Blackwell and her associates did prove themselves. The New York Infirmary grew into a large and thriving hospital which today occupies a modern skyscraper on East Fifteenth Street.

—MARGARET TRUMAN, *Women of Courage*

A visit by the doctor: $1.25. Dental work including a gold crown and five gold fillings: $9.00.

—AUNT MARY'S LEDGER (1899–1903)

What I needed was some new doctors. I found them.

Shortly thereafter, I found myself in the office of one of the new doctors. He listened raptly to my heart as his feet danced a fast tango to its beat. For fear he might dismiss me as having nothing wrong, I confided that what I had was neurocirculatory aesthenia. To my delight he nodded his head. The symptoms, he told me, were a rapid heartbeat and pulse.

I asked if he could give me something for it. He wrote a prescription. At the first drugstore, I was about to hand it to the pharmacist when I read what the doctor had written:

"You have no organic abnormality of the heart, no feeling of breathlessness is dangerous, nothing bad will happen to you." And he had the nerve to sign it. I tore it to shreds and ordered a tube of toothpaste—small size. I knew now I wasn't going to last long.

—GOODMAN ACE, *The Fine Art of Hypochondria*

"If you were marooned on a desert island with a man for the rest of your life, what man would you choose?"

The woman's reply: "The world's finest obstetrician."

Dr. Beall was a homeopath, with idiosyncrasies of his own—a believer in a heavy meal three times a day, a little whiskey to regulate the heart, a cheerful disposition to relax the system, and a sane moderation in exercise and bathing, either of which could kill a man if he didn't watch out. His ancient black medical bag held, in neat rows, dozens of phials containing white pills and powders that looked exactly the same. Coal oil, of course, could be drawn from a lamp in any house in the old days, and next to one on a table in his office he kept a teaspoon, a tablespoon, and a wineglass, and he would fill one or another of them with kerosene, depending on the severity of a patient's ailment. He often took a slug of the stuff himself, and he confounded those who predicted it would kill him by living to be almost ninety.

Old Sam (a neighbor) would have no part of it. When he lay dying, he refused a tablespoonful of lamp oil held to his lips. "I'd ruther die like a man than live like a lamp," he said, and he died like a man.

—JAMES THURBER, *Thurber Album*

There will be a corresponding demystification of medicine in society at large. That means no more doctor as Great White Father, whether kindly or stern—and no more patient as reluctant or willing child. The dashing Dr. Kildares, with their air of secret knowledge and special favor, will have gone for good. Women will have learned to appreciate their bodies in knowledge rather than ignorance, and the medical men and women of the year 2000 will regard their task of caring for the healthy and ailing human body as the ancient Greeks saw it—as both a privilege and a duty.
    —RONA CHERRY, *Woman in the Year 2000*

Two women in conversation. One woman: "You should see my analyst—he's marvelous."
    The other one: "Why should I see your doctor? There's nothing wrong with me."
    The first one: "My doctor's wonderful—he'll find something!"

Young Dr. Anderson hung out her shingle for the first time, but no patient showed up for days. When a man came to her office, she thought it best to impress him. She picked up the phone and in her most professional manner said, "Surgery please, Dr. Anderson here. I've so many patients scheduled, I'm afraid it will be impossible to get over to the hospital for the brain operation before six."
    Then, turning to the man, she asked briskly, "What seems to be paining you, sir?"
    "Nothing's paining me," he said. "I've just come to hook up your phone."

An eighty-year-old obstetrician who has delivered over two thousand babies charged for his services either one hundred or two hundred dollars.
    How did he decide which bill to submit?
    "It's very simple," smiled the doctor. "Every time I deliver a baby, the father is pacing nervously up and down in the waiting room. When I put my hand on his shoulder and tell him, 'Congratulations! You have a beautiful new baby,' he invariably asks me one of two questions. If it's 'Is it a boy or a girl?' I charge him two hundred dollars, but if he asks 'How's my wife?' I only charge him a hundred!"
    —ADAPTED FROM BENNETT CERF, *Stories to Make You Feel Better*

Wherever the art of medicine is loved, there also is love of humanity.
    —HIPPOCRATES

A young woman went to a gynecologist to be fitted with an IUD. It was late spring and the office faced a lovely garden in bloom. As the patient assumed the classic position on the doctor's examination table, a dewy-eyed nurse looked out the window and sighed, "Wouldn't it be nice if we did our work out in the garden?"

For every disease that doctors cure with medicine, they produce ten in healthy people by inoculating them with that virus which is a thousand times more powerful than any microbe: the idea that one is ill.
—MARCEL PROUST

AS FOR DOCTORS

I had no need for drugs, was never ill.
But one unlucky day I had a chill
With just a little twitching in my side,
And, merely thinking of a doctor, died.
—Anon. in LOUIS UNTERMEYER, ed., *Great Humor*

If you treat a sick child like an adult and a sick adult like a child, everything usually works out pretty well.

Dr. Charles Mayo, of the Mayo Clinic, is remembered as a man with a puckish sense of humor. In Omaha he was once approached at the airport by an acquaintance who was looking for free medical advice. The man called attention to a broken blood vessel in one of his eyes. He asked Mayo what he should do about it.

Mayo peered at the eye and cheerfully remarked, "I think I'd have that eye taken out if I were you."

The man got the point and hastened to his own doctor.
—ROBERT MCMORRIS, Omaha *World-Herald*

A famous movie star entered a hospital for a checkup and was fawned upon and babied by every nurse in the institution.

"Now if you want anything at all, you need only pull this cord," one of them told him.

He gave her his patented irresistible smile and said, "Thank you, my dear. What is the cord attached to?"

She smiled back and answered, "Me."

After five months of marriage to a busy intern, I came down with the flu and decided to call my husband at the hospital, hoping to finally get my share of the sympathy and medicine which he generously dispenses to his patients. When I had finished telling him about my symptoms and complete misery, he exclaimed, "Oh, dear!" Then, after a brief pause, he added, "Does that mean you won't be bringing me my dinner tonight?"

A tired physician came home one evening to his resolutely optimistic wife, "I've had a tough day at the office, so I'll welcome particularly this evening the good news you always have for me."

"It's better than ever tonight, darling. You know we have six children—and the wonderful news is that five of them didn't break an arm today."

Many women after childbirth develop insomnia, which is nature's way of making sure they are available to their infants during the night.
> —DR. DEMENT, *Capital Times* (Madison, Wisc.), in "No Comment," *MS*

There was a young man with a hernia
Who said to his surgeon, "gol-dernia,
* When carving my middle,*
* Be sure you don't fiddle*
With matters that do not concernia."
> —HEYWOOD BROUN

My sister-in-law, who is pregnant, told me the other day that she was afraid to bother her gynecologist with questions for fear of "getting on his wrong side."
> —NORA EPHRON, *Crazy Salad*

A patient goes to heaven where he waits around for his wings. A man in a white jacket passes by. "What's going on here?" the patient asks. "Who was that?"
"Ssh!" an angel replies. "That was God. He likes to play doctor."

A rule of thumb in the matter of medical advice is to take everything any doctor says with a grain of aspirin.
> —GOODMAN ACE, *The Fine Art of Hypochondria*

A job-weary woman on vacation sent her psychotherapist a card. She wrote, "Having wonderful time—wish you were here to tell me why."

In my normal seventy-hour week, I have [at home] three things going for me: I have a big freezer, a microwave oven, and good organization. . . .
> —ROSALYN SUSSMAN YALOW, co-winner of the 1977 Nobel Prize in medicine

Margery Albright [practical nurse and midwife] was a woman's woman, who put little faith in the integrity and reliability of the average male. . . . Now and then, in the case of a stubborn pregnancy, she would cut a quill from a chicken feather, fill it with powdered tobacco, and blow the contents up one nostril of the expectant mother. This would induce a fit of sneezing that acted to dislodge the most reluctant baby.
> —JAMES THURBER, *Thurber Album*

The classic female dependency on the obstetrician transfers at childbirth to dependency on the pediatrician—all this in perfect mimicry of the dependency relationship of marital roles. . . .
We feel hesitant to question their procedures, their fees, or their hours,

and often we are simply grateful that we're able to see them at all, particularly if they're well recommended.
—ELLEN FRANKFORT, *Vaginal Politics*

In Memory of
GERTRUDE FIELDING
1910–1978
Beloved Wife and Mother, and Patient
of Doctor Jerome Murdock of Scarsdale
—*Playboy*

... As self-appointed spokesman ... spokeswoman ... for my sisterhood, may I tell you of our gratitude and affection. ... May I herewith propose a toast from the ladies of America in words which are singularly apt ... gentlemen of the profession, BOTTOMS UP!!!
—CORNELIA OTIS SKINNER, in a speech to the American
Gynecological Society

""!!!**
•••

MONEY

There are a handful of people whom money won't spoil—and we count ourselves among them.
—MIGNON MCLAUGHLIN

Once, when Mrs. Truman was out of town, the president invited friends to sail down the Potomac, and asked Mrs. Sharpe, the housekeeper, to supply food from the White House kitchen. Mrs. Sharpe decided that serving a large ice-cream cake that a friend had sent over would save money and please Mrs. Truman, and she ordered dry ice to pack the cake for the trip.

When Mrs. Truman was going over that month's bills, she called in Mrs. Sharpe. "How did we happen to spend twenty-five cents for dry ice?" she asked.
—MARY LYNN KOTZ, *Upstairs at the White House*

I don't like money, actually, but it quiets my nerves.
—*The Trib*

Money is like a sixth sense without which you cannot make a complete use of the other five.
—W. SOMERSET MAUGHAM

Accounting procedures make facts hard to find
Figures are extrapolated, projected, refined
Depreciation doubled, depletion straight-lined
They boggle the books and juggle the mind.
  —JUDGE HARVEY SMITH

You can never be too thin or too rich.
  —MRS. WILLIAM (BABE) PALEY

Those who believe money can do everything are frequently prepared to
do everything for money.
  —ANON.

By sponsoring weekly bingo games, churches and synagogues across the
land have long enjoyed the tribute that vice can be made to pay to virtue.
Their example has led to "Las Vegas Nights," on which such pastimes
as blackjack, roulette, and even craps are turned to worthy purposes.
Clearly, the vistas of vice are vast: pot parties for the benefit of the
American Cancer Society perhaps; after-hours clubs run by Alcoholics
Anonymous; massage parlors to finance Planned Parenthood. . . . The
cause of moral uplift would be well served.
  —*NYT* editorial

If you complain about farmers, don't talk with your mouth full.
  —*Billboard*

I bought my eggs from a woman who lived five miles out in the country.
She usually delivered the eggs to my home, but occasionally I would stop
at her little farm to buy eggs and chat awhile. For some reason the eggs
cost more when I picked them up at the farm than when she made the
five-mile trip to deliver them at my home. I asked her one day to explain
her pricing system. It was disarmingly simple and logical. Her reply was:
"When you come to my farm, you need eggs. When I go to your house, I
need money."
  —W. H. SILL, JR.

I'm tired of Love, I'm still more tired of Rhyme,
But money gives me pleasure all the time.
  —HILAIRE BELLOC

My niece married a Greek who had taken out his U.S. naturalization
papers and was very proud of his new status. They recently purchased
a home; and when the deed came, he looked it over solemnly, then
grinned and broke into a little dance step. "I'm a real American now," he
exclaimed. "I'm in debt!"
  —MRS. R. M. FEE, *Reader's Digest*

Alvin Silverman, Washington correspondent for a Cleveland newspaper, makes it a practice to lay out his daughter Janie's weekly allowance each Sunday night so she'll find it when she gets up on Monday morning. One Sunday night, he forgot to leave the allowance. When he got home from work Monday evening, he found this note from his daughter: "I hate to accuse you of this, but I think you are guilty of delinquency in contributing to a minor."
—BILL GOLD, *Washington Post*

... I am really a poor businessman and bad at figures ... I wish that things were different in this world, that there was an Art Exchange where the artist just deposits his works of art, and receives compensation as needed. As it is, one has to be half a businessman on top of it, and how can one accomplish that. . . .
—LUDWIG VAN BEETHOVEN, in a letter to his publisher (1801)

It's a kind of spiritual snobbery that makes people think they can be happy without money.
—ALBERT CAMUS

Inflation is bringing us true democracy. For the first time in history, luxuries and necessities are selling at the same price.
　　They say kids don't know the value of a dollar. They certainly do know the value of a dollar. That's why they ask for five.
—ROBERT ORBEN

All right, so I like to spend money! But name one other extravagance!
　　—Encyclopedia of Jewish Humor

To be merely marriageable, a girl had to have a fine large bottom or a fine large dowry. If she happened to have both, she was really sitting pretty.
—STELLA J. REICHMAN, *Great Big Beautiful Doll*

We must be prudent and live on our income even if we have to borrow money to do it.
—ARTEMUS WARD

When it is a question of money, everybody is of the same religion.
—VOLTAIRE

The prestige accorded to math has given economics rigor, but alas, also mortis.
—ROBERT HEILBRONER

People are always saying, "I'll do anything to keep my health. It is the greatest treasure in the world." Well, don't believe it.

I have concluded that their money means more to them than their health.

A woman customer called, sobbing, and said. "My best friend stole my husband. What do I do?" I asked her, "Who has the vault?"

The jilted woman had the vault. "Don't do anything rash," I told her. In a while she called and said he had come back.

    —SAYRA FISHER LEBENTHAL, stockbroker

George V of England received a letter from his son, the future Edward VIII, who was attending university, asking for funds. The king answered sternly. He expounded on the virtues of sound financial management, and said that he wanted his son to learn the value of money. Two days later, he received this reply: "Father, I have taken your advice. Have just sold your letter to a collector for twenty-five pounds."

A lot of people can't handle prosperity—but then, most people don't have to.

    —*Modern Maturity*

My wife and I came to the conclusion that today is the tomorrow we were worrying about yesterday, that it's always now. We also did some arithmetic, and figured out that about 40 percent of all the money I'd been working hard to make was earmarked for a tomorrow, for nonreality.

For instance, all the money we'd been spending on insurance—banking on the chance that I'd have the good luck to die young. But if I was unlucky, and lived to a ripe old age, the money would be lost to us. So we canceled the life insurance.

Same thing with fire insurance. Now, if the house burned down tomorrow, we would take it as a sign from God that it was time to move on.

    —ORSON BEAN, actor

It was President Carter on the line, wishing his mother a happy seventy-ninth birthday. The president asked Mrs. Carter for a copy of the book she was autographing, *Away From Home—Letters to My Family,* collected by Gloria Carter Spann. "Listen, Honey," she told the president, "you've got to buy one. We don't give 'em away."

    —ALBIN KREBS, *NYT*

A woman's pleasure in a good bargain is akin to the rapture engendered in the feminine bosom by successful smuggling. It is perhaps a purer joy. The satisfaction of acquiring something one does not need, or of buying an article which one may have some use for in the future, simply because it is cheap or because Mrs. X. paid seventeen cents more for the same thing at a bargain sale, cannot be understood by a mere man.

So she goes on hunting bargains, or rather profiting by those that come in her way, for generally it is not necessary to search for them. These

little snares of the merchant are only too common in this age, when everything from cruisers to clothespins and pianos to prunes may often be had at a stupendous sacrifice.
—MARSHAL P. WILDER, *Wit and Humor of America* (1909)

Someone once asked the famous prima donna Amelita Galli-Curci why she let herself slide off the pitch so often. She replied, "Why should I learn to sing in tune when I have made millions singing out of it?"

Queen Elizabeth II received £ 1,665,000, or about $2,863,800 at the current rate of exchange under the Civil List Act. This sum, while not really a salary but compensation for expenses, still makes her the highest paid woman executive in the world—with twenty-five years of experience.
—*Working Woman*

If consumers are asked to make greater sacrifices than industry, this country is going to have its greatest shortage of all—a shortage of consumers.
—BETTY FURNESS

Small feminist: "So what if Columbus discovered America? Queen Isabella gave him the money."
—Adapted from *Working Woman*

New York is a quiet sort of place, where nobody much knows anybody else, the people work hard or pretend to, and go to bed with a glass of hot milk, having previously hotted up a hamburger in an immaculate five-thousand-dollar kitchen.
—LORD KINROSS, *Punch*

If you're offered an *honorarium* for a speech, you can be sure the money is of no *consequencium.*
—MERLE MILLER

Mrs. Lorraine Joswick, her husband and two grown children spent forty days tearing up the house to find the ticket [for the $5,000 lottery]. She had forgotten where she hid it after finding out it was a winning ticket. The subsequent search involved ripping moldings and paneling from the wall, renting a metal detector hoping it would sense the ticket's foil covering and even trying a hypnotist to jog her memory. Finally, she found the ticket. "It was pasted onto the back of a mirror in my daughter's room," she said. "I don't even remember being in there that night."
—ALBIN KREBS, *NYT*

Jack Dempsey's manager, Jack Kearns, was promised a large sum of money if he would stage a fight in Shelby, Montana.

The day before the fight, Kearns visited the people behind it, asked for some of the promised money and was told that there was no advance gate in hand, since all the people who would come were still out in the field drilling for oil. Kearns told the town fathers, "No money, no fight."

The next morning Dempsey was skipping rope in the freight car when he heard a noise outside. He peered through the sliding door and discovered that the car was solidly encircled by roughnecks from the oilfields. In the middle of the circle were two men holding a rope. And one of them was fashioning a hangman's noose.

"That," Dempsey told me, "was the first time I found out money wasn't everything."

—PETER MAAS, *Daily News*

If someone says, "It's not the money, it's the principle," you can be sure it's the money.

—ANON.

It's our own money and we're free to spend it any way we please. It's part of this campaign business. If you have money, you spend it to win. And the more you can afford, the more you'll spend. It's something that is not regulated. Therefore, it's not unethical.

—MRS. JOSEPH P. KENNEDY

Never make the unpardonable error, then, of thinking that it is romantic to be poor. For youth, which has the riches of health, it is less important; but for age, which has lost them, it is all-essential to compensate with artificial riches.

—CAITLIN THOMAS

The psychiatrist asked his nurse to send in the new patient. He looked at the man who came in and to his amazement the man had a turnip in his ear.

"Doctor, you must help me—I'm at a loss—I can't do my work—people laugh at me—it's awful," he moaned.

The doctor reassured him that they'd talk it through and solve the problem of the turnip.

The man returned the following week still with the turnip in his ear. And the same occurred the next time. The third week the man arrived —this time with a carrot in his ear.

The doctor scolded, "We've spent all this time working on the turnip —and now you have a carrot in your ear—what's the idea!"

The man answered, "Have you noticed the price of turnips lately?"

—JOE URIS

MORES MANNERS LIFE-STYLE

Colonial society took a dim view of unmarried women. One North Carolina newspaper of 1790 described these hapless spinsters in various terms, calling them "ill-natured, maggotty, peevish, conceited, disagreeable, hypocritical, fretful, noisy, gibing, canting, censorious . . . good for nothing creatures."

—LINDA DE PAUW and CONOVER HUNT, *Remember the Ladies*

Letter from Eliza Southgate to her cousin Moses Porter (1800):
. . . I do not esteem marriage absolutely essential to happiness, and that it does not always bring happiness we must every day witness in our acquaintance. A single life is considered too generally as a reproach; but let me ask you, which is the most despicable—she who marries a man she scarcely thinks *well* of—to avoid the reputation of an old maid—or she, who with more delicacy, than marry one she could not highly esteem, preferred to live single all her life. . . .

—CLARENCE COOK, ed., *A Girl's Life Eighty Years Ago*

A SORROWFUL DITTY

Come gentle, come simple, come foolish, come witty—
Come don't let me die a maid, take me out of pitty.
I have a sister Sally, she's younger than I am—
She has so many sweethearts she's oblig'd to deny them.
I never was guilty of denying any;
You all know my heart, I'd be thankful for any.

—EIGHTEENTH-CENTURY SONG

The youth of America is their oldest tradition. It has been going on now for three hundred years.

—OSCAR WILDE

I cannot but smile sometimes, to observe the ridiculous figure of some of our young gentlemen, who affect to square their conduct by his Lordship's principles of politeness—they never tell a story unless it be very short—they talk of decorum and the *etiquette*—they are on the rack if an old man should let fall a proverb—and a thousand more trifling affectations, the ridicule of which arises, not so much from their putting on this foreign dress, as from their ignorance or vanity in pretending to imitate those rules which were designed for an English nobleman.
—SARAH WENTWORTH MORTON, *The Power of Sympathy* (1790)

This time like all times is a very good one if we but know what to do with it.
—RALPH WALDO EMERSON

ALCESTE: *All are corrupt; there's nothing to be seen*
In court or town but aggravates my spleen.
I fall into deep gloom and melancholy
When I survey the scene of human folly,
Finding on every hand base flattery,
Injustice, fraud, self-interest, treachery. . . .
Ah, it's too much; mankind has grown so base
I mean to break with the whole human race.
—MOLIÈRE, *The Misanthrope,* (1666) trans. by Richard Wilbur

When you blow your nose or cough, turn round so that nothing falls on the table.
—A THIRTEENTH-CENTURY ITALIAN ETIQUETTE BOOK

The fork was far from an instant success. When an eleventh-century Venetian doge married a Greek princess who used "little golden forks with two prongs" to carry food to her mouth, clerics denounced her pretentious eastern habit and thought her suitably punished when she contracted "a repulsive illness."
—NORBERT ELIAS, *The Civilizing Process*

The rich need good manners because of the "finish and éclat thus given to their wealth and their homes," the middle class need manners to "gain admission to the homes of the rich," and the poor need them "as solace for the sting of poverty."
—FOREWORD, *Never Give a Lady a Restive Horse* (1873)

The perpetual obstacle to human advancement is custom.
—JOHN STUART MILL

There is nothing that costs less than civility.
—DON QUIXOTE

To establish oneself in the world, one does all one can to seem established there already.
— FRANÇOIS DE LA ROCHEFOUCAULD

A gentleman . . . never suffers his hands to be bare for a moment. The ungloved hand is the cloven foot of their vulgarity.

When you salute a lady . . . in the street, you should take your hat entirely off and cause it to describe a circle of at least ninety degrees from its original resting place.

When a man rises from the seat to give it to a woman, he silently says, in the spirit of true and noble manliness . . . "I offer you this, madam, in memory of my mother, who suffered that I might live, and of my present or future wife, who is, or is to be, the mother of my children."
— ETIQUETTE COLLECTION, Arthur and Elizabeth Schlesinger Library, Radcliffe College

We vacationed on historic Wampum Island. Everybody felt superior.

The people who live year-round on the island felt superior to the summer visitors. The people who were born on the island felt superior to the people who were not born on the island, even though they lived year-round on the island.

The summer people who owned houses felt superior to the summer people who rented houses, and the summer people who rented for the entire season felt superior to the people who rented only for the month.

The people who rented for the month felt superior to the people who rented for two weeks. The people who rented for two weeks felt superior to the people who rented space in rooming houses.

Everybody felt superior to the people who came by boat in the morning and left by boat in the afternoon. These people were called "the day trippers." The day trippers felt superior to the people who had to stay back in the city.
— RUSSELL BAKER, *NYT Mag.*

It's a very selfish decade. It's all me. People who experienced profound disappointment trying to change the system are jogging and growing vegetables and concentrating on brightening their corner of the world.
— TOM HAYDEN

The art of our era is not art, but technology. Today Rembrandt is painting automobiles; Shakespeare is writing research reports; Michelangelo is designing more efficient bank lobbies.
— HOWARD SPARKS, *The Petrified Truth*

"I wish I understood Americans," said Charles-Eduard. "They are very strange. So good and yet so dull."

"What makes you think they are so good?"

"You can see it, shining in their eyes."

"That's not goodness, that's contact lenses—a kind of spectacle they wear next the eyeball. I had an American lover and I used to tap his eye with my nail file. He was a very curious man. Imagine, his huge, healthy-looking body hardly functioned at all by itself. He could only digest yogurt and raw carrots, he couldn't sleep without a sleeping draught or wake up without benzedrine, and he had to have a good strong blood transfusion every morning before he could face the day."

"You had him in the house?"

"For the central heating, dearest," she said apologetically. "It was that very cold winter. Americans have no circulation of their own; even their motors are artificially heated in winter and cooled in summer. . . ."

> —NANCY MITFORD, *The Blessing,* in J. B. Priestley, *English Humor*

"Have fun" is a thoroughgoing imperative.

Have fun driving your own car; have fun going by bus and leave your parking worries behind. Have fun with a filter; have fun with the honest taste of a *real* cigarette. Have fun by calling your relatives long distance; have fun with your mother-in-law living in. Most of all, have fun with fashion. . . . Pleasure turns into a daily grind as the invitation to have a good time presses on all fronts.

Proctor and Gamble have restrained themselves in their claims for Joy, the liquid detergent. Their slogan is that "it makes dishwashing *almost* fun."

> —EVE MERRIAM, *Figleaf*

If today's average American is confronted with an hour of leisure, he is likely to palpitate with panic. An hour with nothing to do! So he jumps into a dither and into a car, and starts driving off fiercely in pursuit of diversion.

. . . We "catch" a train. We "grab" a bite of lunch. We "contact" a client. Everything has to be active and electric. . . . We need less leg action and more acute observation as we go. Slow down the muscles and stir up the mind.

> —DON HEROLD

In the old days, if a person missed the stagecoach, he was content to wait a day or two for the next one. Nowadays, we feel frustrated if we miss one section of a revolving door.

> —*Modern Maturity*

Good manners have much to do with the emotions. To make them ring true, one must feel them, not merely exhibit them.

> —AMY VANDERBILT, *New Complete Book of Etiquette*

Only a blind man would deny that characteristic traits of present life are a mad scramble for material commodities, a devotion to attainment of external power, and an insensate love of foolish luxuries and idle display.

> —JOHN DEWEY

Sign on entrance to Manor Villa, Austin, Texas:
Attention Visitors:
DO NOT ENTER
IF OFFENDED BY LIBERATED LIFE
STYLE (INCLUDES NUDITY, CAVORTING
IN THE POOL, CONSENSUAL FROLICKING, ETC.)

This country has gone mad for gossip, TV, newspapers, radio, movies, books, magazines, all our media are obsessed with private lives. Prying, spying, eyeing—the hounding of public figures has reached such proportions that we may have to declare open and closed hunting seasons.
    —SHANA ALEXANDER, *Talking Woman*

A fad is an epidemic of taste, constantly changing, and success is its kiss of death.
    —JOAN KRON, *NYT*

From the first of this century the dining room of the rich and middle class tended to be the largest room of the house, an elaborately decorated place where the family gathered. Gradually this space diminished, and the dining foyer, the dining platform, and the dinette began to appear, followed, after World War II, by the so-called dining L.
    Today, even that corner has been cut, and builders refer to the "dining area," meaning the corner of the living room nearest the kitchen.
    —ANDREW ALPERN, *Apartments for the Affluent*

the cockroaches are not
the only insects
that are demanding more
consideration
i met a flea
last evening who
told me that he had come
into contact with
a great deal of unrest
lately and a mosquito remarked
to me only this
morning there is darned
little justice in this world the
way the human beings
run it seldom do i
meet a person who will hold
still long
enough for me to get a meal

    —DON MARQUIS, *The Lives & Times of Archy & Mehitabel*

Life never becomes a habit to me. It's always a marvel.
—KATHERINE MANSFIELD

LIMERICKS LONG AFTER LEAR

Said a fervent young lady of Hammels,
"I object to humanity's trammels!
  I want to be free!
  Like a bird! Like a bee!
Oh, why am I classed with the mammals?"

—MORRIS BISHOP

When Melinda was prevented from swimming with friends in the pool at a country club that excluded Jews, her father wrote the club president an indignant, highly publicized letter in which he said, "Since my little daughter is only half-Jewish, would it be all right if she went in the pool only up to her waist?"
—*NYT*

Social integration is no more widespread in Georgia today than it is anywhere else in America, though the penalties for attempting it may be harsher. Not long ago, a schoolteacher in a small east-Georgia community who invited two black couples lost her job for her effrontery, and then, when her husband lost some of his insurance clients, also lost her husband. It was hard in that town to know afterward just who was at the controversial meal and who wasn't, because people who had it in for other people would spread the word that they'd attended it whether or not they had.
—E. J. KAHN, *The New Yorker*

There is none so loyal as a southerner to the South when he is away from home.
—THOMAS WOLFE

MOTHERS

A MOTHERS' MEETING

"Where's the maternal parent of
  This boy that stands in need of beating,
And of this babe that pines for love?"
  "Oh, she is at a Mothers' Meeting!"

"Fair daughter, why these young tears shed,
For passion's tale, too sweet and fleeting,
Lonely and mute, uncomforted?"
"My mother's at a Mothers' Meeting."

"Man, whom misfortunes jeer and taunt,
Whom frauds forsake, and hope is cheating,
Fly to your mother's arms." "I can't—
You see, she's at a Mothers' Meeting."

Alas, what next will women do?
Love, duty, children, home, maltreating,
The while she, smiling, rallies to
The roll-call of a Mothers' Meeting!

> —MADELINE BRIDGES, *Lippincott's Magazine* (c. 1900)

"Woman, it is thy badge of shame!" replied the stern magistrate. "It is because of the stain which that letter indicates, that we would transfer thy child to other hands."

Hester caught hold of Pearl, and drew her forcibly into her arms, confronting the old Puritan magistrate with almost a fierce expression.

"God gave me the child," cried she. "He gave her in requital of all things else which He had taken from me. She is my happiness!—she is my torture, none the less! Pearl keeps me here in life! Pearl punishes me too! See ye not, she is the scarlet letter. Ye shall not take her! I will die first!"

> —NATHANIEL HAWTHORNE, *The Scarlet Letter*

"Mama, Mama," I said happily, "I think I've met a man I could marry." My mother was ecstatic—at first; I was, after all, twenty-six years old and in Jewish families mothers have long since begun to despair when their babies reach that age unmarried.

"There's a small problem, though, Mama," I said. "What is it, sweetheart?" "He's still married," I said. "He has three children, he's thirteen years older than I, and he's not Jewish." Mama burst into tears: "Why does everything have to happen to my baby?"

> —BEVERLY SILLS, *Bubbles*

It is our claim that maternity is no bar to the highest and broadest lifework which lies within the ability of any woman to achieve. Motherhood carries with it its own widening and strengthening of the feminine character. . . . A mother's child is but an incident in her life. Love it as she will, it will grow up; and in a few years it is gone. But a lifework remains for a lifetime!

> —ANTOINETTE BROWN BLACKWELL, "On Marriage & Work" (1875)

All I am, or can be, I owe to my angel mother.

> —ABRAHAM LINCOLN

A mother is not a person to lean on but a person to make leaning unnecessary.
> —DOROTHY CANFIELD FISHER

Weary of the constant disorder in her sons' room, a mother laid down the law: For every item she had to pick up off the floor, they would have to pay her a nickel!

At the end of a week, the boys owed her sixty-five cents. She received the money promptly—along with a fifty-cent tip and a note that read, "Thanks, Mom; keep up the good work!"
> —*Modern Maturity*

Belle-Mere
The French chose this word to give to the mother-in-law. It means: beautiful mother.

I wish all nations would adopt it.

And it would be nice if comedians could get along without their tired, tasteless jokes about mothers-in-law. It would be especially nice for mothers-in-law.
> —MARLENE DIETRICH, *ABC's*

Here is a wedding, flower-decked, musical, and sedate, the kind of traditional scene that brings tears of joy to most women's eyes and especially to a grandmother's. And here is the grandmother of the bride, tearful and smiling as one would expect. And—surprise, surprise!—in her lap she has a baby, the bride's baby and her own great-grandchild.

Grandmother remarks, "Isn't it nice when they decide that they want to get married after all!"
> —RUTH GOODE, *A Book for Grandmothers*

When a cake was in the oven an aura of mystery fell over the house. The shades were drawn, windows shut, neighbors informed. Mama moved cautiously about in house slippers. She knew nothing about thermodynamics. She knew only that a sponge cake is supposed to rise slowly and that the slightest sneeze within an area of twenty miles could cause a collapse.

Happy Sammy would come home from school, slam the door, and hear a horrible scream from the kitchen: "Murderer! You killed my cake!"
> —SAM LEVENSON, *In One Era & Out the Other*

Mom is organization-minded. Organizations, she has happily discovered, are intimidating to all men, not just to mere men. They frighten politicians to sniveling servility and they terrify pastors; they bother bank presidents and they pulverize school boards. . . .

The mealy look of men today is the result of momism and so is the pinched and baffled fury in the eyes of womankind.
> —PHILIP WYLIE

He was short of news that spoke ill of his mother.
   —J. GILCHRIST LAWSON, *The World's Best Proverbs and Maxims*

Sarah Franklin Bache, daughter of Benjamin Franklin, was told by the headmistress of her children's school that pupils were to be seated according to their parents' social rank. Indignant, Mrs. Bache sent the headmistress a cursory message informing her that "in this country there is no rank but rank mutton."
   —ADAPTED FROM PAUL ENGLE, *Women in the American Revolution*

Abe Balaban, in his first movie house, around 1916, instituted a service by which sleeping babies were left in tagged baby buggies on the sidewalk while the mothers went inside to enjoy the show. If the baby cried during the performance a slide would be flashed on the screen, "Mother Number 47, your baby is crying."
   —ARTHUR MAYER, *Merely Colossal*

As a woman was walking down the street with her three grandchildren, a friend stopped her and remarked, "My what beautiful grandchildren." Beaming, the grandmother replied, "That's nothing. Wait until I show you the pictures."

For the black woman who literally covered the holes in our walls with sunflowers:

They were women then
My mama's generation
Husky of voice—Stout of
Step
With fists as well as
Hands
How they battered down
Doors
And ironed
Starched white
Shirts . . .
To discover books
Desks
A place for us
How they knew what we
Must know
Without knowing a page
Of it
Themselves.

   —ALICE WALKER, *Working It Out*

Instant availability without continuous presence is probably the best role a mother can play.
—LOTTE BAILYN

It is a curious reflection on Freud's conception of the Oedipus complex that nowadays it is often the mother that the son wants to kill by breaking her heart, while she, so far from being the object of his desire, has to seduce him into filial sentiments and healthy aggressions.
—ANATOLE BROYARD, *NYT*

When you came into the world, my last born, Minet-Cherie, I suffered for three days and two nights. When I was carrying you I was as big as a house. Three days seems a long time. The beasts put us to shame, we women who can no longer bear our children joyfully. But I've never regretted my suffering. They do say that children like you, who have been carried so high in the womb and have taken so long to come down into the daylight, are always the children that are most loved, because they have lain so near their mother's heart and have been so unwilling to leave her.
—COLETTE, *My Mother's House and Sido*

ONE WEPT WHOSE ONLY CHILD WAS DEAD

One wept whose only child was dead,
New-born, ten years ago.
"Weep not; he is in bliss," they said.
She answered, "Even so,

"Ten years ago was born in pain
A child, not now forlorn.
But oh, ten years ago, in vain,
A mother, a mother was born."

—ALICE MEYNELL

MOVIES

The great moguls of vaudeville persisted in regarding living pictures as a temporary fad whose novelty would soon be exhausted. They were used in the vaudeville houses as "chasers" between shows to drive out the patrons. Indeed, the history of motion pictures might well be summarized to date as starting with drive-outs and culminating with drive-ins.
—ARTHUR MAYER, *Merely Colossal*

The automobile is an extension of the house. Young people used to court in the parlor, then on the front porch, then in the automobile—the porch-on-wheels. Today, the porch-on-wheels may be observed at the local drive-in movie "house."
—R. BUCKMINSTER FULLER, *I Seem to Be a Verb*

Hollywood: a mining-camp in lotus land.
—F. SCOTT FITZGERALD

It is hard to laugh at the need for beauty and romance, no matter how tasteless, even horrible, the results of that need are. But it is easy to sigh. Few things are sadder than the truly monstrous.
—NATHANAEL WEST, on first seeing Hollywood architecture

Hollywood is a nice place if you happen to be an orange.
—FRED ALLEN

I think my grandfather . . . and the rest of them [film-makers] invented the happy American family and put it into movies to drive everyone crazy.
—JILL ROBINSON, author

Hollywood is a great place. I mean great like a sausage factory with lots of system that turns out fine sausages. In Italy I have no sausages but I have freedom.
—ROBERTO ROSSELLINI, Italian film director

In transitions from sadness to dumbness to openmouthed total despair nothing is held in reserve. [Lillian] Gish gives the impression she is playing her final scene, the final one of her entire life. . . . As she travels between cliché and self, from a stock situation to the uniqueness of context . . . . she demonstrates a dynamics basic to great screen acting.
—CHARLES AFFRON, *Star Acting*

Greta Garbo sees not only her own life, but everybody else's before it has been lived. This fatalism has happily passed over into her technique. . . . The chief excitement is to watch how perfectly she now sees backward, like a perpetually drowning woman, not only her life but her past. . . . : The way—years ahead of the acting textbooks—she hides a broken moment not with a cute nose-dive into cupped palms, but with the five inadequate fingers of one bony hand;—her gestures, too, therefore have the same anxiety to treat people with perhaps too much care at the moment, because she knows what's going to happen to them in a year or two.
—ALISTAIR COOKE, *Garbo and the Night Watchmen*

When *The Covered Wagon* was being made, around 1922 or '23, Jesse Lasky, who was making it, told me he received a wire from his boss, Adolph Zukor, advising him to discontinue work on it as exhibitors were complaining that too many Westerns were being made. Lasky wired back, "Wagon not a Western. It is an epic." To this he received the reply, "In view of fact it is an epic and not a Western, kindly proceed without further delay."
—ARTHUR MAYER, *Merely Colossal*

You don't learn to be effective from film, but from life. Actors who watch themselves tend to become mannered. The less you think about how effective you are, the more effective you are. If you *try,* what finally shows is the effort.
—MARLON BRANDO, in Shana Alexander, *Talking Woman*

Do you believe a major newspaper in this most sophisticated city in the world ran a story on me that read, "Robert Redford is standing around the streets in a stocking cap!"? I ask you, is that news?

Last week I attended a vitally important energy conference, but not one paper printed a word about it. But my stocking cap gets into the headlines. Famous is not so great. Ralph Waldo Emerson once wrote, "Even a hero becomes a bore at last."
—ROBERT REDFORD, *Book Digest*

Sanford Meisner, acting teacher, taught me to walk into a scene with purpose. He taught me how to listen to another actor, not just to his lines. If a scene was bad, he'd always yell, "You're faking it!"

I've seen him in the audience frequently. But never, ever in all these years has he told me that I was good. I'm so sure I'll never get his approval I even dream about it.

It goes like this:

I am in Grand Central Station. For some reason, I'm throwing up. A large crowd has formed. The crowd parts and out steps Mr. Meisner. He opens his mouth, pauses, then yells:

"You're faking it, Randall!"
—TONY RANDALL, *Daily News*

All great actors, if not essentially comic, are gifted with an appreciation for paradox that is one of the roots of comedy. Olivier has this. So do Ralph Richardson, Marlon Brando, Dustin Hoffman and, I suspect, Robert De Niro. At the peak of her form in a film like *The Little Foxes,* Bette Davis was funny—dishonest and stingy and mean, but also funny. One doesn't necessarily laugh, but the awareness of the wit within a performance is one of the pleasures of both the cinema and theater.
—VINCENT CANBY, *NYT*

Back in the fifties you had to be sexy, glamorous, and if you were those things then you could become successful as an actress. Women weren't like a James Dean, a Montgomery Clift, or a Marlon Brando who said, "Screw that stereotype. I'm going to be what I am." Women didn't have enough power to do that. So I opted to become what they told me I should become if I was going to be a successful actress. And to my amazement it worked. Then you begin to realize, so what? I'm not the actress I should have been. People whom I respect don't respect me. My father was very loyal, but he didn't approve of some of the films I did. And suddenly I'm thirty years old and what am I doing with my life anyway?

You can be a privileged movie star, or you can commit yourself to the idea that people can change their lives and can change history. I want to make films that will make people feel stronger, understand more clearly, and make them move forward—women and men. That's what I'm interested in.

—JANE FONDA, *Newsweek*

Kooky was a word I would never escape, and one I seemed to have grown up with. The closest the dictionary comes to its derivation is: Kookaburra, *Australia.* It means the laughing jackass.

For the fan magazines and gossip columnists, I was fresh copy.

She lives in a one-room shack at the beach.

She's never even swum in a Hollywood swimming pool.

She doesn't own a formal dress or a piece of fur.

Sometimes the cop at the gate turns her away in the morning, saying the casting calls are filled for the day.

—SHIRLEY MACLAINE, *Don't Fall Off the Mountain*

Once, while filming his movie, *The Producers,* the volatile Mel Brooks began to shout at leading man Zero Mostel. The star raised an interrupting finger and in a calm, if booming voice, said, "I am now going into my dressing room. When your tantrum is over, you may knock on my door. I will then return to the set."

"You are going into your *dressing room?*" Brooks shouted. "You mean to stay there while thousands of dollars' worth of shooting time drains away, and not come back till my tantrum is over and I *knock on your door?*"

Mostel nodded.

Brooks held up his hand and, suddenly tranquil, said, "My tantrum is over."

—LAURIE MANDEL

Fellini gives great interviews; he has turned into the Italian Orson Welles. He talks such a remarkable movie that maybe he doesn't need to make it. He has become the work of art.

—PAULINE KAEL

I love close-ups. To me they are a challenge. The closer a camera comes, the more eager I am to show a completely naked face, show what is behind the skin, the eyes; inside the head. Show the thoughts that are forming.
—LIV ULLMANN, *Changing*

Power is another fantasy I live in. The truth is, I am weak. My goal is to find the strength to stop acting. It's not a profession for a real man. I find myself on top of a woman making love, and I am really on top of a chair. The actress has gone home and the camera is shooting me making love to a chair. It's an insane profession.
But it buys a lotta pizza.
—GIANCARLO GIANNINI

Overheard at a theater where an X-rated art film is playing:
WOMAN: [*Rushing up to man who apparently has been waiting in the lobby*] Oh, I'm sorry I'm late. I guess the picture has started.
MAN: That's all right. We only missed about three minutes of the foreplay.
—"METROPOLITAN DIARY," *NYT*

Yesterday I saw a movie that was so embarrassing, I asked the lady in front of me to put her hat back on again.
—ROBERT ORBEN

Columnist Abigail Van Buren recently informed her twin sister, Ann Landers, that she'd been to her first X-rated movie. "How did you have the nerve?" Ann asked her.
"I just put on my Ann Landers wig and went," said Abby.
—NEIL MORGAN, San Diego *Tribune*

Someone said that the art of acting is relaxing. Of course this basic principle can be applied to all the arts, but an actor especially must have restraint and an inner containment. No matter how frenzied the scene, the technician within the actor should be calm and relaxed, editing and guiding the rise and fall of his emotions—the outer man excited and the inner controlled. Only through relaxation can an actor achieve this.
—CHARLES CHAPLIN, *My Autobiography*

Acting is standing up naked and turning around very slowly.
—ROSALIND RUSSELL, *Life Is a Banquet*

GOLDWYNISMS

Sam was warned not to produce *The Captive* because its leading character was a lesbian. "We'll get around that," said Sam. "We'll make her an American."

One of Sam's publicity staff created an ad for a forthcoming movie. It read: "The directorial skill of Mamoulian, the radiance of Garbo, and the genius of Goldwyn have united to make the world's greatest entertainment." "That," Sam said, "is the kind of ad I like. Facts. No exaggeration."

Sam was strolling through a gorgeous Hollywood garden when he paused in front of a bronze sundial. "What is that?" asked Sam of his host. The man replied, "That's for telling the time." Sam shook his head. "Well, well, what won't they think of next."

Suspiria is really quite funny, during those isolated interludes when nobody is bleeding.
—JANET MASLIN, film critic, *NYT*

Reporters ask how I make it as a director in a man's world. If I have to answer that silly question, I say through humor. Through humor you establish a serious relationship more quickly.

A good director, a good writer, is hermaphrodite. The director loves all the women, loves all the men, loves all the characters.
—LINA WERTMULLER, *MS*

Joan Darling, film director, was asked if women directors would someday have casting couches. She looked at the small love seat in her dressing room. "It's too small," she said. "But . . . next picture?"
—*NYT*

BARBARA WALTERS: Can you actually believe that you've been married seven times?
ELIZABETH TAYLOR: I really can't. My family background made me believe that marriage was necessary when you were in love. So actually, I married seven times for *moral* reasons.
—INTERVIEW ON ABC-TV

MUSIC

Music is most detrimental to the modesty befitting the female sex, as it distracts from more proper actions and occupations; and on account of the dangers to those connected with it, instructors as well as listeners, no young girl, married woman, or widow, though for educational purposes, or else in convents or music schools under any other pretext, although studying music to the end of performing it in these convents, shall be

permitted to take lessons in singing or any kind of instrument from men teachers.
—EDICT ISSUED IN ROME (1686)

So much is spoken about music, and so little really said. I strongly believe that words are insufficient. They appear to me so many sided, so vague, so open to misunderstanding as compared to some good music, which fills our soul with a thousand better things than words.
—FELIX MENDELSSOHN, in reply to a request to explain the "meaning" of several of his *Songs Without Words* (1842)

A true music lover is one who, on hearing a soprano singing in the bathtub, puts his ear to the keyhole.
—ANON.

Just before a concert, a clarinetist came to Toscanini and said his E-natural key was broken, and he wouldn't play [the symphony program] that night. The maestro shut his eyes for a moment and said, "It's all right; you don't have an E-natural tonight."
—SCOTT BEACH, *Musicdotes*

It is nice to write your own libretto. When I have a musical idea that does not fit my poem, I can cut or change it—without pain.
—THEA MUSGRAVE, British composer and conductor, *Opera News* (1977)

Opera is an exotic and irrational entertainment.
—DR. SAMUEL JOHNSON

Jenny Lind's Swedish herdsman's song was singularly quaint, wild, and innocent—the joyful laugh, the echo—as if her singing had brought the very mountains there. Her singing of the national prize song, "Greeting to America," had a soul in it, coming from her lips:

And long as the waters shall gleam in the sun
And long as the heroes remember their scars
Be at the hands of thy children united as one
And peace shed her light on this banner of stars!

The audience exploded, yelling hoarsely and tossing bouquets of flowers on stage.
—*Mirror of the Times* (1850)

Puccini's opera *Madame Butterfly* is an Italian fantasy. It has little real connection with the Orient, of which he knew very little. Japanese ladies do not wear their hearts on their kimono sleeves. They contain their reactions. But Puccini's Butterfly expresses her emotions freely, like the *buona Italiana* she is. Japanese women do not strew

flowers about the house, but Puccini liked the idea. Puccini wants it—
I do it!

    —RENATA SCOTTO, Metropolitan Opera soprano, in *Opera News*

What an improbable scenario. Even a militant feminist editor might
reject it as just too much. One of the world's most lionized conductors
[George Solti] scheduled to lead one of the great orchestras in a Carnegie
Hall performance of Mahler's most complex and philosophically ambi-
tious symphony, injures an arm and is forced to withdraw at the last
moment. His place is taken by his woman assistant [Margaret Hillis] and
she conducts a triumphant performance that wins her a standing ova-
tion.

    If all the foregoing does not yet strike you as the fevered dream of a
novelist, consider in addition that this is a symphony that closes with
a Mystical Choir singing the final, famous words of Goethe's *Faust:*
"Das Ewig-Weibliche zieht uns hinan"—"The Eternal Feminine leads
us on."

    —DONAL HENAHAN, *NYT*

All I did was my job. There's something that has to do with staying power.
I've never been discouraged. I love music, and I get back from it more
than I ever gave to it.

    —MARGARET HILLIS, conductor and Chicago Symphony choral
       director

Women ruin music. If the ladies are ill-favored the men do not want to
play next to them, and if they are well-favored, they can't.

    —SIR THOMAS BEECHAM

Children have inspired me in the search for songs . . . to satisfy their
insatiable demands for energetic and creative expression in music . . .
folk songs born in the hearts of people rather than the minds of scholars,
and that have come down to us only because they were loved and shared.

    —BEATRICE LANDECK, *Songs To Grow On*

On the night violinist Jascha Heifetz was to open in New York, many
fellow musicians came to hear him play. Among them were piano virtuoso Josef Hofmann and violinist Mischa Elman. Hofmann sat
transfixed with admiration, but Elman could not sit still, and was constantly taking out his handkerchief to wipe his brow.

    Finally, Hofmann asked what was wrong. Elman, whose face was
beaded with sweat, said, "Awfully hot in here, isn't it?"

    Hofmann smiled and replied, "Not for pianists."

I only know two tunes. One of them is "Yankee Doodle" and the other one
isn't.

    —U. S. GRANT

Swans sing before they die. 'Twere no bad thing
Should certain persons die before they sing.
—SAMUEL TAYLOR COLERIDGE

A conductor stopped a rehearsal to rhapsodize: "The music should sound as if you were playing on top of a high mountain, overlooking a bank of clouds. You are fanned by the winds . . ."
   "Look," said the concertmaster, "just tell us whether you want it played loud or soft."
—SCOTT BEACH, *Musicdotes*

The aim and final end of all music should be none other than the glory of God and the refreshment of the soul. If heed is not paid to this, it is not true music but a diabolical bawling and twanging!
—JOHANN SEBASTIAN BACH

Ah Mozart! He was happily married—but his wife wasn't.
—VICTOR BORGE

For a long time, players have acted against nature in seeking to give equal power to each finger. On the contrary, each finger should have an appropriate part assigned to it. . . . There are, then, many different qualities of sound, just as there are several fingers. The point is to utilize the differences; and this, in other words, is the art of fingering.
—FRÉDÉRIC CHOPIN

Franz Liszt, in the mid-1800s, was invited to the court of Nicholas I, emperor of Russia. As the great composer and pianist began to play, the emperor began conferring with an aide at his side. Liszt continued playing, hoping that the emperor would soon be silent. Exasperated, he finally gave up playing.
   The emperor inquired why Liszt had stopped performing. Liszt replied discreetly, "When the czar speaks, others must be silent." The emperor took the hint.

Education is to bring people to be themselves, and at the same time, know how to conform to the limits. Remember what Stravinsky said: "If everything would be permitted to me, I would feel lost in this abyss of freedom." But with discipline there must also be intuition and love.
—NADIA BOULANGER, famed teacher of composition

Grandmother's costliest possession was a small wonder case, containing a slip of paper written by Goethe's own hand: "To the great artist, Clara Wieck." Goethe considered this little girl of ten years old [a piano prodigy] as a great artist.
   "This message of Goethe's is my most precious possession," she said reverently to me as I looked long at this autograph. Grandmother wears

on her little finger a blue enamel ring, which is a small locket containing hair of Mendelssohn.

—REMINISCENCES OF CLARA SCHUMANN, from *The Diaries of Her Grandson, Ferdinand Schumann*

My playing is getting all behindhand, as is always the case when Robert is composing. I cannot find one little hour in the day for myself.

—CLARA SCHUMANN, in B. Litzmann, *Clara Schumann*

Music hath charms to soothe a savage breast,
To soften rocks, or bend a knotted oak.

—WILLIAM CONGREVE, *The Mourning Bride*

Medieval life was artful, exquisite, and short. I think the shortness contributed to their living intensely.

Music was used in therapy to promote wound-healing and to eliminate lower-back-pain sciatica. Music was used in banquets and bedrooms. It was essential for good digestion. In medieval bedrooms it was an erotic stimulus.

There was music to rise by and to drowse by, for laving and loving. Communal bath parties splashed amorously to the lilt of viol and shawm.

—PROF. MADELEINE PELNER COSMAN, founder of the Institute for Medieval and Renaissance Studies of City College of New York

Sweetest the strain when in the song
The singer has been lost.

—ELIZABETH STEWART

In opera, anything that is too stupid to be spoken is sung.

—VOLTAIRE

Who does not know the power, the soul, which Mlle. Falcon threw into this glorious personation? . . . The eagle eye sparkles with liquid flame; the form of steel is pliant in its strength; the complexion is brown and warm; the long hair of raven black floats in the breeze, free from that pale and sickly shade which the climates of the north give to the skins and locks of their daughters.

—REVIEW OF MLLE. FALCON IN F. HALEVY'S *La Juive* (1835) in George P. Upton, *Woman in Music*

Sarah Caldwell, opera conductor and director, decided that Rosina in *The Barber of Seville* should carry a mechanical bird in a miniature cage. And so one afternoon Beverly Sills found herself in a shop looking at rare music box birds.

"I found a bird, but it cost $185," Sills recalls. "At that price, I decided to call Sarah. Sarah said, 'Could you bring the bird close to the telephone?' So I brought it close and wound it up. Then she said, 'Now *you* sing.' I said, 'I'm in a store full of people on Madison Avenue!' "

Sarah explained that she wanted a bird that sang a cadenza Sills could imitate. So Beverly chirped into the phone. The mechanical bird was bought, and on opening night almost stole the show.

—*Time*

In an odd way, Mr. Bing [Rudolph Bing, Metropolitan Opera manager] made my career by keeping me out of the Met so long. Nothing infuriates the American public quite as much as the notion of a haughty, foreign-born aristocrat being mean to one of its native-born girls.

—BEVERLY SILLS, *Bubbles*

Will you permit me to suggest that Trifler Hall is immensely large and that with proper precautions, you might certainly avoid selling tickets to speculators and at the same time put the prices within reach of the people at large. If you can do so, you will greatly oblige me.

—JENNY LIND, in a letter to P. T. Barnum (1850)

When going to a dinner party at a private home, there is a monster to be encountered: hi-fi.

They look through their record collection, stack the changer high, and subject their guests to a program that turns the boeuf à la royale to ashes and the Lafite '66 to vinegar.

The point about music to eat by is that it should be good music and, at the same time, neither demanding on the one hand nor offensive on the other. The great composers of dinner music well knew this. Mozart was not going to waste his best and most creative ideas on music intended to amuse his friends while eating. He—and Lully and Haydn and the others —merely wrote light, attractive material that did not have to be heard with any great degree of concentration.

Of music in our own time, a medley of the best from Broadway, played by a skilled pianist, will cause no heartburn.

—HAROLD SCHONBERG, *NYT*

It needs no gift of prophecy to predict that Berlioz will be utterly unknown a hundred years hence to everybody but the encyclopedists and the antiquarians.

—Boston *Daily Advertiser* (1874)

As for Tchaikovsky's *Slavic March,* one feels that the composer must have made a bet, for all that his professional reputation was worth, that he would write the most hideous thing that had ever been put on paper, and he won it, too.

—Boston *Evening Transcript* (1883)

The music of Stravinsky's *Le Sacre du Printemps* baffles verbal description. Practically it has no relation to music at all as most of us understand the word.

> —London *Musical Times* (1913), all from Nicolas Slonimsky, *Lexicon of Musical Invective*

Sweet sounds, oh, beautiful music, do not cease!
Reject me not into the world again.

> —EDNA ST. VINCENT MILLAY, "On Hearing a Symphony of Beethoven"

Give me the making of the songs of a people. I care not who makes their laws.

> —ANON.

I look at people like musical instruments, I set people to music.

> —ELIZABETH SWADOS, composer

We were married in 1940 and in the first month we had four children. I sometimes phone the lazy ones early in the morning and tell them, "I'm glad I woke you up. Why aren't you practicing?"

> —IVAN GALAMIAN, famous violin teacher, speaks of his students

Life is something like this trumpet. If you don't put anything in it you don't get anything out. And that's the truth.

> —W. C. HANDY

We depend largely on tricks, we writers of songs. There is no such thing as a new melody.

> —IRVING BERLIN

Don't ever let anyone give you a singing lesson. It'll ruin you.

> —GEORGE GERSHWIN, advising Ethel Merman

I quit high school at fifteen. There wasn't any rhythm for me in algebra. . . .
    Concentrate on the melody. If it's good, you don't have to shoot it out of a cannon. You got to hang on to the melody and never let it get boresome.

> —FATS WALLER, jazz pianist and composer

If you have to ask what jazz is, you'll never know.

> —LOUIS ARMSTRONG

Because of Vernon Duke's haunting song "April in Paris," I decided one year that I must see Paris in April. It was disastrous. The weather was cold, and it rained every day. Later that summer, I saw Vernon and told him that I had gone to Paris in April.

"Why did you do that?" he asked. "The weather is terrible then." I looked at him in astonishment.

"But, Vernon," I exclaimed, "I went because of your song!"

"Well," replied Vernon, "we really meant May, but the rhythm required two syllables."

—L. ARNOLD WEISSBERGER, *Famous Faces*

Frank Sinatra was in the audience at a concert, and afterward went backstage to be greeted by the players. Someone asked the violist, "Do you know Frank Sinatra?" "Sure I know the Franck Sonata. But who is this?"

—SCOTT BEACH, *Musicdotes*

I didn't know anything at all about Roosevelt. I think the first time I ever heard his name was a couple of months ago when somebody was in my dressing room, and they repeated this saying of his: You have nothing to fear but fear itself. When I heard that I said, "That's *marvelous!*" They said, "You mean you never heard that before?" I said, "No, I never have, what's it from?" They told me Franklin Roosevelt said that, and I said, "Well, I don't know anything about him but he must have been a brilliant man to have had such a powerful thought." You have nothing to fear but fear itself! I took an eyebrow pencil and wrote it on my mirror so I'd remember it.

—DIANA ROSS, interview in *Rolling Stone*

The nuns hated me. They hated the way I talked about boys. I was too giggly and wore too much lipstick and dressed too sexy. I came on too strong. I still do.

We had this young priest in catechism—you had to pass catechism. We used to write the answers to the catechism on our legs, up real high. We would slide up our dresses, and he would turn his face away, and we would copy down the answers.

—LINDA RONSTADT, *Time*

Rock began as a scandal. It was underclass music, a hybrid of Hank Williams's country and western, Memphis rockabilly and blacker rhythm and blues sounds that were euphemistically called "race music."

And it was rampantly sexual.

Adults hated it. Especially when a rockabilly singer named Elvis Aron Presley put it all together and exploded into America's homes via the *Ed Sullivan Show.* They censored Elvis's pelvis right off the TV.

—ABE PECK, *N.Y. Post*

Both Crosby and Presley were creations of the microphone. It made it possible for people with frail voices not only to be heard beyond the third row but also to caress millions. Crosby was among the first to understand that the microphone made it possible to sing to multitudes by singing to a single person in a small room.

Presley cuddled his microphone like a lover. With Crosby the microphone was usually concealed, but Presley brought it out on stage, detached it from its fitting, stroked it, pressed it to his mouth. It was a surrogate for his listener, and he made love to it unashamedly.
—RUSSELL BAKER, *NYT*

Most people think that the entertainer sees the world. But, after the twenty-sixth city, especially if you're doing one-nighters, your hotel room is your world.
—STEVIE WONDER

There is some prejudice in jazz, and some of it's reverse prejudice. But that's natural, you see, because jazz *is* our music. That doesn't mean that Stan Getz can't play or that Bunny Berigan can't. But your playing is so much a part of you that your early life has to come out in your music. Every now and then you hear a teety-teety-teety from a trumpet player and you know it's a white musician. But music is music—you're dealing with the same notes.
—DIZZY GILLESPIE

The trombones crunched redgold under my bed, and . . . the trumpets three-wise silver-flamed, and there by the door the timps rolling through my guts and out again crunched like candy thunder. Oh, it was wonder of wonders. And then, a bird of like rarest spun heavenmetal . . . came the violin solo above all the other strings. Then flute and oboe bored, like worms of like platinum. . . .
—ANTHONY BURGESS, *A Clockwork Orange*

""‖**
•••
POLITICS

While others argued the equality of women with men, I proved it, successfully engaging in business; while others sought to show that there was no valid reason why women should be treated, socially and politically, as inferior to men, I boldly entered the arena. . . .

I have deliberately and of my own accord placed myself before the people as a candidate for the presidency of the United States, and having the means, courage, energy, and strength necessary for the race, intend to contest it to the close.
—VICTORIA WOODHULL (1872)

Sensible and responsible women do not want to vote. The relative positions to be assumed by man and woman in the working out of our civilization were assigned long ago by a higher intelligence than ours.
> —GROVER CLEVELAND, in *Ladies' Home Journal* (1905)

I felt at the time that the first woman [in Congress] should take the first stand, that the first time the first woman had a chance to say *no* to war she should say it.
> —JEANNETTE RANKIN (1883–1973) in casting her solitary vote against World War I

There is not one woman in the Senate today. A stag Senate is stagnation.
> —BELLA ABZUG

After visiting the House of Representatives, a farmer took his daughter to the gallery of the Senate. As they entered, the chaplain of the Senate was starting to talk.
"Does the chaplain pray for the Senate, Daddy?" asked the little girl.
"No," chuckled the farmer. "He comes in, looks at the senators, and then prays for the country."

The learned asses of the masculine sex . . . would like to lower woman to "general culture," indeed even to newspaper reading and meddling with politics.
> —FRIEDRICH NIETZSCHE

CONNECTICUT CAN'T AFFORD A GOVERNESS
Opposition bumper sticker when Governor Ella Grasso was running for office.

Carol Bellamy gained a reputation for independence in the New York State Senate, where she was ranking Democrat.
Responding to the abstention of five senators from voting on a checking-account bill on the ground of possible conflict of interest, Miss Bellamy, who had no outside source of income, quipped: "The next time there's a poverty bill, I'll have to abstain."
> —*NYT*

Maryland Congresswoman Barbara Mikulski gives the woman's-eye view of how the old boy network operates. "Pete Preppy looks through his yearbook, calls up Mike Macho, and says, 'Got anyone good for State?' 'Sure,' answers Mike. 'Try Tom Terrifico.'"
> —*Time*

A woman's place is in the House, and the Senate.
> —FROM A T-SHIRT

During the last presidential campaign, I was asked questions about the economy rather than about menus. I credit the influence of the women's movement for that. Thank you for liberating us political wives from our juggling act, and for giving us the freedom to try our own wings.

> —JOAN MONDALE, wife of Vice-President Walter Mondale, in an address to the National Women's Political Caucus

I handled my mid-life crisis by resigning my job at public television and running for office.

> —RONNIE ELDRIDGE, Political Candidate

You do not seem to understand who I am. I am a black woman, the daughter of a dining-car worker. I am a black woman who could not buy a house eight years ago in parts of the District of Columbia.

If my life has had any meaning at all, it is that those who start out as outcasts can wind up as being part of the system. Maybe others can forget what it was like to be excluded from the dining rooms in this very building, Senator, but I shall not forget.

> —PATRICIA ROBERTS HARRIS, secretary of housing and urban development, testifying before the Senate Committee during her confirmation hearing

A candidate running for Congress hired two assistants: one to dig up the facts and the other to bury them.

> —ANON.

Bette Lowrey was discovered in Dayton [Ohio] in a search for the "typical voter" by Scammon and Wattenberg, Washington journalists.

Scammon asked her about inflation. Mrs. Lowrey said, "It's an expensive depression." He asked her if he could use the phrase. "Sure," she replied. "All the words are in the dictionary."

Mrs. Lowrey is offended by the "Mrs. Average" tag. "It's not good, it's not bad. Average really is the wrong word. Typical is better. I represent not myself but the majority, which is female, Democratic, and lives in small suburban towns."

She says she enjoys the publicity: "Before this, the only other time I made the paper was for my pet bullfrog."

> —JONATHAN MILLER, *New Republic*

On one occasion, when President Woodrow Wilson had to travel through Missouri, he requested a stop in Hannibal, the place where Twain grew up. The president wandered through the town feeling nostalgia for his own boyhood, when he first had read Twain's stories.

Chancing upon a general store, Wilson entered and addressed the proprietor. "Pardon me. I'm a stranger in these parts. Could you tell me where Tom Sawyer was supposed to live?"

"Never heard of him," the storekeeper muttered.

"Well, how about Huck Finn?" asked the president.

The local man simply said, "Never heard of him neither."

"How about Puddinhead Wilson?"

"I heard of *him* all right," the proprietor suddenly said with vigor. "In fact, I even voted for the durn fool."

It is excellent to have a giant's strength,
But it is tyrannous to use it like a giant.

  —SHAKESPEARE

Charles Evans Hughes, U.S. Supreme Court justice, was the Republican presidential candidate against Woodrow Wilson in 1916. Hughes led in the early returns, and retired around midnight. Then the California returns started to come in, and in a dramatic reversal, they were heavily for Wilson. A reporter for a New York paper telephoned Hughes's hotel suite and asked to speak to him. He was told, "The president cannot be disturbed." The reporter said it was urgent. Would he care to leave a message? "Yes," said the reporter. "When the president wakes up, just tell him he isn't president."

  —TOM MCMORROW, *Daily News*

Bad officials are elected by good citizens who do not vote.

  —GEORGE JEAN NATHAN

I heard Willkie's [Wendell Willkie, Republican candidate for president in 1940] speech to organized labor in Pittsburgh over the radio. He said all the right things. "I will appoint a secretary of labor directly from the ranks of organized labor." Very good. Lots of applause. Willkie obviously loved it so he tried for a second hand. "And it will not be a woman, either," he told them. That was a boner! He not only took a swipe at my Labor Secretary, Frances Perkins, but at every woman in the United States. I knew right then that if we didn't do anything to break the spell, Wendell would talk himself out of enough votes to reelect me. It was a close race, but as an old politician, I considered that a turning point.

  —FRANKLIN D. ROOSEVELT, after his successful 1940 presidential
   campaign; in Howard Teichman, *Smart Aleck*

Here, richly, with ridiculous display,
The Politician's corpse was laid away.
While all of his acquaintances sneered and slanged,
I wept: for I had longed to see him hanged.

  —HILAIRE BELLOC

I am no politician and still less can I be said to be a party man; but I have a hatred of tyranny and a contempt for its tools; and this feeling I have expressed as often and as strongly as I could. . . . I deny that liberty and

slavery are convertible terms, that right and wrong, truth and falsehood, plenty and famine are matters of perfect indifference. That is all I know of the matter; but on these points I am likely to remain incorrigible.
—WILLIAM HAZLITT

A conservative is a person who does not think that anything should be done for the first time.
—FRANK VANDERLIP

Newspaperman Horace Greeley once spent three months serving in Congress.

In conversation one day during that time, a fellow legislator announced pompously, "I am a self-made man."

To this remark Greeley replied, "That, sir, relieves the Almighty of a great responsibility."

Democrats think of government as an art form. They practice it, relish it; they're schooled in it. For them it's a life's work. The Republicans think of government as a charity. They have a Junior League attitude. "I will give four years of my time." You never feel they enjoy it.
—LIZ CARPENTER

Edward M. Kennedy is the youngest majority whip in the history of the U.S. Senate. He landed there in 1962 after a race in which his mother, Rose Fitzgerald Kennedy, was perhaps his best campaigner. Her pitch was an exquisite blend of politics and religion.

In answer to the charge that Ted Kennedy was too young, she said, "You're right about Teddy. He's too young for that old Senate. As a matter of fact, I always wanted him to enter the priesthood. I thought for a time that Teddy would become one," she'd say with a catch in her voice that moved her audiences. "But he wanted to start out as a bishop," she would finish, bringing down the house.
—BOB CONSIDINE, Hearst Headline Service

Dorothy Detzer, prominent pacifist lobbyist, was denounced by a crowd in Concord, Mass., as "a Communist." Miss Detzer, after denying the charge, turned on one accuser and said, "And you are a nudist."

"No I'm not," said the man.

"Prove it," she retorted, finishing the exchange.

Have you ever seen a candidate talking to a rich person on television?
—ART BUCHWALD

This is the first convention of the space age—when a candidate can promise the moon and mean it.
—DAVID BRINKLEY

In politics as on the sickbed people toss from one side to another, thinking they will be more comfortable.
—GOETHE

Liberty will not descend to a people, a people must raise themselves to liberty.
—EMMA GOLDMAN

""!!!
•••

THE PRESS

The basis of our government being the opinion of the people, the very first object would be to keep that right; and were it left to me to decide whether we should have a government without newspapers, or newspapers without a government, I should not hesitate to prefer the latter.
—THOMAS JEFFERSON (1787)

The journalist in us was amused to read again that anecdote, no doubt apocryphal, about the American reporter who cabled an article to London in which the phrase "So's your old man" was used. An editor, a Cockney we are told, corrected the copy to read, "Your father is also."
—PAUL and QUINTANILLA, *Intoxication Made Easy*

"Dear Sir, I have two subscriptions to your newspaper," reads a recent letter received by our circulation department. "One paper is placed under the doormat and the other is tossed on the porch, where it blows away. Please cancel the subscription to the one that blows away."
—CHARLIE HOUK, Milwaukee *Journal*

The art of newspaper paragraphing is to stroke a platitude until it purrs like an epigram.
—DON MARQUIS

After the Civil War, young Mark Twain headed west to begin his literary career as a newspaper journalist. His first editor would not print any fact if the reporter could not vouch for its veracity.

Covering the society events new reporters are often tested on, Twain came back with this careful report:

"A woman giving the name of Mrs. James Jones, who is reported to be one of the society leaders of the city, is said to have given what purported to be a party yesterday for a number of alleged ladies. The hostess claims to be the wife of a reputed attorney."

Gypsy Rose Lee invited me to lunch, and so a terrified sixteen-year-old cub reporter arrived at her splendid town house. . . . When I finally blurted out, "Miss Lee, after the birth of your child, do you intend to resume your career?" she favored me with the one thing she knew could save me—a good quote.

"Honey," she said, "I can't have everything going out and nothing coming in."
—SHANA ALEXANDER, *Talking Woman*

Concerning the more stringent regulations of the CIA's relationships with journalists, one CIA old-timer commented, "The pendulum will swing and someday we'll be recruiting journalists again.

"When that day comes," he added confidently, "I will have no problem recruiting. I see a lot of them, and I know they're ripe for the plucking."
—JOHN M. CREWDSON

There ain't any news in being good. You might write the doings of all the convents of the world on the back of a postage stamp, and have room to spare.
—FINLEY PETER DUNNE

The English smear campaign is still the best in the world.
—JOHN DAVIES, *Punch*

A young woman graduate of a college of journalism arranged for an interview at a newspaper office. The interview over, she asked the personnel director when she should expect to hear from him. "A year from July," he answered. Later that same day, she telephoned him. "You forgot to tell me whether to come in the morning or the afternoon," she said.

Dead news like dead love has no phoenix in its ashes.
—ENID BAGNOLD

My title seemed to be clear enough—Press Secretary and Staff Director to the First Lady. But when people asked me to clarify it, I just said, "I help her help him." And that covered everything.

You are the bridge between those two separate worlds: the First Family and the press, the participants and the critics, the hunted and the hounds.

We came to work early, and if we didn't, we might as well have, because Lyndon Graham Bell himself was on the phone, bolting us out of bed with some gentle wakener, like: "Have you read page three of the *Washington Post?*"

My years with Lyndon Baines Johnson were anything but placid. They were eventful, frustrating, exhausting, exhilarating, hilarious—in short, the best years of my life. An old friend who served in the Roosevelt

administration warned me, "When you've worked in the White House, the rest of your life is like playing poker for matchsticks."
—LIZ CARPENTER, *Ruffles and Flourishes*

An American reading the Sunday paper in a state of lazy collapse is perhaps the most perfect symbol of the triumph of quantity over quality. . . . Whole forests are ground into pulp to minister to our triviality.
—IRVING BABBITT

I keep reading between the lies.
—GOODMAN ACE

There were literally dozens of problems arising from being female in that world [CBS News], and from the stereotype expected of women. To take a trivial example, if a male correspondent complained, he was merely analyzing the situation; if I were to do so, I was automatically "a bitch."
—NANCY DICKERSON, TV reporter, *Among Those Present*

First, the morning paper. Not, of course, these current sheets full of lies and vulgarity. I always read the *Gaulois,* the issue of March 22, 1903. It's by far the best. It has some delightful scandal, some excellent fashion notes, and, of course, the last-minute bulletin on the death of Leonide LeBlanc. She used to live next door, poor woman, and when I learn of her death every morning, it gives me quite a shock. I'd gladly lend you my copy, but it's in tatters.
—JEAN GIRAUDOUX, *The Madwoman of Chaillot*

When the great developments in American society can take place almost unnoticed by major American newspapers and broadcasters, and when important institutions and processes find the American press mostly indifferent to their functioning, it's hard to make the case for that press as a superpower.
—TOM WICKER, "On Press," *NYT*

RELIGION

I count religion but a childish toy,
And hold there is no sin but ignorance.
—CHRISTOPHER MARLOW, *The Jew of Malta*

There lives more faith in honest doubt,
Believe me, than in half the creeds.

>   —QUOTED BY ELIZABETH CADY STANTON in Preface to *The*
>   *Woman's Bible* (1898)

A minister's wife asked George Bernard Shaw which denomination
he belonged to. "I'm an atheist and I thank God for it," snapped
Shaw.

>   —RUDOLF FLESCH, *The Book of Unusual Quotations*

Dialogue between waitresses talking across the counter during the after-
lunch lull in a coffee shop:
   The Blonde one: "Hey, on the day I die do you think they'll close up this
shop?"
   The Gray-Haired One: "Yeah, sure. For a whole month."
   The Blonde One [*suddenly glum*]: "Well I don't want to talk about
it."
   The Gray-Haired One: "Listen, don't worry. You think when you go up
there [*pointing heavenward*] you're gonna have to rush around carrying
plates of hamburger? Oh, no—it's gonna be nice. When you get there you
can just fly around and do what you want. You won't even have to set your
hair."

>   —LENORE BLUMENFELD, "Metropolitan Diary," *NYT*

Know ye not that a little leaven leaveneth the whole lump? Purge out
therefore the old leaven, that ye may be a new lump.

>   —ST. PAUL, I Corinthians 5:7

I cannot praise the Doctor's eyes;
I never saw his glance divine;
He always shuts them when he prays,
And when he preaches he shuts mine.

>   —GEORGE OUTRAM, in Ralph L. Woods,
>   *Third Treasury of the Familiar*

Whenever I noticed a romantic twinkle in the eye of a woman in my
congregation, I always checked to make sure it wasn't caused by a reflection from the gleam in my own.

>   —LETTER FROM A MINISTER to "Dear Abby" (Abigail Van Buren),
>   Chicago Tribune-New York News Syndicate

O Lord, in thy grace and favor look upon the people of the Greater and
Lesser Cumbraes, and in thy mercy do not forget the inhabitants of the
adjacent islands of Great Britain and Ireland.

>   —A MINISTER'S PRAYER on the tiny islands off the coast of
>   Scotland, in Sir Walter Scott, *Diary* (1827)

A Mrs. Hummock gave her church a stained-glass window to commemo-
rate her late husband, and the vicar, to be sure he credited her properly,
rhymed her name in his mind with "stomach." It was perhaps inevitable
that in his thanks from the pulpit she came out as "our beloved patroness
. . . Mrs. Kelly."
—ADAPTED FROM WILLARD R. ESPY, *Words at Play*

The old rabbi, surrounded by his disciples, was nodding sleepily. They
began to praise him—how fortunate they were to be studying with a
teacher so wise, so learned, with so brilliant a mind. They paused for a
moment. The old man opened one eye and said, "And how about my
modesty?"

Ministers have a real problem. They're still against sin, but they're no
longer sure what qualifies.
—ORBEN'S COMEDY FILLERS

We must gird up our loins and fulfill God's will.
—BRIGHAM YOUNG, second president of the Mormons, on
polygamy

Jewish women live in a twilight zone of myth.
They are programmed to be enablers, to do whatever they have to do
—housework, cooking, taking care of the children—to enable Jewish men
to do their thing. They do it because of the myth that they have this
honored and important role in Jewish survival, and that if they don't the
Jewish people are going to fall apart.
—AVIVA CANTOR ZUCKOFF, ed., *Hadassah*

The woman who most attracts our attention in the Book of Judges is
Deborah, priestess, prophetess, poetess, and judge. What woman is there
in modern or in ancient history who equals in loftiness of position, in
public esteem and honorable distinction this gifted and heroic Jewish
creation? . . . She was consulted by the children of Israel in all matters
of religion and of war. Her judgment seat was under a palm tree, known
ever after as "Deborah's Palm." Though she was one of the great judges
of Israel for forty years, her name is not in the list, as it should have been,
with Gideon, Barak, Samson and Jephthah.
—CLARA B. NEYMAN, *The Woman's Bible*

If we accept the Darwinian theory, that the race has been a gradual
growth from the lower to a higher form of life, and that the story of the
fall is a myth, we can exonerate the snake, emancipate the woman, and
reconstruct a more rational religion for the nineteenth century, and thus
escape all the perplexities of the Jewish mythology as of no more importance than those of the Greek, Persian and Egyptian.
—ELIZABETH CADY STANTON, Summation, *The Woman's Bible*

More tears are shed in playhouses than in churches.
—TYRONE GUTHRIE

There's no need for funless people committed to social justice.... Let us try to heed the advice of whoever it was who said, "Take yourself lightly, so that, like angels, you may fly."
—REV. WILLIAM SLOANE COFFIN

Many bring their clothes to church rather than themselves.
—ANON.

There is something impressive, awful, in the simplicity and terrible directness of the book of Esther. Esther stands before her wicked lord. She knows her life is in his hands; there is no one to protect her from his wrath. Yet, conquering her woman's fear, she approaches him, animated by the noblest patriotism, having but one thought: "If I perish, I perish; but if I live, my people shall live." . . .

[And] Ruth is so loyal and gentle-hearted, we cannot help loving her, as she stands with the reapers amid the waving corn. Her beautiful, unselfish spirit shines out like a bright star in the night of a dark and cruel age. Love like Ruth's, love which can rise above conflicting creeds and deep-seated racial prejudices, is hard to find in all the world.
—HELEN KELLER, *The Story of My Life*

Jesus defied convention to teach that there are no distinctions between male and female. But within fifty years of his crucifixion, a strong strain of anti-feminism surfaced among his followers and the position of women in the Church began to decline. Thereafter, the priesthood was limited to men.
—SISTER ELIZABETH CARROLL, Catholic Sister of Mercy, *Woman's Almanac*

Do not be afraid. Trust in God. She will protect you.
—EMMELINE PANKHURST, English suffragist

Though most women continue to think of God as "He," a surprising 38 percent expressed the view that God was neither male nor female.
—GALLUP POLL—1976, *Woman's Almanac*

Haven't chosen yet!
—IMOGEN CUNNINGHAM, the photographer, in her nineties, when asked three days before her death to state her religion on a hospital form

"If you had not lost your faith death would not terrify you so," wrote the devout, with rancorous commiseration [for Mother's death]. Well-intentioned readers urged, "Disappearing is not of the least importance: Your

works will remain." And inwardly I told them all that they were wrong. Religion could do no more for my mother than the hope of posthumous success could do for me. Whether you think of it as heavenly or as earthly, if you love life, immortality is no consolation for death.
—SIMONE DE BEAUVOIR, *A Very Easy Death*

There is no excuse for secondary sexism, put in gratuitously by translators. The Greek wording said, "If anyone" and the translation came out "If a man." When Moses talked of "God, who bore you," the translators made it "begot." There was clearly a feminine reference in the original.
We are in a language bind. I see no way to change the Lord's Prayer to "Our Parent, Who art in heaven."
—DR. WILLIAM HOLLADAY

[Let's] start praying to "Our Mother, Who art in heaven," and see how it sounds for the next week.
—DR. BEVERLY HARRISON, *NYT*

I couldn't handle 500 anxieties anymore.
—A RABBI who gave up his congregation

Atheists have an excellent longevity record because we have no place to go after we die, so we take good care of ourselves and our world while we are here.
—MADALYN MURRAY O'HAIR

A diplomat asked the Pontiff how many persons worked at the Vatican. Winking an eye, Pope John XXIII replied: "Oh, no more than half of them!"
—RALPH L. WOODS, *Third Treasury of the Familiar*

On a New England April: "What a misnomer in our climate to call this season spring, very much like calling Calvinism religion."
—LYDIA MARIA CHILD, in Seth Curtis Beach, *Daughters of the Puritans*

THE PREACHER: RUMINATES BEHIND THE SERMON

I think it must be lonely to be God.
Nobody loves a master. No. Despite
The bright hosannas, bright dear-Lords, and bright
Determined reverence of Sunday eyes. . . .

Perhaps—who knows?—He tires of looking down.
Those eyes are never lifted. Never straight.

Perhaps He tires of being great
In solitude. Without a hand to hold.

—GWENDOLYN BROOKS

The pope one day told his cardinals that he had good news and bad news. The good news: "I've just received a phone call from Jesus, who has returned to earth." The bad news: "He was calling from Salt Lake City."

—MSGR. GENO BARONI, quoted in *The Wall Street Journal*

It's going to be fun to watch and see how long the meek can keep the earth after they inherit it.

—KIN HUBBARD

Say not, if people are good to us, we will do good to them, and if people oppress us we will oppress them; but resolve that if people do good to you, you will do good to them, and if they oppress you, oppress them not again.

—MOHAMMED

I NEVER SAW A MOOR

I never saw a moor,
I never saw the sea;
Yet know I how the heather looks,
And what a wave must be.
I never spoke with God,
Nor visited in heaven
Yet certain am I of the spot
As if the chart were given.

—EMILY DICKINSON

I did not merely observe the Sufi dancers, I whirled too. I did not just read about Zen, I "sat," I chanted with the Hare Krishnas. I stood on my head . . . and spent hours softly intoning a mantra to myself. . . .

[Americans] through chanting, meditating and exercise, wanted an immediacy of experience, without the intervention of intellectual concepts. Some were looking for authority, or charisma, and some of the women were looking for relief from the male domination of Western faiths . . . I expect this Westernized pseudo-Oriental pastiche to spread. . . . We can expect to see the growing use of meditation and eventually of any religious discipline . . . to enhance the exploration and realization of the insatiable Western self.

—HARVEY COX, *The Promise and Peril of the New Orientation*

IN THEIR EDEN

ADAM: "Do you love me, Eve?"
EVE: "Who else?"

God Himself dare not appear to a hungry man except in the form of bread.
—MAHATMA GANDHI

A southern Negro was refused entrance into an all-white church. The sexton told him to go back to his own church and pray to God.

The next Sunday he was back to tell the sexton, "I took your advice and prayed to God—and He told me, 'Take it easy, Sam, I've been trying to get into that church for years and haven't made it yet.' "
—JOEY ADAMS, *Son of Encyclopedia of Humor*

George Bernard Shaw would have understood my feeling about souvenirs. When he went to the Holy Land in 1931, his old friend, the Abbess of Stanbrook, asked him to bring her something from Calvary. Disgusted with commercial souvenirs, Shaw brought her a small stone he had found on a road in Bethlehem. "Heaven knows whose footprints may be on the stone," he wrote her. He presented it to her in a silver reliquary.

Now that's what I call a souvenir.
—MARY Z. GRAY

At a sermon being preached in a country church all fell a-weeping—all but one. When she was asked why she did not weep with the rest, she replied, "I belong to another parish."
—ADAPTED FROM LOUIS UNTERMEYER, ed., *Great Humor*

God gives every bird its food, but he does not throw it into the nest.
—J. G. HOLLAND

A minister famous for his abstinence was persuaded to take one small glass of cherry brandy. Then, after two more had been consumed and enjoyed, his host promised to send him a couple of bottles provided the reverend gentleman acknowledge the gift in the parish newsletter. The next bulletin contained the following announcement: "Your minister wishes to acknowledge and express his thanks for the most welcome gift of fruit and the spirit in which it was given."
—SYLVIA L. BOCHIN, ed., *After-Dinner Laughter*

This afternoon there will be a meeting in the south and north ends of the church. Children will be baptized at both ends.

The service will close with "Little Drops of Water." One of the ladies will start quietly and the rest of the congregation will join in.

On Sunday, a special collection will be taken to defray the expenses of the new carpet. All those wishing to do something on the carpet please come forward and get a piece of paper.

The ladies of the church have cast off clothing of every kind, and they may be seen in the church basement on Friday afternoon.

Thursday at 5:00 P.M. there will be a meeting of the Little Mothers Club. All wishing to become little mothers will please meet the minister in his study.

Wednesday, the Ladies Literary Society will meet. Mrs. Johnson will sing "Put Me in My Little Bed" accompanied by the preacher.

    —FROM A COLLECTION OF CHURCH BULLETINS by Rev. Stanley H.
       Conover, in *Modern Maturity*

""!!!**
...
SCIENCE

What this meant for me at the time was that my [scientific] research was in jeopardy. There were experimental conditions I needed to run that simply could not be done without a computer. So there I was, doing research with stone-age equipment, trying to get by with wonder-woman reflexes and a flashlight, while a few floors below, my colleague was happily operating "his" computer. It's as if we women are in a totally rigged race. A lot of men are driving souped-up, low-slung racing cars, and we're running as fast as we can in tennis shoes we managed to salvage from a local garage sale.

    —NAOMI WEISSTEIN, SARA RUDDICK and PAMELA DANIELS, eds.,
       Working It Out

The marvels of modern technology include the development of a soda can which, when discarded, will last forever—and a $7,000 car which, when properly cared for, will rust out in two or three years.

    —PAUL HARWITZ, in *The Wall Street Journal*

Thomas Edison loved gadgets of all kinds, and filled his home with mechanisms for many purposes.

His summer home had an incredibly difficult turnstile in front of the house. It took a mighty force to push it. A friend asked him, "Why is everything so perfect here except that awful turnstile?"

Edison smiled. "Shh!" he said. "Everybody who pushes the turnstile pumps eight gallons of water into the tank on my roof!"

"I accept the Universe," Margaret Fuller told Carlyle. "Egad, you'd better," he answered.

It soon may be possible for a couple to rent a young lady's womb as an incubator for their child. Cow wombs are cheaper. That too is a coming possibility.

    —VANCE PACKARD, *The People Shapers*

Science is a first-rate piece of furniture for a man's upper chamber if he has common sense on the ground floor.

    —O. W. HOLMES, *The Poet at the Breakfast Table*

Now that women astronauts are moving into the space program, we wonder if spacecraft will be redesigned with rear seats so that the ladies may exercise their rare talents for backseat driving.

    —"NO COMMENT," *MS*

Scientists are conducting research that is attempting to isolate a single chemical that is responsible for sexual attraction. . . . It may just be a primal response to what we smell.

    The Fragrance Foundation even went so far as to put Margaret Mead on the podium for a fragrance seminar. Predictably, the feisty anthropologist slapped the wrists of the cosmetics industry and told them to think more about ordinary smells, and less about making us so unnaturally clean and homogenized, lest they evolve our sense of smell right out of existence.

    —GAYLE BRYAN, *New Dawn*

BETSIE: America's scientists are the greatest in the world.
GRANDMA: What's so great?
BETSIE: Look at their achievements! Computers that can figure out problems that would take a human being a hundred years; spaceships to the planets; mechanical hearts. There is absolutely nothing our scientists can't solve.
GRANDMA: So why don't they invent something we shouldn't have to return to the bathroom to jiggle the hook?

    —*Encyclopedia of Jewish Humor*

His theory of relativity, as worded by Albert Einstein for laymen: "When does Zurich stop at this train?"

Science is really going away at a rapid pace. Now it's only a hundred years behind the comic strips.

    —JOEY ADAMS

The comet that Maria Mitchell (1818–1889) discovered from the roof of her home was named for her. She became the first woman elected to the Academy of Arts and Sciences and a professor of Vassar's first faculty. Dr. Mitchell didn't believe in grades: "You cannot mark a human mind," she would say.

    —*Woman's Almanac*

‘‘’’|||
!!!
•••

SELF-IMAGE
PSYCHOLOGY

Nora asked Helmer, "What do you consider is my most sacred duty?" and when he answered, "Your duty to your husband and children," she replied:

"I have another duty, just as sacred.... My duty to myself.... I believe that before everything else I'm a human being—just as much as you are ... or at any rate I shall try to become one. I know quite well that most people would agree with you, Torvald, and that you have a warrant for it in books; but I can't be satisfied any longer with what most people say, and with what's in books. I must think things out for myself and try to understand them."

 —HENRIK IBSEN, *A Doll's House*

Housewives are beginning to feel they are nothing. If you watch any of the talk shows, like Johnny Carson, where the host meets the audience, you can see it happening live. "Yes, Mrs. Mary Smith, and what do you do?" he asks. Years ago, Mrs. Mary Smith would smilingly say she was a housewife. Today, her response is muffled, even apologetic.

 —RENEE VALENTE, *Working Woman*

There are few good women who do not tire of their role.

 —FRANÇOIS DE LA ROCHEFOUCAULD

... What, after all, is a halo? It's only one more thing to keep clean.

 —CHRISTOPHER FRY

Who can say more than this rich praise, that you alone are you.

 —SHAKESPEARE

No one can make you feel inferior without your consent.

 —ELEANOR ROOSEVELT

You can never have a greater or a less dominion than over yourself.

 —LEONARDO DA VINCI

Despite the penalties for using power in strong ways, a woman has little choice if she wants to be effective. Someday such things as gentleness, empathy, and caring, traditionally feminine ways of thinking and behaving, will come to be recognized as being compatible with competence and expertise.
—*New Woman*

I live alone and sometimes I wish there were a toothbrush in the holder next to mine. I often eat alone, sleep alone, and go to the movies alone, even on Saturday night. Some of my friends live the same way, and we agree that being alone is a tax we pay for the luxury of our freedom.
—*New Dawn*

If only we'd stop trying to be happy, we could have a pretty good time.
—EDITH WHARTON, quoted by Willard R. Espy, in *An Almanac of Words at Play*

Better to have pain than paralysis.
—FLORENCE NIGHTINGALE

Noise proves nothing. Often a hen who has merely laid an egg cackles as if she had laid an asteroid.
—MARK TWAIN, *Pudd'nhead Wilson's Calendar*

Since a lot of our duties are undignified, we learn not to let our self-image depend on what we're doing at the moment—which is picking bubble gum out of the bathroom rug. We can rise above it. Men, however, keep *looking* at themselves. If they see themselves in an apron with a broom, they feel just awful.
—BARBARA HOLLAND, *Woman's Day*

What in God's name is wrong with being feminine?
Feminine is beautiful.
It's refreshing and most important, it's so relaxing.
Have you ever heard a man apologize for being masculine? Of course not. That's always been a good word, a positive word.
Why isn't it feminine to go out and get the story no matter what, beat someone out of it, scoop other reporters, win? All those things I was doing were *not* masculine. They were acts committed by a female in her everyday line of work with the same goal as a man would have—to do well, to win—and therefore feminine.
—SALLY QUINN, *New Woman*

Little girl batter to little boy pitcher: "No, I'm not a tomboy! Are you a tomgirl?"
—*New Woman*

It is the long people, not the short people, who have the hard life. Short people are never accosted by imbeciles who want to know, "How's the weather up there?" Short people never have to sleep with their feet dangling over the end of the mattress.

Male short people do not have to suffer nicknames like "Bones" and "Stork." Female short people never have to lean over to be kissed. Short people do not have to go through life seeing the dust on the top of the refrigerator. . . .

Long people are expected to live in a perpetual stoop. This is one of the baldest injustices of all . . . and as the years of courteous, unselfish stooping begin to bow his back and permanently round his shoulders, people of less altitude deride him for bad posture.

—RUSSELL BAKER, "Sorrows of the Long People"

Negro blood is sure powerful—because just one drop of black blood makes a colored man. *One* drop—you are a Negro! Now, why is that? Why is Negro blood so much more powerful than any other kind of blood in the world? If a man has Irish blood in him, people will say, "He's *part* Irish." If he has a little Jewish blood, they'll say, "He's *half* Jewish." But if he has just a small bit of colored blood in him, BAM!— "He's a Negro." Not "He's *part* Negro." You can have ninety-nine drops of white blood in your veins down South—but if that other *one* drop is black, shame on you. Even if you look white, you're black. That black is really powerful.

—LANGSTON HUGHES, *Simple Takes a Wife*

When an individual is kept in a situation of inferiority the fact is that he does become inferior.

—SIMONE DE BEAUVOIR

Alone in No. 1 dressing room without my closest friends, I developed a star complex, and for a time I was really impossible. Then Pamela came to see me . . . she was in no mood to put up with my fanciful airs. She told me outright that I had become a bore. Thinking it over, I decided I far preferred the company of my friends to the isolated pinnacle implied by the title Prima Ballerina ASSOLUTA. So I climbed down. As a matter of fact, it was partly the fault of those who, with the best will, unwittingly destroy you with such talk as: "People should fall back in awe when you leave the stage door"; "You should be treated like a queen." All of which is, of course, rubbish. Great artists are people who find their way to be themselves in their art. All sort of pretension induces mediocrity in art and life alike.

—MARGOT FONTEYN, *Autobiography*

Before you let yourself go, be sure you can get yourself back.

—ROGER ALLEN, *Grand Rapids Press*

Six people shoved ahead of you the other morning when you were standing in line for the bus. At lunch, it took you twenty minutes to catch the waiter's eye. On the way back to the office, you wanted to buy some shampoo, but you finally stalked out of the drugstore, the salesman kept ignoring you.

"Well maybe I do slouch a little," you admit. "And of course I don't SHOUT when I talk. But people do pick on me more than others."

The conviction—that people take advantage of you and that there's nothing you can do about it—is the heart of the problem. What your actions are saying is, "I'm so helpless, world. Take care of me."

A Chronic Victim, experts agree, really relishes the "Woe is me" role. It's a way of dealing with the world.

You have to understand why you're acting the way you are and realize you're victimizing yourself. When your feelings change, your behavior will, too.

> —DR. ERNEST BEIER, quoted by Constance Rosenblum, *Daily News*

Fear less, hope more, eat less, chew more, whine less, breathe more, talk less, say more, hate less, love more and all good things will be yours.
> —SWEDISH PROVERB

Compulsive neatness can mask internal confusion. The woman who fears her life is crumbling may have the most meticulously ordered desk; the man at sea about his future may maintain a dazzling file system.

One reason this behavior is so insidious is that it takes on a fierce moral cast. For the compulsively neat, it's dirty socks, not good intentions, that pave the way to hell.
> —CONSTANCE ROSENBLUM, *Daily News*

A young woman, an assistant bank manager, under considerable stress on her job consulted a psychotherapist who suggested she take tranquilizers every four hours.

On the next visit she was asked, "Have the pills relaxed you?"

"Oh, yes," replied the young woman.

"And how do you feel about your job?" continued the psychotherapist.

"Who cares?" said the patient.

The most noticeable thing about her [Cicely Tyson] was her sense of herself. She was her own measuring stick. And she didn't look to the left or the right or talk about how unfair it was for blacks in the arts. She's just right for these times, and she won't take anything less than what she is. She's a very special—a very seldom—lady.
> —VINNETTE CARROLL, drama teacher, *MS*

All this talk of painless life has disturbing implications. . . .

Do away with the sensation of pain, not the situations that cause pain, these psychologies tell us, and get back to business as usual.

. . . Should we follow this prescription, we would place ourselves in considerable danger. For we would lose the important, if unpleasant, virtue of pain [and] . . . the impulse to real change.
—SUZANNE GORDON, *Lonely in America*

We cannot live in the afternoon of life according to the program of life's morning. For what was great in the morning will be little at evening, and what in the morning was true, will at evening have become a lie.
—CARL JUNG

Psychoanalysis is the creation of a male genius, and almost all those who have developed his ideas have been men. It is only right and reasonable that they should evolve more easily a masculine psychology and understand more of the development of men than of women.
—KAREN HORNEY, *Feminine Psychology*

It was like a revelation to me, taking complete responsibility for one's own actions. I thought, "I'm unscrewing myself." That's why people use the phrase, "all screwed up."
—CARY GRANT, interviewed in *NYT Mag.*

Worry is a thin stream of fear trickling through the mind. If encouraged, it cuts a channel into which all other thoughts are drained.
—ARTHUR SOMERS ROCHE

You never realize what a good memory you have until you try to forget something.
—FRANKLIN P. JONES, *Quote*

He jests at scars that never felt a wound.
—SHAKESPEARE

What an excellent name for a psychoanalyst is Schrenk-Notzing. For truly they shrink from nothing.
—CHRISTOPHER MORLEY

Fear is static that prevents me from hearing my intuition.
—HUGH PRATHER, *Notes to Myself*

Fortunately analysis is not the only way to resolve inner conflicts. Life itself still remains a very effective therapist.
—KAREN HORNEY, *Our Inner Conflicts*

A teen-ager was going through a psychological testing procedure.
A psychiatrist showed her an ink blot. "What does it remind you of?" he asked. "Boys," she answered.

He showed her another ink blot. "What does this remind you of?"
"Boys," she answered. He showed her a third ink blot. "What does this
remind you of?"
"Boys!"
"All you seem to think about is sex," the psychiatrist said.
The girl was indignant. "All *I* seem to think about? Who's showing the
dirty pictures?"

A neurotic is a person who builds a castle in the air. A psychotic is
the person who lives in it. A psychiatrist is the one who collects the
rent.
—JEROME LAWRENCE

What I don't understand is that with so many of us stuck with these
clichéd feminine/masculine, submissive/dominant, masochistic/sadis-
tic fantasies, how are we ever going to adjust fully to the less thrilling but
more desirable reality of equality?
—NORA EPHRON, *Crazy Salad*

The psychic task which a person can and must set for himself is not to
feel secure but to be able to tolerate insecurity.
—ERICH FROMM

What wound ever healed but by degrees?
—SHAKESPEARE

Nostalgia is recalling the fun without reliving the pain.
—*National Enquirer*

In [our] psychological society the concept of sin has given way to the
concept of sick . . . privacy has become a serious victim . . . [Americans]
will tell their life stories to professionals, paraprofessionals, even laymen
who will listen. They will spill out their secret resentment, problems, and
sex lives to a dozen strangers called a group.
—MARTIN L. GROSS, *The Psychological Society*

When you have to make a choice and don't make it, that is in itself a
choice.
—WILLIAM JAMES

Spotted on the wall near the office of the Psychology Department at
Columbia University:
"Does the name Pavlov ring a bell?"
—"METROPOLITAN DIARY," *NYT*

SEX!

Believe me, the pleasure of love is not to be rushed, but gradually elicited by well-tempered delay. When you have found the place where a woman loves to be fondled, don't you be ashamed to touch it any more than she is. You will see her eyes gleaming with a tremulous brightness like the glitter of the sun reflected in clear water. Then she will moan and murmur lovingly, sigh sweetly, and find words that suit her pleasure. But be sure that you don't sail too fast and leave your mistress behind, nor let her complete her course before you. Race to the goal together. Then pleasure is complete, when man and woman lie vanquished side by side. This tempo you must keep when you dally freely, and fear does not rush a secret affair. When delay is dangerous, then it is useful to speed ahead with full power, spurring your horse as she comes.
> —OVID (43 B.C.–17 A.D.)

After drinking, my thoughts turned to Venus, for as surely as cold causes hailstones, a liquorous mouth makes a lecherous tail.

A wise wife who knows what's good for her will be able to convince her husband that the little gossipy bird is crazy, and arrange for her own maid to bear her witness. . . .

The man who will not allow another to light a candle from his lantern is too stingy; his light will not be therefore less, by God. So long as you have enough, you shouldn't complain.

And, therefore, I give everybody this advice; anyone can profit, for everything is for sale; with an empty hand a man lures no hawks.

And, by my faith, I paid them word for word. So help me omnipotent God, if I had to make my last testament right now, I don't owe them a word that is not paid.
> —GEOFFREY CHAUCER, The Wife of Bath's Prologue, *Canterbury Tales*

Woman is man's joy and all his bliss.
> —GEOFFREY CHAUCER, The Nun's Priest's Tale, *Canterbury Tales*

Wandering through the famous house at Nahant where George Sand, mistress of so many famous men, had lived, Henry James said to Edith Wharton: "In which of these rooms, I wonder, did George herself sleep?" To mutter a moment later: "Though in which indeed, my dear, did she *not?*"
> —LOUIS KRONENBERGER, *The Cutting Edge*

REPENTANCE

"Now that poor wayward Jane is big with child.
She has repented and is reconciled
To lead a virtuous life in thought and deed."
So spoke her aunt, and all the girls agreed.

Then one of them, an artless, large-eyed one,
Murmured, "Repentance we would never shun—
But first let's learn to do what Jane has done."

> —JEAN DE LA FONTAINE

The best account I have seen of the causes of this disease [nymphomania] is as follows: all circumstances capable of producing an exaltation of excitement in the brain and nervous system, such as the reading of lascivious and impassioned works, viewing voluptuous paintings, romantic conversations, frequent visits to balls or theaters, the too assiduous cultivation of the fine arts, the abuse of aphrodisiac remedies, or of spiritous liquors, or of aromatics and perfumes, which excite too much the brain and general sensibility.

The causes which act directly upon the genital organs (the exciting causes), and which may afterward act sympathetically upon the brain, are masturbation, the abuse of coition, pruritus of the vulva, inflammation of the nymphae, clitoris, neck of the uterus, and ovaries.

> —WILLIAM A. ALCOTT, *The Young Woman's Book of Health*
> (1855)

'Tis the devil inspires the evanescent ardor, in order to divert the parties from prayer.

> —MARTIN LUTHER

It is a well-established fact that in healthy loving women, uninjured by the too frequent lesions which result from childbirth, increasing physical satisfaction attaches to the ultimate physical expression of love. . . . Love between the sexes is the highest and mightiest form of human sexual passion.

> —DR. ELIZABETH BLACKWELL, *The Human Element in Sex*
> (c. 1870)

The apathy of the sexual instinct in woman is caused by the enslaved and unhealthy condition in which she lives. . . . Healthy and loving women are destroyed by being made bond-women, having no spontaneity, and bearing children more rapidly than they ought, and in unhealthy condition.

> —T. L. NICHOLS, M.D., and MRS. MARY S. GOVE NICHOLS, *Marriage:*
> *Its History, Character & Results, Its Sanctities, and Its*
> *Profanities; Its Science & Its Facts* (1854)

Masturbation causes convulsions, emaciation, and pain in the membranes of the brain; it deadens the senses, particularly the sight, gives rise to dorsal consumption, and various other mental and bodily disorders.

—Dr. Morrill, *Physiology of Woman and Her Diseases* [1855] in Nancy Cott, *The Roots of Bitterness*

A well-bred woman does not seek carnal gratification, and she is usually apathetic to sexual pleasures. If women were as salacious as men, morality, chastity, and virtue would not exist and the world would be but one vast brothel.

—DR. O. A. WALL, *Sex and Sex Worship* (1932)

The seventh commandment states: "Thou shalt not commit adultery." The seventh commandment does not say "Thou shalt not commit fornication," which is sexual relations between unmarried men and women. Premarital lovemaking was common in [eighteenth-century] Puritan New England. . . .

—PAGE SMITH, *Daughters of the Promised Land*

MACDUFF: What three things does drink especially provoke?
PORTER: Marry, sir, nose-painting, sleep, and urine. Lechery, sir, it provokes and unprovokes. It provokes the desire, but it takes away the performance; therefore, much drink may be said to be an equivocator with lechery; it makes him and it mars him; it sets him on, and it takes him off; it persuades him, and disheartens him; makes him stand to and not stand to; in conclusion, equivocates him in a sleep, and, giving him the lie, leaves him.

—SHAKESPEARE, *Macbeth,* II, 3

Chastity—the most unnatural of the sexual perversions.
—ALDOUS HUXLEY

Chastity—perhaps the most peculiar of all sexual aberrations.
—REMY DE GOURMONT

When the candles are out all women are fair.
—PLUTARCH, Conjugal Precepts (c. 350 B.C.)

When the candles are out, all cats are gray.
—HEYWOOD'S PROVERBS (1546)

When a woman has lost her chastity, she will shrink from no crime.
—TACITUS

Chastity is tagged, like a packet of cigarettes, with the warning that it can damage your health.

There is no evidence that sex is a categorical imperative like food or oxygen; and there is no evidence that voluntary abstention from it leads to neurosis or emotional disturbance.

—ELAINE MORGAN, *The Listener*

Much of man's sex is in his mind, while woman's is more centrally located.

—PAGE SMITH, *Daughters of the Promised Land*

Sex: In America an obsession. In other parts of the world a fact.

—MARLENE DIETRICH, *ABC's*

A friend of young Samuel Hopkins Adams once showed him an invitation he had received to a nudist party. Adams said he thought the idea sounded like fun. Laughing, his friend dared Adams to go, and so he did.

When the two met again, the friend asked Adams how the gathering had gone.

"They didn't do things by halves," said the adventurer. "Even the butler who opened the door for me was completely nude."

"If he wasn't uniformed, how did you know it was the butler?" wondered the friend.

"Well," reflected Adams, "it certainly wasn't the maid."

A little theory makes sex more interesting, more comprehensible, and less scary—too much is a putdown, especially as you're likely to get it out of perspective and become a spectator of your own performance.

—ALEX COMFORT, *The Joy of Sex*

The lusty, lascivious, impulsive, selfish, carefree brigand that women often envision, to the clandestine delight of men, is not a man at all—he is a satyr, a myth. Most men still choose marriage.

—ANTHONY PIETROPINTO, M.D., and Jacqueline Simenauer, *Beyond the Male Myth*

The men came behind their wives like shadows. They had less color, less distinctiveness, less personality. They were like the males in pornographic movies: The film is written, directed, and produced by them, includes male figures, and is intended for them, intended to please men. But the whole film focuses on the female, upon her body, her joy.

—MARILYN FRENCH, *The Woman's Room*

I don't know why I'm here. I'm only nude because there's nothing to do here with your clothes on.

—CLIENT AT A SWINGER'S CLUB, *Time*

The human body is not obscene, sexuality is not obscene.

But [pornography] is not sex, it is violence. It encourages acceptance of the idea that violence is a legitimate part of sexuality.
        —GLORIA STEINEM

A survey was taken on the nocturnal habits of men. The results showed that 5 percent of the men get up to drink a glass of water, 10 percent to go to the bathroom, and 85 percent get up to go home.
        —JOE URIS

The more I was treated as a woman, the more woman I became. I adapted willy-nilly. If I was assumed to be incompetent at reversing cars, or opening bottles, oddly, incompetent I found myself becoming. If a case was thought too heavy for me, inexplicably I found it so myself. . . .
        —JAN MORRIS (formerly James Morris), *Conundrum*

Whoever called it necking was a poor judge of anatomy.
        —GROUCHO MARX

The act of sex, gratifying as it may be, is God's joke on humanity. It is man's last desperate stand at superintendency.
        —BETTE DAVIS

An amorous fellow hotly wooed a pretty young wife. "Pray cease," said she. "I have a husband that won't thank you for making him a cuckold."
        "No, madam," replied the young fellow. "But you will, I hope."
        —LOUIS UNTERMEYER, ed., *Great Humor*

The myth of Casanova's Retribution—the belief that sexual "excess" wears you out young and leaves you gasping from exhaustion by age forty-five—is precisely 180 degrees wrong.
        —CAROL TAURIS, social psychologist, *MS*

If strict monogamy is the height of all virtue then the palm goes to the tapeworm, which has a complete set of male and female sexual organs in each of its 50–200 proglottides or sections and spends its whole life copulating in all its sections with itself.
        —FRIEDRICH ENGELS, *The Origin of the Family*

As soon as Mathilde [the milliner] arrived in Lima she attained her dream. Men approached her with flowery words, disguising their intent with great charm and adornments. This prelude to the sexual act satisfied her. She liked a little incense. In Lima she received much of it, it was a part of the ritual. She was raised on a pedestal of poetry so that her falling into the final embrace might seem more of a miracle. She sold many more of her nights than hats.
        —ANAIS NIN, *Delta of Venus*

We don't pose men as sex objects. We think of it more as something of social value.

The first thing I look at are his eyes. If someone has dead eyes then, no matter how good his body is, I won't choose him. I believe that the eyes are the mirror of the soul, and that everything else is secondary.

—TONI HOLT, centerfold-coordinator for *Playgirl*

To err is human—but it feels divine.

—MAE WEST

A suave-looking chap invited a young lady to go home with him and see his stamp collection.

The girl smiled, shook her head, and said, "Philately will get you nowhere."

—AL ROTONDO, quoted by Norton Mockridge

I already know How—what I want to know is When.

—FROM A ST. VALENTINE'S DAY CARD

One guy to the other, at a singles' bar:

"I think she's really interested in me. She asked if I've had a vasectomy."

—*New Woman*

Dear Collector: We hate you. Sex loses all its power and magic when it becomes explicit, mechanical, a bore.

No two hairs alike, but you will not let us waste words on a description of hair; no two odors, but if we expand on this you cry Cut the poetry.

There are so many minor senses, all running like tributaries into the mainstream of sex, nourishing it.

—ANAIS NIN, in a letter to the old man who paid writers and poets a dollar a page for writing erotica, Preface to *Delta of Venus*

I see how every day Eve is punished again for man's anguish over Paradise Lost—and for her childbearing abilities.

Male emotions of rage, outrage, jealousy, and shame—toward more powerful men—are laid to rest, or acted out, in women's beds or in pornographic sexual fantasies.

—PHYLLIS CHESLER, *About Men*

Homosexuality is natural, but it isn't *as natural* as heterosexuality.

A fig tree, under ordinary conditions, grows up round. On a windy slope, it may take other shapes, and in a garden the gardener may espalier it—train it flat against a sunny wall. The wind-swept tree and the espaliered tree aren't "unnatural," as a genetically deformed tree is; they have just developed in ways that are different from the usual way because of special influences at work. But in one sense the round tree is the more natural one; it has the shape most likely to develop in most conditions in which the tree lives and grows.

    —MORTON HUNT, *Gay*

Making love is a mental illness that wastes time and energy.

    —CHINESE COMMUNIST PARTY SLOGAN

One might say that the activity of ova involves a daring and independence absent, in fact, from the activity of spermatozoa, which move in jostling masses, swarming out on signal like a crowd of commuters from the 5:15.

    —MARY ELLMAN, *Thinking About Women*

FOR A PRAYING MANTIS, STANDING IN THE NEED OF PRAYER

The Male (or Lesser) Praying Mantis is
A victim of romantic fantasies.
He cries, "My angel, let me prove
A mantis' life well lost for love!"
He takes her in his tender arms;
He soothes her virginal alarms—
Pours all his love and longing in her,
While she is having him for dinner.
He reassures her that they'll wed;
Meanwhile, she's gnawing off his head.
He soothes her gastric pains with Borax,
As she is working on his thorax;
And when there's nothing left above,
Still doth the Lower Mantis love.

This system, as needs scarcely saying,
Makes little Mantises . . . all praying.

    —WILLARD R. ESPY

Consider the marvelous symmetry of the human edifice, the shoulders and the haunches and the breasts flowering from one side to the other on the bosom, and the ribs arranged by pairs, and the navel in the middle of the softness of the stomach. . . . Consider the shoulder blades stirring under the silky skin of the back, and the spine which descends toward the cool and twin luxuriance of the buttocks and the great branches of the vessels and the nerves which pass from the torso through the ramifications of the armpit, and how the structure of the arms corresponds to that of the legs. Oh, the sweet regions of the interior joining of the elbow and the back of the knee, with their abundance of organic refinements under their cushions of flesh. What an immense feast to caress them, these delicious places of the human body. A feast after which one would die without regret! Yes, my God, let me smell the odor of the skin of your kneecap, under whose ingenious articular capsule a glistening oil is secreted! Let me touch devoutly with my lips the femoral artery which throbs in the front of your thigh and divides lower down into the two arteries of the tibia!

> —HANS CASTORP TO MME. CHAUCHET, in Thomas Mann, *Magic Mountain*

Think of all the time and energy spent in the search and consummation —and the hangovers of sex. Think of the books I could have written, the photographs I could have taken.

Sure, there have been terrific moments, but when you boil them down, they amount to thirty seconds, all told. My fondest wish is to be an asexual.

> —SHAUN CONSIDINE, *Village Voice*

It doesn't matter what you do in the bedroom as long as you don't do it in the street and frighten the horses.

> —MRS. PATRICK CAMPBELL

In today's chaotic world it's best to know one's self before playing musical beds. Freedom can be an excuse for the immature woman to waste a lot of time being a sex object.

> —AVODAH K. OFFIT, M.D., *The Sexual Self*

One more drink and I'll be under the host.

> —DOROTHY PARKER

I am sixty years old and they say you never get too old to enjoy sex. I know, because once I asked my grandma when you stop liking it and she was eighty. She said, "Child, you'll have to ask someone older than me."

> —LETTER TO CAROL TAVRIS, social psychologist, *MS*

THE TURTLE

The turtle lives 'twixt plated decks
Which practically conceal its sex.
I think it clever of the turtle
In such a fix to be so fertile.

> —OGDEN NASH, *The Face Is Familiar*

During a discussion on the Mike Douglas TV show, actress Patty Duke was asked to comment on sex education in the schools. She unhesitatingly responded, "I think it's a wonderful idea, but I don't think the kids should be given homework."

I can only tell you his Who's Who is six inches long.
> —MINNIE GUGGENHEIM, civic leader, introducing a prominent political figure

""!!!**
SPEECH
SPEAKING

Nature has given us two ears, two eyes and but one tongue, to the end that we should hear and see more than we speak.
> —SOCRATES

Let thy speech be better than silence, or be silent.
> —DIONYSIUS, the Elder

A word fitly spoken is like apples of gold in pictures of silver.
> —PROVERBS 25:11

Out of the abundance of the heart the mouth speaketh.
> —MATTHEW 11:34

HOW JOAN OF ARC ANSWERED HER INQUISITORS (1431)

INQUISITOR: Are you sure that you are in a state of grace?
JOAN: If I am not in it, may God put me there; and if I am in it, may God keep me there.
ANOTHER INQUISITOR: What did Saint Michael look like when he appeared to you?
JOAN: I didn't see any crown on him, and I don't know anything about his garments.
INQUISITOR: Was he naked?
JOAN: Do you think Our Lord had nothing to clothe him with?
INQUISITOR: Did he have hair?
JOAN: And why, pray, would they have cut it off?
> —ABRIDGED FROM BARROWS DUNHAM, *Heroes and Heretics*

There is no such thing as a sphere for a sex. When Angelina Grimké and Lucretia Mott [hold forth in public] with eloquence and power on slavery and women's rights, who shall tell us that these divinely inspired women are out of their sphere?
> —ELIZABETH CADY STANTON (1848)

Eloquence is saying the proper thing and stopping.
—FRANÇOIS DE LA ROCHEFOUCAULD

Last night we had the first meeting of the class in elocution. It was very pleasant, but my deficiency of ear was never more apparent to myself. We had exercises in the ascending scale, and I practiced after I came home, with the family as audience.
—MARIA MITCHELL, astronomer (1853)

SPEECH ACCOMPANYING PRESENTATION OF A WATCH TO A CLERGYMAN

With a deep sense of your many benefactions, those assembled here have requested me, in their name, to present to you this watch, as a token of our mutual and increasing admiration and esteem for yourself, and of our gratitude for your labors in our behalf. We ask you, dear sir, to accept it as freely as we offer it; for it is fitting that you who are daily and hourly preparing us for the joys of Eternity, should bear about you this monitor of passing Time, ever marking, as we sincerely hope, hours, days, and many years of happiness for you and yours.
—*Hill's Manual,* handbook of etiquette (1873)

While Judy Garland was waiting for a train in the station master's office, the dispatcher wandered by and complained that he was having an awful time announcing trains lately. His throat hurt all the time.
"You're probably not using your voice right," Judy said. "Take a deep breath and I'll show you." The mink-coated star took hold of the startled dispatcher and pushed hard against his belly. "Feel it? *That's* where your power comes from." She gave him a light punch in the diaphragm. "And be careful of those loud *eee* sounds. They'll give you a bleeding throat unless you keep your teeth open."
—SHANA ALEXANDER, *Talking Woman*

As a frequent speaker myself, I am still trying to learn. So many things can lose an audience: a monotonous rhythm, a one-level voice dwelling on one point too long, or including too many.
You begin to develop a special sense: the awareness of losing your listeners and of drawing them back. Changes of pace and mood, serious to humorous, challenging to empathizing; these can break tensions, refresh interest.
The conviction that what you are saying is not only true for you but important to them must never leave you. You are not asking them to agree, only to listen.
—MARYA MANNES

Public speaking changes you; the applause, the stance, you become a different person—the audience has this effect.
—WILFRID SHEED, on *Dick Cavett Show*, PBS

When you want to win your audience, tell a "true" story on yourself. Depict yourself in an embarrassing situation. For example, "The other night after I had finished making a speech I overheard a lady say to her husband, 'That certainly was an inspirational speech, wasn't it?' And her husband said, 'It was all right, but thirty minutes of rain would have done us a lot more good.'"

> —WINSTON PENDLETON, *How to Win Your Audience with Humor*

The other day my twelve-year-old daughter went to the library and said to the librarian, "I want to learn something about the Nile River for school. Can you help me, please?" The librarian said she would be glad to help. After about twenty minutes she had assembled a stack of books about two feet high. "There," she said, "that will tell you all about the Nile River." My daughter stood and looked at the stack of books and said, "I certainly do thank you for all of your trouble, but I don't want to know that much about the Nile River." I have been asked to tell you about my business. I could talk all afternoon about my company, but I am sure you are like my little girl. You don't want to know that much about it. So for the next five minutes I'll. . . .

> —WINSTON PENDLETON, *How to Win Your Audience with Humor*

In a general way, psychiatrists were able to establish on a wide basis what many of them had always felt—that the most telling cues in psychotherapy are acoustic, that such things as stress and nagging are transmitted by sound alone and not necessarily by words.

> —ROSEMARY BLACKMON, *Vogue*

The further we get from the harem, the more open and honest becomes women's talk.

> —J. B. PRIESTLY, *Talking*

Half the sorrows of women would be averted if they could repress the speech they know to be useless—nay, the speech they have resolved not to utter.

> —GEORGE ELIOT

A woman who had just been ordained was given a flowery introduction before her first sermon. She opened her remarks with "May the Lord forgive the deacon for his excesses of praise, and me for enjoying them so much."

My advice to the Women's Clubs of America is to raise more hell and fewer dahlias.

> —WILLIAM ALLEN WHITE

Speak no evil and cause no ache;
Utter no jest that can pain awake;
Guard your actions and bridle your tongue;
Words are adders when hearts are stung.
> —ANON.

At a Fourth of July celebration in Wisconsin, a platform was quickly constructed in a shaded grove where Lucy Stone delivered "the first Women's Rights address and Anti-slavery speech ever given by a woman in the great Northwest." During her rousing speech, the platform suddenly crumbled, and Lucy fell. Struggling to her feet the clever Lucy adlibbed, "So will the nation fall unless slavery is abolished!"
> —ADAPTED FROM LYNN SHERR and JURATE KAZICKAS, *American Woman's Gazetteer*

A word isn't a bird; if it flies out you'll never catch it again.
> —RUSSIAN PROVERB

When the three goldfish in the control room are laughing, I know that my little talk is a good one.
> —GILBERT HIGHET, radio program *People, Places and Books*

I am the most spontaneous speaker in the world because every word, every gesture, and every retort has been carefully rehearsed.
> —GEORGE BERNARD SHAW

A child in nursery school fills a bucket with a hose. Teacher says, "Hey, wow, that's almost full to the top!"

A child shows his mother old toys he has been given by another child. The mother whoops with joy.

A child shows his father a crude wooden truck he has made. Father says, "Hey, that's really something, isn't it?"

Gee, boy, and *gosh* are words that adults use in conversation with children, not with each other.

The researchers found that parents often persist in addressing, say, eight-year-olds with the speech common at four, much to the dismay of the children.

Of course, some parents never do seem to understand the angry signals and continue telling their children to wash behind the ears until they are thirty-five.
> —DRS. MICHLER and GLEASON, psychologists, *NYT*

Marie-France Pisier holds a master's degree in law and is called Marie-Pensee (Thinking Marie) by her fellow French film star, Jean-Paul Belmondo. She especially likes speaking English for a change. Says Thinking-Marie: "You use fewer facial muscles."
> —*Time*

On rising to talk, omit the Birds-Eye Frozen Smile. Be what you've had a lifetime of practice being: yourself. Loudness is often accepted as conviction. Let your voice emphasize particular points. But to stress everything is of course to stress nothing. Vary volume. A well-placed whisper can drown out surrounding shouts. Pause frequently. Within reason, *pause* equals *poise.* Indeed, moments in a speech filled with silence can say more than those filled with words. Don't let rigor mortis set in. Via a little choreography, be your own visual aid. Move around a bit, gesture, look here and there, lean on the lectern, draw yourself up to full height, as you feel like it.

    —*The Madison Avenue Speech Book*

The reason there are so few good talkers in public is that there are so few thinkers in private.

    —*Woman's Home Companion*

If one could only teach the English how to talk and the Irish how to listen —society would be quite civilized.

    —OSCAR WILDE

Well, I found out early in life that you didn't have to explain something you hadn't said.

    —CALVIN COOLIDGE in reply to someone twitting him for his
       habitual silence

A CAUTION

If you your lips
    Would keep from slips,
     Of these five things beware:
Of whom you speak,
To whom you speak,
    And how, and when, and where.

    —ANON.

Speakers intent on sugar-quoting their speeches, who can't find quotes that make the points they want them to, have been known to make them up. These they sometimes attribute to G. K. Chesterton, since nobody's sure quite what all G. K. Chesterton said.

    —*The Madison Avenue Speech Book*

I am actively trying to remove some of the "feminisms" that typify women's speech from my own communication style. At the same time, I have been helping others [transsexual males in the process of physically and mentally becoming women] to adopt the traditional "woman's language." Women's voices are more animated—our highs are higher, our lows lower. Women tend to be more hyper-correct in pronunciation.

A woman will make a statement and then add a question. "It's very amusing, don't you think?" Women almost exclusively use intensifiers. "Such a nice day." Or a qualifier, "It's rather windy." Women tend to maintain more eye contact—head nodding, puzzled looks, injections such as "mhmm" or "umm."
—MAUREEN O'CONNOR, speech therapist

Without notes or cue cards, Jimmie Carter, the man who once hired a Georgia radio announcer to give him elocution lessons, spoke for five or six minutes about films and film stars and their place in American society and their influence on his own life. When he had finished, even some of the veteran thespians on hand, like James Stewart and Henry Fonda, were quite impressed.
"It was so good and so—so spontaneous," Olivia de Havilland said. "That's why I like him. He's so—so spontaneous."
But as she would understand, there was more to what he said than met her ear.
His remarks were scripted for him by Peter Stone, the author of the Broadway musical *1776*, and brought to him at the White House in late afternoon. In no time at all, he had committed them to memory.
—JAMES T. WOOTEN

Audiences are nicer than people, easier to talk to. They won't talk back or challenge you at every turn, at least not until the question period, and by then you've had your say. Besides, there's the nice attentive hush before you start. Can you count on that in a living room or in the office lounge?
—DOROTHY URIS, *A Woman's Voice*

It is good speaking that improves good silence.
—DUTCH SAYING

Women are the source and fountain of language, pouring it forth at the time when we most need language, in the earliest years of childhood.
—JOHN MACY, *About Women*

The program director really wasn't sure how I'd do tonight. I asked him the capacity of this room. He said, "It sleeps three hundred."
—ROBERT ORBEN

THE TONGUE

"The boneless tongue, so small and weak,
Can crush and kill," declared the Greek.

"The tongue destroys a greater horde,"
The Turk asserts, "than does the sword."

A Persian proverb wisely saith,
"A lengthy tongue—an early death."

"The tongue can speak a word whose speed,"
Says the Chinese, "outstrips the steed";

While Arab sages this impart,
"The tongue's great storehouse is the heart."

From Hebrew was the maxim sprung,
"Though feet should slip, ne'er let the tongue."

The sacred writer crowns the whole;
"Who keeps the tongue doth keep his soul."

—PHILLIPS BURROWS STRONG

A woman will entertain endlessly, but she will not get recognition until she gets up and speaks.
—DOLORES WHARTON, director of two multinational corporations and two large Michigan companies

First sit up straight, then put your feet together and raise them about one inch off the floor. It takes so much concentration that you're bound to stay awake.
—*Manufacturing Chemists Association Newsletter,* giving prescription for staying awake while a speaker has his say

Talk does not cook rice.
—CHINESE PROVERB

SPORTS

Running requires no special skills. It is often more beneficial to jog around the psychiatrist's building than to enter—and cheaper than a couch.
—MARATHON MOTHER, quoted by Red Smith, *NYT*

I have always sensed the exhilaration and independence of being self-propelled. Besides, you can jog while pushing a baby carriage. Maybe I'm a product of Wonder Woman comic books.
—NINA KUCSIK, marathoner, *Newsweek*

My first try, children were passing me, fat ladies, old men. Pretty soon I heard this putt-putt behind me and it was the policeman on his motorcycle bringing up the rear. I was the rear.

    —JAMES F. FIXX, *The Complete Book of Running*

For workers-wives-mothers-runners, 3,000 meters is a breeze compared with:

Carrying a thirty-five-pound youngster in one arm and juggling a twenty-pound bag of groceries in the other.

Dragging a fifty-pound bag of dog food and a twenty-five-pound bag of cat litter into the house from the station wagon.

Or lugging loads of wet laundry up from the basement.

These women could tell the International Olympic Committee a thing or two about what is and what isn't strenuous for them.

    —JULIA WARD, sports columnist, *NYT*

It is a great art to saunter.

    —HENRY DAVID THOREAU

Hockey is the most difficult sport I've ever tried.

You think you've got it mastered, and then it doesn't work anymore; you have to make it better. But when it works, when you're playing with a team without talking, when you know where they are without looking, when you know what they're going to do before they do it, it doesn't really matter what the caliber of the team is; it's working together.

    —JULIE STAVER, *WomenSports*

Some proverbial excuses that nonticket holders use, attempting to crash a stadium:

- "I came 750 miles from Indianapolis. The clubhouse attendant was going to leave me four."
- "My wife is in the hospital, and I came all the way here from Brooklyn with my son."
- "I came from Los Angeles with three tickets. My girl friend got angry and tore them all up. Look!"
- "You got tickets for Congressman Whelan of North Carolina?"
"No," the guard said, "where is he?"
"He's outside."
"OK, bring him in, and we'll see if we can find some!"

    —TONY KORNHEISER, *NYT*

The kind of caving we are doing is more than just walking through passages. We are the intruders in the dark, the cold, the wet.

In vertical caving, there is no way to get people up above you to rescue you if something goes wrong. By the time they'd reach you, you'd be dead of exposure.

There may be wilderness in the mountains, but airplanes still fly overhead. It is known. Underground—that's wilderness.

    —CHERYL JONES DAVISON, *WomenSports*

How much happiness is gained, and how much misery escaped, by frequent and violent agitation of the body.
   —SAMUEL JOHNSON

The inept are a vast fraternity. One of my friends dislocated her knee in
a modern dance class while trying to be interpretive about autumn. A
roommate actually shot herself in the arm during archery practice. Another friend trying to master the overhand tennis serve had bruises
across both shins for weeks when she failed to control her follow-
through. The list could go on and on.
   We inept are appreciative spectators. Invite us along to admire your
prowess or dexterity, to applaud your wins, or even to keep your score. But
please, folks, don't ask us to play too.
   —DR. MARY D. KRAMER, *WomenSports*

The widely held belief that women athletes developed bulging muscles
turned out to be scientifically unprovable—a woman's physique is genetically determined at birth, and no amount of exercise and training can
radically change it. When women began to train strenuously for serious
athletics in the eighties, it turned out that with the same amount of
training they developed less musculature than men, and instead used a
higher percentage of already-existing fiber. Those shot-putters with
bowling-ball shoulders turned out to have had the basic bulges in the first
place.
   —LUCINDA FRANKS, in Maggie Tripp, ed., *Woman in the Year
   2000*

Historically, the menstrual cycle has been the root of discrimination
against women in sports. . . . The menses did not interfere with the
American Olympic swimmer who broke a world record and won three
gold medals at the height of her period.
   —JANICE DELANEY et al., *The Curse*

Mr. and Mrs. Muldowney teamed up to race low-budget stockers, then a
gas dragster, and finally a Funny Car. "I went racing because I didn't dig
having the cleanest wash on the block," said Mrs. M.
   She was driving a Funny Car at Indianapolis in 1973 when the engine
exploded in a ball of fire. The flames got inside her goggles and burned
her eyes. "My eyelids were welded shut," Muldowney recalls, "but the
first thing I did when they got me out was pull off my false eyelashes."
   —*Sports Illustrated*

Golf is a good walk spoiled.
   —MARK TWAIN

You wake up in the morning saying, "Where am I? What city is this?
What day? What month?"
   Soon life became nothing more than a mattress, a box spring, a bath-

room, and four walls. You say to yourself, "Is that all there is?" and you cry a lot.

There are cliques, but why not. The top players have earned the right to sit together. Some other kids come along for the ride, eat at McDonald's, rent a caddy, shoot a ninety, and eventually disappear.

  —JOANN WASHAM, professional golfer

Show me a man who is a good loser and I'll show you a man who is playing golf with his boss.

  —*Nebraska Smoke-Eater*

The bridge expert, Charles Lochridge, once watched his partner murder a hand. "How would you have played it?" the partner asked him afterward. Said Lochridge: "Under an assumed name."

He that leaveth nothing to chance will do few things ill, but he will do very few things.

  —HALIFAX

After swimming through dead bodies in the Nile and decaying cow carcasses in the Ganges, I hardly noticed the water was dirty in the East River. Once a sea lion swam with me all the way through a thirty-five-mile race in Argentina. At first I thought it was a shark, but it was a race, so I kept on going.

  —DIANA NYAD, world's champion woman swimmer, *Glamour*

If you wish to drown, do not torture yourself with shallow water.

  —BULGARIAN PROVERB

Benjamin Franklin was America's first swimming master. When he was eighteen, he traveled to London and while there swam a three-and-a-half-mile course in the Thames. Few Europeans had much interest in swimming, since bathing was infrequent and swimming through the deep was considered an activity only for fish. There also was a great fear of drowning.

Franklin pondered remaining in London to open a swimming school but finally decided against the idea. He admitted later that if he had had more time to consider, he would have given it a try.

  —WELLS TWOMBLY, *200 Years of Sport in America*

There's a girl out in Center Moriches
Who keeps all the neighbors in stitches;
 She swims down to Islip
 And borrows a dry slip,
And bicycles home without breeches.

  —LOUIS UNTERMEYER, ed., *A Subtreasury of American Humor*

Before the turn of the century, the most daring escapade involving the Niagara Falls was a walk above them on a tightrope. That wasn't enough for Annie Edson Taylor. Eager for a change of career, the forty-three-year-old schoolteacher from Bay City, Mich., saw real possibilities in an entirely original vaudeville act starring herself, a wooden barrel, and the Horseshoe Falls. On October 24, 1901, as thousands of spectators cheered her on, she climbed into her barrel and plunged over the edge. The trip was bumpy but swift. Within minutes, the dazed voyager emerged from her battered barrel into the welcoming arms of her admirers. She thus became the first person to navigate—and survive—such a trip.
    —*American Woman's Gazetteer*

As a hustler, W. C. Fields was magnificent. While practicing, he couldn't seem to make a shot even if the ball stood an inch from a pocket, but the moment a sucker challenged him, he started running the table.
    He always installed a pool table in his house, which he used for recreation, therapy and gambling. He described it as "a beautiful sight for sore eyes, this greensward."
    —CARLOTTA MONTI, *W. C. Fields and Me*

Whenever a fellow fisherman gives the hysterical cry "The white bass are running!" [my husband] grabs his boots and does the same.
    Actually I have never known the white bass to do anything else but run. They certainly never stop long enough to nibble at the bait. The reasons they give for the fish not biting are enough to stagger the imagination.
· The fish aren't biting because the water is too cold.
· The water is too hot.
· The fish are too deep.
· It is too early.
· It is too late.
· They haven't stocked it yet.
· They're up the river spawning.
· The water skiers and motorboats have them stirred up.
· They've been poisoned by pollution.
· They just lowered the lake level.
· They haven't been biting since the Democrats have been in power.
    —ERMA BOMBECK, *At Wit's End*

This is the story about a man
With iron fists and beautiful tan.
He talks a lot and boasts indeed
Of a power punch and blinding speed.

Archie's been living off the fat of the land.
I'm here to give him his pension plan.
When you come to the fight, don't block the door,
'Cause you'll all go home after Round Four.
    —MUHAMMAD ALI

Not everything that is more difficult is more meritorious.
> —SAINT THOMAS AQUINAS

The need for exercise is a modern superstition, invented by people who ate too much, and had nothing to think about.
> —GEORGE SANTAYANA

If you come here thinking you are the big I Am, you learn fast there is no big I Am. You have to grow with success, not swell with it.
> —ED TEMPLE, coach of the famous Tennessee State Tigerbelles basketball team

Bess Truman enjoyed hunting, fishing, skating, riding, tennis, and swimming. She played a crackerjack third base and could beat all the boys at mumblety-peg. She was the star forward in the Barstow School's 22-10 basketball triumph over Independence, Mo. . . . One contemporary remembered Bess Truman as "the first girl I ever knew who could whistle through her teeth."
> —*WomenSports*

There is no logical reason why girls shouldn't play baseball. It's not that tough. Not as tough as radio and TV announcers make it out to be. . . . Some can play better than a lot of guys who've been on that field. . . . Baseball is not a game of strength; hitting is not strength.
> —HENRY AARON, home-run record holder, San Francisco *Examiner & Chronicle*

The baseball mind is a jewel—a stone of special beauty, rare value, and extreme hardness. It resists change as a diamond resists erosion.
> —RED SMITH

We will be out again next Sunday as every Sunday—old people reaching for youth and young people reaching for line drives. And everybody catching something.

Laughs, not hits, are essentials of what the game is all about.

The philosophic thrust of the game is inherent in the pitcher's obligation to make a hitter of the batter. It is a choose-up game and the sides are different each week.

I don't know how Abner Doubleday would have felt about the game, but Laurel and Hardy would have loved it.
> —HARVEY ARONSON, *NYT*

When a ranking tennis player asked for yet another raise, the association official scolded, "Do you realize, Liz, that you're asking for more money than President Carter made last year?"

"I know," she countered. "But I had a better year than Carter."

Virginia Wade expresses concern over maintaining her femininity. "It doesn't do girls any good to be stuck around together all the time," she says. "They become desexed, a terrible thing." But Rosie Casals simply refuses to consider any hang-ups about being a woman athlete. "If someone says it's not feminine," she snaps, "I say screw it."

And from Billie Jean King, "We come off the court sweating, hair dripping. You don't see many femmes fatales in tennis dresses."

—*Newsweek*

"If I could only have a transsexual operation," I told my wife, "I know I could improve my forehand." She was very sympathetic: "Do it if you think it will help your game."

"But if I had the operation and then women started beating me, instead of men, it would make me sick."

"Women beat you now," she said.

"With an operation I might be able to psych them out. It could make them so nervous they might double fault and lose their nerve, particularly if I didn't shave my legs."

"If you had the operation and you still kept losing at tennis, there would be no way of going back, if you know what I mean," said my wife.

"I've thought of that," I said. "But it did wonders for Dr. Renée Richards's game."

"But she was a good player as a man. She's just become better as a woman. If you're a lousy player as a man, there is no guarantee you'll play better as a woman. Wouldn't you feel more comfortable taking tennis lessons?"

—ART BUCHWALD

"When I married Nancy [Chaffee, tennis star], I vowed I'd beat her at tennis one day," said Ralph Kiner, the baseball great. After six months, she beat me 6—2; after a year, it was 6—4. After a year and a half, I pushed her to 7—5. Then I did it—she had a bad day and I had a good one, and beat her 17—15. "Good for you, Ralph," said his friend. "Was she sick?" "Of course not!" Kiner was indignant. "Well," he added, "she was eight months pregnant."

Losses are always a relief. They take a great burden off me, make me feel more normal. If I win several tournaments in a row I get so confident I'm in a cloud. A loss gets me eager again.

—CHRIS EVERTS, *Sports Illustrated*

Sometimes, I get out on the court and think, "Big deal—this little plot of land. How significant, really, is this?" But something still makes me strive to perfect a shot and to give people a perfect performance. And I still get that aesthetic value—that absolute thrill and sensation—from hitting the ball just right.

—BILLIE JEAN KING, *Newsweek*

Nancy Lopez, the amazing rookie pro golfer, hit a spectator in the head recently, teeing off on the 10th hole. As she rushed up to him, gripping the gold cross around her neck, tears welling up in her walnut brown eyes, the injured man mumbled to a friend kneeling beside him, "At least I'll get to meet her now." . . . Still crying, Nancy teed off on the next hole —and birdied it.

    —GRACE LICHTENSTEIN, *NYT Mag.*

""!!!**
TELEVISION

As if to breathe away a supposedly "liberal" fear of the broadcasting business as Big Brother, a new concept has lately been put forward which asserts that commercial television is a merely neutral force, "another utility, like the telephone." Because of commercials, and the public's responses to commercials, it is the mass public that exerts the controlling force on broadcasting. There is some merit in trying to demystify television in this country, but that is not the same as saying that it is a neutral appliance—that neutral forces somehow combine and produce neutral sequences of information, which are then acted on subjectively only in our own heads. The fact we are all stuck with is that television is an authority, and the evidence of this century is that there has been no such thing as a *neutral* authority.

    —MICHAEL J. ARLEN, *The New Yorker*

Broadcaster Joe Garagiola spends a lot of time away from home doing TV shows. One day he walked into the house and his daughter yelled excitedly, "Mother, here's Daddy!"

  "Good," said Mom. "On what channel?"

    —PUTT POWELL, in Amarillo *News*

Think of the possibility of two women anchors on a network news broadcast, and you'll understand we're still in the Ice Age.

    —LYNN SHERR, *Time*

Television is a communication art first, an entertainment source second.

  Effective communication can package anything from product to personality. But the success factor in reaching and touching people is to remain part of the audience yourself. You can't step outside the consumer's circle and expect to have a realistic viewpoint. I think television programming today, except for the too few documentary films, is out of step—and out of reality.

    —JACQUELINE C. WARSAW, *Working Woman*

This season the only things worth watching on TV seem to be the trage-
dies and comedies—the news and the commercials.
>—ANGIE PAPADAKIS, quoted by Earl Wilson

Nothing reveals more about the insecurity of many creative people than
the avalanche of awards that sprouts on television like a fungus. Why is
there a show biz obsession with self-congratulation?

Other trades don't do it. Glue makers consider prizes tacky. Butchers
do not loin-ize each other. Awards would rub furriers the wrong way. And
we all remember the candidate for Best Waiter who said, "If elected, I
will not serve."

But in show biz, there is no end to it. Emmys, Grammys, Tonys. Do
bakers give out Crummies?

Hardly any awards are as silly as Emmys, which aside from having the
most grotesque statuette, have the most categories.

So let's put an end to it all.

Let us invoke the statuette of limitations.
>—GENE SHALIT, "Man About Everything," NBC

Not only are women now openly having sex on the tube, but they are even
able to admit they don't always like it. That's liberation. We've come a
long way since the days when Lucy Ricardo couldn't say "pregnant" on
the air.
>—*Daily News*

The mass arena of fame is TV, which, more than personality-oriented
magazines like *People* or *Us* or gossip columns, is responsible for the
current fame age. TV cuts across lines of triumph and disaster, defining
our existence for us, showing us power and fame in a kind of soft blur.
>—CANDACE LEEDS, *Daily News*

Yesterday's sensation is today's routine.
>—DAVID BRINKLEY, NBC News

What would Aristotle, whose *Poetics* is a prevailing Bible for writers of
drama, have thought of the soaps?

The soaps strictly obey Aristotle's mandate that "plot is the soul of
drama." Character in the soaps is totally subservient to the demands of
the story.

The upcoming plot complications of any soap opera are a closely
guarded secret. Even the actors don't know what's going to happen more
than a few days in advance.

Soaps conform to Aristotelian specifications in another important
sense: They provide their audiences with carefully orchestrated moments of emotional catharsis, purging them of anxieties by allowing
fictional scapegoats to suffer in their stead.

But on one important point Aristotle would have turned thumbs down
on the soaps: his insistence that all drama possess a distinct beginning,
middle, and end. On a long-running soap opera, almost nothing is ever

decisive. [It] caters to those whose belief in a better future (every cloud has a silver lining, etc.) overrides any evidence to the contrary. In Greek tragedy, characters always submit to the gods, but the characters on soap operas are subject to the commandments of only one god, the great god Nielsen.
— ROGER COPELAND, *NYT*

THE DISCONTENT OF OUR WINTER

Dear Lord, to mitigate the freeze,
This single favor grant us, please:
Consign to Hades, if you can,
The cheerful TV weather man,
Or douse him, please, in lukewarm oil,
Then gently bring it to a boil.
And let him, though he shriek and wail,
Sizzle. (On the Celsius scale.)
— ARNOLD AUERBACH, "Metropolitan Diary," *NYT*

When you do twenty-four shows as we do, you just know going in that four of them are not going to be up to snuff. And you put your head down, and the week goes by—it's the slowest week in the world. Because we're rehearsing something we don't believe in.
— BOB NEWHART, *Newsday*

When comedian Joey Bishop was host of *The Tonight Show,* he was plagued with autograph seekers. One day, when someone stopped him on the street and asked if he was Joey Bishop, he smiled politely and replied, "No, I only look like Joey Bishop."

Then, on second thought, he asked the woman if she was a fan of Joey Bishop's. She smiled politely and replied, "No, I only *look* like a fan of Joey Bishop's"—and walked away.
— *The Tonight Show*

Teacher recommendations of a documentary, such as the National Geographic series, are ignored by two-thirds of the children, according to teachers in Limerick, Pennsylvania. The typical excuse: "My father was watching *Bionic Woman."*
— NANCY LARRICK, *NYT*

I have never seen a bad television program, because I refuse to. God gave me a mind, and a wrist that turns things off.
— JACK PAAR, in *TV Guide*

"What do you think of radio?" Fred Allen once asked Titus Moody. And Titus replied, "I don't hold with furniture that talks."

It's funny, but when I think about who would have made it without whom, I guess I would have made it without Mary Tyler Moore. But without me, she probably would have become secretary of state.
—LOU GRANT, in *New Woman*

What would public television be if the British didn't speak English?
—LAURENCE GROSSMAN, president, PBS

I see television as a consciousness-raising machine, invented in the nick of time as a survival tool. If we don't get to know one another, we perish. TV is saving us.
—JAMES LEO HERLIHY, author

A couple of years ago a network was going to do a series on the Ten Commandments. The entire project was ultimately canceled, probably because it was too radical. But the thing that really amused me was the fact that the network only took five of the commandments from me with an option on the other five. That, my friend, is television.
—HUBERT SELBY, JR., author

No matter how nasty you see me acting, I'm holding back a little.
—FLIP WILSON, comedian

Perhaps the crime situation would be improved if we could get more cops off television and onto the streets.
—BILL VAUGHAN, Kansas City *Star*

My success on television was because, as an only child, I got into the habit of going for long walks and talking to myself. Television is a form of soliloquy.
—KENNETH CLARK, *Civilization, PBS-TV*

His first polysyllabic utterance was "Bradybunch." He learned to spell Sugar Smacks before his own name. Recently, he tried to karate chop his younger sister after she broke his Six Million Dollar Man bionic transport station (she retaliated by bashing him with her Cher doll). His nursery-school teacher reports he is passive, noncreative, and possessed of an almost nonexistent attention span—in short, very much like his classmates.
—*Newsweek*

Awakened one night at 2:30 by the phone, I groped to pick it up. The operator was saying, "Long distance calling—will you accept the charges?" "Yes," I managed groggily.
A woman's voice came on. "Mr. Field, as president of the Ellenville Utah Naturalist Society, it is my great pleasure to inform you that the membership has voted you Weatherman of the Year."

"Thank you, I'm honored," I replied. Then citing two other network weather people, I asked, "Why didn't you call them?"

"Oh, I did," she answered, "but they wouldn't accept the charges."
— FRANK FIELD

REFLECTIONS DENTAL

How pure, how beautiful, how fine
Do teeth on television shine!
No flutist flutes, no dancer twirls,
But comes equipped with matching pearls.
Gleeful announcers all are born
With sets like rows of hybrid corn. . . .
M.C.s who beat their palms together,
The girl who diagrams the weather,
The crooner crooning for his supper—
All flash white treasures, lower and upper,
With miles of smiles the airwaves team,
And each an orthodontist's dream.

'Twould please my eye as gold a miser's—
One charmer with uncapped incisors.

— PHYLLIS MCGINLEY

THEATER

Stage direction from the play *The Group* (1775), used as propaganda for the American Revolution:

The Group [Hutchinson and his henchmen] enter attended by a swarm of court sycophants, hungry harpies, and unprincipled danglers . . . hovering over the stage in the shape of locusts, the whole supported by a mighty army and navy from Blunderland for the laudable purpose of enslaving its best friends.
— MERCY OTIS WARREN (1728–1814), playwright (under pseudonym)

There was but one person in the world, male or female, who could, at that time, in my opinion, have written *The Group;* and that person was Madam Mercy Warren, the historical, philosophical, poetical, and satirical consort of the Colonel, since General James Warren of Plymouth.
— JOHN ADAMS, in a letter to Mercy Warren

"You know what's going to make this show?" asked a producer—"Mouth to mouth!"
> —HARVEY SABINSON, *Darling, You Were Wonderful*

Why should *anyone* write for the theater? The theater is a necropolis of ideas. One goes there to mourn the loss of life, and to numb the backside. Occasionally we hear laughter, but only because an old man in the street has slipped on a banana peel.
> —ROSALYN DREXLER, playwright

My mother keeps wanting to know why I don't write a play every year the way Neil Simon does. I have explained to her that (a) I don't have Neil Simon's talent, and (b) I don't have Neil's wife. The question is forgivable coming from a mother and the answer is the God's truth, but not the whole truth. I could conceivably find the energy to write a play if not every year, perhaps every third year. I don't mean a good, bad, or even acceptable play, just a play—something that Peter de Vries describes as having "a beginning, a muddle, and an end."

The presence of a skillful director, a tasteful producer, and a talented cast seems only to increase my paranoia, because now I have to face the notion that if the play is a disaster I must take *all* of the blame.

My heart goes out to the playwright who was sprawled in what S. J. Perelman has called the Anguish Room of the Warwick, and he said: "When I get through with this, I shall have a nervous breakdown. I worked for it, I deserve it, and nothing shall deprive me of it."
> —JEAN KERR, playwright

When a playwright tells you that the reviews of his new show were "mixed," he means they were "good and rotten."
> —GEORGE S. KAUFMAN, playwright

CONVERSATION BACKSTAGE AT THE SHUBERT THEATRE, PHILADELPHIA

SHE: Do you think I ought to have my nose fixed, y'know what I mean?
ME: No, Barbra, if you do, you'll be just another pretty face from Brooklyn.
> —HARVEY SABINSON, *Darling, You Were Wonderful*

The theatrical press agent is a resilient amalgam of glue and guile, chutzpah and heartburn, optimism and imagination.
> —ROBERT BERKVIST, *NYT*

The Cherry Sisters, billed as "the world's worst sister act," was considered so bad it was good. The late nineteenth-century vaudeville act consisted of Elia, Jessie, Lizzie, Addie, and Effie Cherry, who often had to perform behind a wire screen to shield themselves from fruit and eggs hurled at them by spirited audiences. Once, in a courtroom, to prove that they had been unfairly attacked by a newspaper, they performed for the judge. When His Honor saw their act, he upheld the newspaper report.

—ADAPTED FROM LYNN SHERR and JURATE KAZICKAS, *American Woman's Gazetteer*

For those of us who have gone through a number of opening nights, there are certain members of the audience recognizable to all.

First there is the Discreet Choker. Handkerchief pressed to his lips and deeply embarrassed, the Discreet Choker makes a dash up the aisle and crashes through the double doors at the back in order not to further disturb the audience.

The second and more common category is the Straight Cougher. The Straight Cougher confines himself to short controlled barks. He knows, without ever having seen the play before, precisely the key word in a scene or joke to cover most effectively.

The Snoozer is no serious threat. But beware if you have any sudden, startling noise in your play such as a gunshot, because the startled Snoozer will awake with a loud snort. Startled Snoozers have also been known to cry out things like, "Ethel, there's someone in the room!"

—MIKE NICHOLS, director

American actress Cornelia Otis Skinner was widely acclaimed for her performance in Shaw's *Candida*. The playwright sent her a telegram stating, "Excellent. Greatest."

The actress was so honored, she wired back, "Undeserving such praise."

Humorously, Shaw sent another cable which said, "I meant the play." Miss Skinner was annoyed. She retorted by wire, "So did I."

Uncle Matthew went with Aunt Sadie and Linda on one occasion to a Shakespeare play, *Romeo and Juliet*. It was not a success. He cried copiously, and went into a furious rage because it ended badly. "All the fault of that damned padre," he kept saying on the way home, still wiping his eyes. "That fella what's 'is name, Romeo, might have known a blasted papist would mess up the whole thing. Silly old fool of a nurse too, I bet she was an R.C., dismal old bitch."

—NANCY MITFORD, *The Blessing*

As soon as I suspect a fine effect is being achieved by accident I lose interest. I am not interested, you see, in unskilled labor. An accident— that is it. The scientific actor is an *even* worker. Anyone may achieve on some rare occasion an outburst of genuine feeling, a gesture of imperishable beauty, a ringing accent of truth; but your scientific actor knows how he did it. He can repeat it again and again and again. He can be depended on. Once he has thought out his role and found the means to express his thought, he can always remember the means.

—MINNIE MADDERN FISKE, from Alexander Woollcott, *Mrs. Fiske* (1917)

You have to upset yourself. Unless you do, you cannot act. And there comes a time in one's life when you don't want to do it anymore. You know a scene is coming where you'll have to cry and scream and all those things, and it's always bothering you, always eating away at you . . . and you can't just walk through it. . . .

Actors *have* to observe. They have to know how much spit you've got in your mouth, and where the weight of your elbow is. . . .

I've always tried to run acting down, tried to be very tough about it, and I don't know why. . . . It's a perfectly reasonable way to make your living. You're not stealing money, and you're entertaining people.

—MARLON BRANDO, in Shana Alexander, *Talking Woman*

I construct a compressed accuracy, a character essence that is as true and real as I can get it. I don't go for laughter. I never play for a joke, per se. If the joke gets in the character's way, I take it out.

—LILY TOMLIN, *Time*

I can make any fantasy come true. I can be anything I want. I can change my age, I can change my looks—I can change my sex. I can become these women and speak from another planet. When I'm Peggy Lee I can speak from Venus. When I'm Carol Channing, I can speak from—Detroit.

—CRAIG RUSSELL, in Andrew Kopkind, "The King/Queen of Drag," *NYT*

From extreme left upstage Eleanora Duse [the famed Italian actress] unobtrusively entered through an archway. A murmur went through the house, and my attention immediately centered on her. She slowly walked diagonally downstage and sat in an armchair by the fireplace and looked into the fire. Once, and only once, did she look at the young man, and all the wisdom and hurt of humanity was in that look.

She spoke calmly as she looked into the fire. Her delivery had not the usual histrionics; her voice came from the embers of tragic passion. I did not understand a word, but I realized I was in the presence of the greatest actress I had ever seen.

—CHARLES CHAPLIN, *My Autobiography*

The school of acting which I call the "Looking-for-the-other-shoe method" employs nonarticulation to help the "naturalness" along. The L.F.O.S. method gets its name from the attitude of the actor, who, let's say, plays a proposal scene sitting on a bench. He never looks the girl in the eye—turns his head away from her, bends over, looks to all sides and almost under the seat while delivering his lines hesitantly, as though his entire concentration was being absorbed by the search for the other shoe.

—MARLENE DIETRICH, *ABC's*

Eugene Field on Creston Clarke's portrayal of King Lear: "Mr. Clarke played the king as though under momentary apprehension that someone else was about to play the ace."

Howard Dietz on Tallulah Bankhead: "A day away from Tallulah is like a month in the country."

George Oppenheimer objected to a geriatric drama: "I don't like plays," he said, "in a varicose vein."

An aspiring playwright asked Carl Sandburg, "How could you sleep through my dress rehearsal when you knew how much I wanted your opinion?" "Young man," said Sandburg, "sleep *is* an opinion."

> —WILLARD R. ESPY, *An Almanac of Words at Play*

Reviewing a play, Walter Kerr said of one of the actors: "He has delusions of adequacy."

> —LOUIS KRONENBERGER, *The Cutting Edge*

I sat in back of a woman at one of my plays. She laughed and cried throughout the play. As the curtain went down she turned to her friend. "Well, it wasn't bad," she said.

> —NEIL SIMON, playwright

There have been many accounts written of the opening night of *The Threepenny Opera*. . . .

People who scornfully had passed up that opening night began to lie about it, to claim to have been there. Even now, anybody who passed through the Berlin of that period, and who comes backstage to see me years later in New York, feels compelled to cry, "Of course I was there that opening night!" And though I remember that the theater had less than eight hundred seats, I nod. Why not, after all? Sometimes, remembering all that madness, I'm not even sure I was there myself.

> —LOTTE LENYA, star of *The Threepenny Opera*

I don't become a character. I show a character . . . I *share* a character. I share it not only with the audience but with myself.

> —LIV ULLMANN, *Newsweek*

Bernard Shaw wrote to Winston Churchill: "I'm sending two tickets to the opening night of my new play for you and a friend, if you have a friend."

Churchill answered, "Sorry, can't come to the opening night but I'll be glad to come the second night, if you have a second night."

""!!!**
TRAVEL
LEISURE

Be careful when asking directions. Many Latin Americans will give you the wrong answer rather than admit they do not know; this may be partly because they fear losing face, but is also because they like to please!

If you are unlucky enough to be bitten by a venomous snake, spider, scorpion, or sea creature, always try (within limits) to catch the animal for identification.

 —*South American Handbook*

With only four cabins to fill, the manager has a screening method as folksy as the cabin site. She uses the instincts of Chip, her half-Labrador, half-German shepherd.

"If Chip doesn't wag his tail, I don't even let them get out of the car. I just yell out, 'We're full up.' "

She is tolerant, however, of illicit couples.

"You can always spot them. Usually the man comes to the office alone. You know the woman with him isn't his wife, because a wife would look over the cabin too. Or sometimes the woman just sort of hides in the car, and comes sneaking in a few minutes later. Usually they only stay a couple of hours.

 —*NYT*

[I loathe] this sad commerce. The lowest peasant of the Danube would stick at letting strangers into his house for a fee but our dukes, marquesses, earls, viscounts and baronesses not only do this incredible thing, they glory in it.

 —NANCY MITFORD

Tourist: person who travels a thousand or more miles to have his picture snapped beside his car, then doesn't remember where it was taken.

 —*Modern Maturity*

Bad weather had made for a number of flight delays at the airport. One passenger was growing increasingly impatient. When a further thirty-minute delay was announced, he walked up to a ticket agent and said, "I don't see why you people even bother publishing a flight schedule."

The agent replied, in her usual calm, professional tone, "Well, sir, we have to have something to base our delays on."
　　　　—MICHAEL I. POFF, *Reader's Digest*

"Try to hold on," a year-round neighbor muttered a day or so ago. "Just a few more days now, and They'll have to give the Island back to us."
　　Says a policeman: "Stand by for the all clear. Any minute now."
　　Says one of four hitchhikers: "You live here all year?"
　　Yup. That's Yankee.
　　What's it like off-season?
　　Some peaceful. Some beautiful. Yankee too is the intensifier, "some."
　　"I imagine you'll be glad when we're gone." Was that a statement or a question? They wanted an answer. We all do. Who doesn't wonder how the world will be after we're gone?
　　Glad to see the hosts of summer dissolve away?
　　Keep it curt. Keep it cool. Keep it Yankee.
　　Nope.
　　　　—*Vineyard Gazette,* Martha's Vineyard

The weather forecasts always lie when it's cold or rainy in Miami. The TV stations show a picture of a bright sunny day, blue skies with suntanned people playing happily at games.
　　　　—KENNETH TYNAN, on *Dick Cavett Show,* PBS

I don't understand the Parisians
Making love every time they get a chance.
I don't understand the Parisians
Wasting every lovely night on romance.
Any time and under every tree in town
They're in session two by two.
What a crime with all there is to see in town
They can't find something else to do.
　　　　—GIGI, *Town & Country*

If I hear the name of Titian, I have to lie down.
　　　　—HELEN BELL, after a long tour of European art galleries, in
　　　　　Louis Kronenberger, *The Cutting Edge*

WHY DO I TAKE BOOKS TO THE BEACH

Where human wisdom is collected
*　Here is the best we have to teach*
No great book was read nor written
*　While sunning on the beach*

　　　　—LOUIS PHILLIPS

I don't suppose there is anything to be added about the Taj Mahal; more than of any other building in the world, it has all been said. Never, especially in architecture, was there similar tribute by man of his love for a woman. The literal and physical aspect of the affection is generally affirmed by the fact that Mumtaz Mahal died while giving birth to her fourteenth child.
—JOHN KENNETH GALBRAITH

When all were arranged in order Solomon told the wind where he wished to go, and the carpet, with all its contents, rose in the air and alighted at the place indicated.
—*Brewer's Dictionary of Phrase and Fable*

The skipper of a sinking boat out of Chesapeake Bay radioed for help.
"We're on our way," replied the Coast Guard. "What is your position? Repeat. What is your position?"
"I'm executive vice-president of the First National Bank," answered the yachtsman. "Please hurry!"
—E. T. HENRY, *Weight Watchers*

It's not my place
  To run the train
The whistle I can't blow
  It's not my place
To say how far
  The train's allowed to go
It's not my place
  To shoot off steam
Nor ever clang the bell
  But let the damn thing
Jump the track . . . And see
  Who catches hell.
—ON THE WALL OF THE STATIONMASTER'S OFFICE,
  Grand Central Terminal

People on a chartered tour appear to be a homogeneous lot. But the appearance is deceptive. Certain types of tourists inevitably assert themselves.

The Firsts

These people spend their vacation doing everything before everyone else. They're the first off the plane, first on the bus, first on line at the buffet barbeque.
Their command of logistics is awesome.

The One-ups

These tour members spend their trip doing everything better than any-one else. You bought the straw basket in a tourist shop for $20? They paid $15 for a more authentic specimen at the local craft cooperative.

The Do-it-alls

Do-It-Alls don't need to plan their activities. The tour brochure is their Bible, and they know it by heart. They'll take you under their wing with a zeal surpassed only by that of missionaries. They never miss the group picture, the free tour of the city, or the complimentary cocktail.

The Inside Scoops

Inside Scoops spend little time with the group, although they are soon on a first-name basis with the waiter, the hotel owner, and the guide's moth-er-in-law. They can drive fellow tourists to distraction; while the Firsts are waiting on the dock and the One-Ups are packing their own box lunch of pâté and champagne, the Inside Scoops are loafing around the pool. They know that the tour boat sank last night.

The Casuals

The Casuals are forced to order from room service every day because they never make it down in time for breakfast. They have to sun them-selves on the cement patio around the pool because all the towels and chaises are taken. Whatever they order for dessert is always gone.

If your path crosses that of a Casual, it means that you've missed the bus.
    —BARBARA KLAUS, *NYT*

Once Mark Twain checked into a hotel and was asked to sign the register. He saw that the arrival just before him was a titled man who had regis-tered, "Baron von So-and-so and valet."

Twain took pen in hand and scrawled his own entry in the register. "Mark Twain and valise," he wrote.

A California tour guide: "That house on the left with the three green doors belongs to Steve McQueen."

A few minutes later another bus slows and its driver announces, "That house on the left with the three green doors belongs to Paul Newman."

Each day the tour guides gossip and learn new stories to tell their passengers. What they're being told is often untrue, but probably they don't care. One guide pointed out Angel Island. "That was one of the Hawaiian Islands until 1948, when it was bought by a Southern Califor-nia oil millionaire and towed to San Francisco. He's going to move it to Arizona and open it as a resort."
    —San Francisco *Examiner & Chronicle*

It's so expensive even the birds aren't going South.
    —ROBERT ORBEN

Study a map of the Caribbean with a magnifying glass. When you find an island almost impossible to make out, you've got it made.

Safer than Japan these days is Australia. Few Americans go there, and that's what makes it so valuable. Think of "I'll never forget sunset at that little sheep station in Goulburn." Or laugh with pleasure at your recollection of "the fair dinkum weekend we spent noodling at Coober Pedy."

Refer not to cities but to districts. For all their Hertzing around, Americans seldom absorb the names of English counties or French provinces.
    —JOHN T. BEAUDOUIN and EVERETT MATTLIN, *The Phrase-Dropper's Handbook*

It's wonderful to be in Florida this time of the year. You can open the windows in the morning and listen to the birds coughing.
    —ROBERT ORBEN

During the day the Thais till the soil, at night they are performers in stunning costumes and masks; they sing, they dance. If I had lived in Thailand, I'd have starved to death.
    —CHARLES CHAPLIN on his return from the Orient

From bar mitzvah on, I had longed to qualify as a Jewish Robert Louis Stevenson.

In Israel: In Tel Aviv I came across a brand of perfume called Chutzpah. ... Not a soul in history from Helen of Troy to Helena Rubinstein had ever thought of pure unadulterated gall as a cosmetic.

In Iran: The demented thoroughfares in Teheran are terrifying; as a result, there are only two kinds of pedestrians ... the quick and the dead.

In the Soviet Union: Yalta contains sanitariums that ignite more hypochondria in the onlooker than the Magic Mountain . . . that Chekhov managed to glean any literary nuggets from Yalta is merely added proof of his stature.

    —S. J. PERELMAN, *Eastward Ha!*

Vacations are a little like love: anticipated with relish, experienced with inconvenience—and remembered with nostalgia.
    —*The Pennant*

Too often travel, instead of broadening the mind, merely lengthens the conversation.
    —ELIZABETH DREW

Customs officials are like doctors—they see people's most personal belongings, and they have to be prepared for anything.

One woman at Kennedy Airport insisted she had bought nothing abroad.

"Are you quite sure that you have nothing to declare?" the customs agent asked her.

"Absolutely sure," she said firmly.

"Am I to understand, then," smiled the agent, "that the fur tail hanging from under your dress is your own?"

—LOUIS KRONENBERGER, *The Cutting Edge*

The hell-clicking authoritarian Germans who fill our television screens are nowhere to be found in Germany. The Italians have become rather boring. The Dutch have even evinced wit. We ourselves [the British] have taken to cringing and whining, pouring out ghastly intimacies to strangers.

—QUENTIN CREW, *British Vogue*

One was married to someone. That one was going away to have a good time. The one that was married to that one did not like it very well that the one to whom that one was married then was going off alone to have a good time and was leaving that one to stay at home then. The one that was going came in all glowing. The one that was going had everything he was needing to have the good time he was wanting to be having then. He came in all glowing. The one he was leaving at home to take care of the family living was not glowing. The one that was going was saying, the one that was glowing, the one that was going was saying then, I am content, you are not content, I am content, you are not content, I am content, you are content, you are content, I am content.

—GERTRUDE STEIN, *Storyette H.M.*

Fashions in landscapes change like any others, and today the hideous part of an otherwise beautiful country is the one to be sought: bone-bare Mykonos, the bleak chic of Port' Ercole and Porto Santo Stefano on what is perhaps the only really plain strip of Italian coast.

—ELEANOR PERENYI, *Vogue*

SOUR GRAPES SONG

Lugging their baggage for want of a porter,
Fleeced by a driver for want of a word,
Timetable-haunted and Baedeker-blinded,
Part of the avid American herd.

Let them off with their farewells and flurry;
I'll stay behind in my peaceful old groove,
Secretly nursing a gnawing desire
To follow my fellows—the fools on the move.

—MARYA MANNES, *Subverse*

"""!!!**
...

WAR AND PEACE

LYSISTRATA: Women of Sparta, Corinth, Thebes, and our Athenians, you ask me why I've sent for you—it's not an easy thing to tell. We must do something we have never done before, my friends. Something no woman, since the beginning of time, has dreamed of doing. . . .

My sisters, to compel our men to sign a pact of peace, we must make war—but not as men make war. Yet, be prepared for a great sacrifice. Oh, have no fears, it's not your lives you must give up. You'll only promise never to lie . . . to lie with any man, until the war is ended. Never to let a soldier home on leave, starved for your soft white arms and the great embrace of love, have joy of you. . . . If you tell them: "Never until the war is over"—*they'll make peace!*

—ARISTOPHANES, *Lysistrata* (411 B.C.), translated and adapted by Gilbert Seldes

Why should we [women] pay taxes when we do not share in the offices, honors, military commands, nor, in short, the government, for which you fight between yourselves with such harmful results? You say, "because it is wartime." When have there not been wars? . . . Let war with the Celts or Parthians come, we will not be inferior to our mothers when it is a question of common safety. But for civil wars, may we never contribute nor aid you against each other.

—HORTENSIA, in the Roman Forum (42 B.C.), in Sarah Pomeroy, *Goddesses, Whores, Wives and Slaves*

FROM A LETTER WRITTEN AT THE HEIGHT OF THE REVOLUTIONARY WAR.

You can have no idea of the life of continued amusement I live in. I can scarce have a moment to myself. I am but just come from under Mr. J. Black's hands and most elegantly am I dressed for a ball this evening at Smith's where we have one every Thursday.

I know you are as fond of a gay life as myself—you'd have an opportunity of rakeing as much as you choose either at plays, balls, concerts, or

assemblies. I've been but three evenings alone since we moved to town. I begin now to be almost tired.
—REBECCA FRANKS (1778)

FROM A LETTER WRITTEN AFTER THE REVOLUTIONARY WAR

... Both my Sons, their wives and infants were exiled. ... Their estates had been long before sequestered and mine was shattered and ruined, which left me little power to assist them; nor had I in Country or Town a place to lay my head, all was taken out of my possession. But let me forget as soon as I can their cruelties.
—ELIZA LUCAS PINCKNEY, a former loyalist

The British army accepted the presence of "camp wives" for officers, and they had the money to pay for such services. But the American officers would not tolerate adultery among their ranks, and the enlisted men did not have enough money even to keep themselves clothed and fed. Although the hardships of war did drive some women into prostitution, they practiced this profession in the cities occupied by the British, not in American army camps.
—LINDA DE PAUW and CONOVER HUNT, *Remember the Ladies*

In our youth our hearts were touched with fire. It was given us to learn at the outset that life is a profound and passionate thing.
—OLIVER WENDELL HOLMES, JR., on the Civil War

Who will remember, passing through this gate,
The unheroic dead who fed the guns?
Who shall absolve the foulness of their fate—
Those doomed, conscripted, unvictorious ones?
—SIEGFRIED SASSOON

In Peace children bury their parents: War violates the order of Nature and causes parents to bury their children.
—HERODOTUS

Nothing except a battle lost can be half so melancholy as a battle won.
—WELLINGTON

I have bowed myself out of one town after another, as the Federal troops have bowed themselves in; yet you know the old saw, "He that fights, and runs away," etc.; though I can take no comfort in this, as fighting has been my abomination since the war began. I have always, in peaceful times, had an admiration for heroes in brilliant uniforms, and would now, if the

hero could possibly assure me that the brilliant uniform would always be filled with life.
> —MARY ANN WEBSTER LOUGHBOROUGH, wife of a Confederate officer, *Letters and Journal* (1864)

A peace which depends upon fear is nothing but a suppressed war.
> —HENRY VAN DYKE

There is no kind of peace which may be purchased on the bargain counter.
> —CAREY MCWILLIAMS

... [N]ever think that war, no matter how necessary, nor how justified, is not a crime. Ask the infantry and ask the dead.
> —ERNEST HEMINGWAY

It is the blood of the soldier that makes the general great.
> —ITALIAN SAYING

During the Nazi occupation of Paris, a husky storm trooper stepped into a subway car and tripped headlong over the umbrella of a little old lady sitting next to the door. After picking himself up, the bruised Nazi launched a tirade of abuse, then bolted from the car at the next station.

When he was gone, the passengers burst into spontaneous applause for the little old woman.

"I know it isn't much," she said, graciously accepting the compliments, "but he's the sixth one I brought down today."

I can still pick out the Dashiell Hammett lines. One cartoon shows a G.I. in a parka staring at the wet Aleutian weather and saying defiantly: "Go ahead—rain!" Another shows a G.I. pointing out the sights to a newcomer: "There's nothing over there, too." A third shows a couple of soldiers gazing at the snow-covered mountains. "Awright," says the caption, "but there's a limit to what beauty can do for ya."
> —BERNARD KALB, describing *The Adakian,* a World War II Army newspaper

Some recent work by E. Fermi and L. Szilard, which has been communicated to me in manuscript, leads me to expect that the element uranium may be turned into a new and important source of energy in the immediate future. Certain aspects of the situation seem to call for watchfulness and, if necessary, quick action on the part of the Administration. ... This new phenomenon would also lead to the construction of bombs ...
> —EXCERPT FROM ALBERT EINSTEIN'S LETTER to President Roosevelt, October 11, 1939

I am become death, the shatterer of worlds.
> —ROBERT OPPENHEIMER, after a successful test of the A-bomb

The belief in the possibility of a short decisive war appears to be one of the most ancient and dangerous of human illusions.
> —ROBERT LYND

ON LIMITED WARFARE

Don'tcha worry, honey chile,
Don'tcha cry no more,
It's jest a li'l ole atom bomb
In a li'l ole lim'ted war.

It's jest a bitsy warhead, chile,
On a li'l ole tactical shell,
And all it'll do is blow us-all
To a li'l ole lim'ted hell.

> —MARYA MANNES, *Subverse*

When two elephants fight, it is the grass underneath which suffers.
> —AFRICAN PROVERB

Science, which was to be the midwife of progress, became the angel of death, killing with a precision and a rapidity that reduced the wars of the middle ages to the level of college athletics.
> —WILL DURANT

One murder makes a villain;
Millions, a hero.
> —JOHN PORTEOUS

In the name of peace
They waged the wars
*   ain't they got no shame*
> —NIKKI GIOVANNI

The idea of having this weapon under such control with limited applications is the best news I have heard in years.
> —SEN. JOHN C. STENNIS, on the Mini-Neutron Bomb

The world's getting too small: The Near East is too near and the Far East isn't far enough.
> —LOU ERICKSON, in Atlanta *Journal*

Here's what I have learned in this war [Vietnam], in this country, in this city: to love the miracle of having been born.
    —ORIANA FALLACI, *Nothing and So Be It*

We believed in all the myths created by that most articulate and elegant mythmaker, John Kennedy. If he was the king of Camelot, then we were his knights and Vietnam our crusade.
    —PHILLIP CAPUTO, *A Rumor of War*

Hundreds that day were protesting the building of a gymnasium on the memorialized site of the shooting at Kent State. There was loud applause as the parents sat down among them—parents of Sarah Scheuer, one of four students killed by National Guardsmen, and of Alan Canfora, wounded in the shooting (two days after the Cambodian invasion in the Vietnam War).
    "When you get arrested, keep your head up—proud," Mr. Scheuer said softly to the Canforas.
    —*NYT*

To hell with all arms, excepting those grandly grafted to our human bodies, given to do noble and useful work! These arms are all we need to give glory to God and all honor to man.
    —SEAN O'CASEY

We have not yet brought peace to Northern Ireland. We have created a climate for peace to become respectable.
    —BETTY WILLIAMS, co-founder with Mairead Corrigan of the Community of Peace People, on learning that they had won the Nobel Peace Prize

Although my theory holds that anatomy destines males to be trained to be fierce and aggressive if there is war, it denies that anatomy or genes or instinct or anything else makes war inevitable.
    —MARVIN HARRIS, anthropologist

During the Civil War, Mary Bowser, a black spy for the North, pretended to be an illiterate, ignorant servant in the mansion of Confederate President Jefferson Davis. In fact she was intelligent, well-educated, and able to memorize the military reports she read on Davis's desk while she did her daily dusting.
    —*MS*

In 1892 the French crushed the only authenticated Amazon Army—the fighting women of the kingdom of Dahomey in West Africa had been formed into an army in the early eighteenth century and trained into a serious fighting force in the early nineteenth. They carried muskets, blunderbusses, duck-guns, enormous knives, and bows and arrows, and their method of warfare was surprise.... They killed only in self-defense as their aim was to capture slaves to sell and victims for their king's human sacrifices....

—JOAN and KENNETH MACKSEY, *The Book of Women's Achievements*

""!!!

WOMEN ON MEN MEN ON WOMEN

From the beginning the god made the mind of woman
A thing apart. One he made from the long-haired sow;
While she wallows in the mud and rolls about on the ground,
Everything at home lies in a mess.
The next one was made from a dog, nimble, a bitch like its mother.
And she wants to be in on everything that's said or done
Scampering about and nosing into everything.
She yaps it out even if there's no one to listen.
Her husband can't stop her with threats.
Not if he flies into a rage and knocks her teeth out with a rock ...
Not if he speaks to her sweetly when they happen to be sitting
*   among friends.*
No, she stubbornly maintains her unmanageable ways.

—SEMONIDES OF AMORGAS, seventh century, B.C.

Then, if women are to have the same duties as men, they must have the same nurture and education. They must be taught music and gymnastic and also the art of war, which they must practice like the men ... all the pursuits of men are the pursuits of women also; but in all of them a woman is inferior to a man.

—PLATO, *Republic*

It is good for a man not to touch a woman,
  But if they cannot contain, let them marry; for it is better to marry than to burn.

—ST. PAUL

The souls of women are so small,
That some believe they've none at all.
—ANON.

Virginity is a hard matter, and therefore rare. Many begin, few persevere.
> —ST. JEROME

Woman is a necessary evil, a natural temptation, a desirable calamity, a deadly fascination, and a painted ill.
> —ST. JOHN CHRYSOSTOM

By God! if women had written stories, as the clerics have done in their studies, they would have written more about the wickedness of men than all the sons of Adam could make good.
> —GEOFFREY CHAUCER, Wife of Bath's Tale, *Canterbury Tales*

The man's a fool who thinks by force of skill,
To stem the torrent of a woman's will;
For if she will, she will, you may depend on it,
And if she won't, she won't, and there's an end on it.
> —SIR SAMUEL TUKE, seventeenth century

There is something in a woman beyond all human delight; a magnetic virtue, a charming quality, an occult and powerful motive.
> —ROBERT BURTON, *Anatomy of Melancholy*

All the reasonings of men are not worth one sentiment of women.
> —VOLTAIRE

If the heart of a man is depressed with cares,
The mist is dispell'd when a woman appears.
> —JOHN GAY

Most women have small waists the world throughout,
But their desires are a thousand miles about.
> —CYRIL TOURNEUR, *The Revenger's Tragedy* (1607)

O fairest of creation! last and best
Of all God's works!
> —JOHN MILTON, *Paradise Lost*

She is pretty to walk with,
And witty to talk with,
And pleasing too, to think on.
> —SIR JOHN SUCKLING, *The Discontented Colonel*

Genius has no sex!
—MADAME DE STAEL

A man of sense only trifles with [women], . . . humors and flatters them, as he does with a sprightly, forward child; but he neither consults them about, nor trusts them with, serious matters; though he often makes them believe that he does both; for they love mightily to be dabbling in business (which by the way, they always spoil).
—EARL OF CHESTERFIELD, letter to his son (1748)

As the faculty of writing has been chiefly a masculine endowment, the reproach of making the world miserable has been always thrown upon the women.
—SAMUEL JOHNSON

The appointment of a woman to office is an innovation for which the public is not prepared, nor am I.
—THOMAS JEFFERSON, *Letter to Albert Gallatin*

Disguise our bondage as we will,
'Tis woman, woman rules us still.
—THOMAS MOORE

Literature cannot be the business of a woman's life because of the sacredness of her duties at home.
—ROBERT SOUTHEY, *Letter to Charlotte Bronte*

That woman is by nature meant to obey may be seen by the fact that every woman who is placed in the unnatural position of complete independence, immediately attaches herself to some man, by whom she allows herself to be guided and ruled. It is because she needs a lord and master. If she is young, it will be a lover; if she is old, a priest.
—ARTHUR SCHOPENHAUER

[We] Charm by accepting, by submitting sway,
Yet have our humor most when we obey.
—ABIGAIL ADAMS, in a letter to John Adams (1776)

Women are told from their infancy, and taught by the example of their mothers, that a little knowledge of human weakness, justly termed cunning, softness of temper, outward obedience, and a scrupulous attention to a puerile kind of propriety, will obtain for them the protection of man;

and should they be beautiful, everything else is needless, for, at least, twenty years of their lives.
> —MARY WOLLSTONECRAFT, *A Vindication of the Rights of Women* (1792)

Then this little man in black there, he says women can't have as much rights as men, 'cause Christ wasn't a woman! Where did your Christ come from? From God and a woman! Man had nothing to do with Him. . . . Obliged to you for hearing me, and now old Sojourner ain't got nothing more to say.
> —SOJOURNER TRUTH at a Woman's Rights Convention, in Akron, Ohio (1851)

And You, in this disconsolate London square
Flaunting an ill-considered purple hat
And mud-stained, rumpled, bargain-counter coat,
You of the broken tooth and buttered hair,
And idiot eyes and cheeks that bulge with fat,
Sprawl on the flagstones chalking for a vote!
> —T. W. H. CROSLAND, *Votes for Women* (1908)

George Sand smokes, wears male attire, wishes to be addressed as "Mon frère,"—perhaps if she found those who were as brothers indeed, she would not care whether she were a brother or a sister.
> —MARGARET FULLER

Talk to women as much as you can, 'tis the best school.
> —BENJAMIN DISRAELI

Marriage is necessary as a waste pipe for emotion, as security in old age. . . . Yes, I daresay an old family servant would do as well.
> —BEATRICE WEBB

The great question that has never been answered, and which I have not yet been able to answer despite my thirty years of research into the feminine soul, is: What does a woman want?
> —SIGMUND FREUD

Man's superiority will be shown, not in the fact that he has enslaved his wife, but that *he* has made her free.
> —EUGENE V. DEBS

One hair of a woman draws more than a team of oxen.
> —ANON.

An American woman who respects herself must buy something every day of her life. If she cannot do it herself, she must send out some member of her family for the purpose.
—HENRY JAMES, in Leon Edel, *The Complete Tales of Henry James*

There is no life of a man, faithfully recorded, but it is a heroic poem of its sort, rhymed or unrhymed.
—THOMAS CARLYLE

Being a woman is a terribly difficult task, since it consists principally in dealing with men.
—JOSEPH CONRAD

There are two things I have always loved madly: They are women and celibacy.
—NICOLAS CHAMFORT

Women are declared to be better than men, an empty compliment which must provoke a bitter smile from every woman of spirit, since there is no other situation in life in which it is the established order that the better should obey the worse.
—JOHN STUART MILL, *The Subjection of Women*

I wish Adam had died with all his ribs in his body.
—DION BOUCICAULT

To dream of equal rights, equal training, equal claims and obligations: This is a typical sign of shallow-mindedness.
—FRIEDRICH NIETZSCHE, *Beyond Good and Evil*

Man for the field and woman for the hearth:
Man for the sword and for the needle she:
Man with the head and the woman with the heart:
Man to command and woman to obey:
All else confusion
—ALFRED, LORD TENNYSON

DON JUAN: Do you not understand that when I stood face to face with Woman, every fibre in my clear critical brain warned me to spare her and save myself. . . . And whilst I was in the act of framing my excuse to the lady, Life seized me and threw me into her arms as a sailor throws a scrap of fish into the mouth of a seabird.
—GEORGE BERNARD SHAW, *Man and Superman*

Women have more imagination than men. They need it to tell us how wonderful we are.
　　—ARNOLD H. GLASOW

It is getting harder to compliment women. They're tired of empty words, of being compared to flowers, landscapes, climates and other irrelevancies. They've changed, and the descriptions of them will have to change.
　　—ANATOLE BROYARD, *NYT*

In men this blunder still you find,
All think their little set mankind.
　　—HANNAH MORE

Nobody will ever win the Battle of the Sexes. There's just too much fraternizing with the enemy.
　　—HENRY KISSINGER

[Men] forgive us—oh, for many things, but not for the absence in us of their own failings.
　　—COLETTE, *Gigi*

All artists are half man and half woman, and the woman is usually insufferable.
　　—NED ROREM, quoting Pablo Picasso

Sons rebel against mother-rule and submit, mindlessly, to father-rule. More, they blame mothers for whatever guilt or anguish they feel about this. . . . It is women, men tell us, who are bitchy, belittling, dangerous, and demanding. Not other men. Never their fathers.
　　—PHYLLIS CHESLER

He is every other inch a gentleman.
　　—REBECCA WEST

Four stars—close your eyes and waves crash, mountains erupt and flowers bloom;
Two stars—don't worry about his dirty feet; they hang off the end of the bed;
One star—Lazy;
Turkey—"I did it!" he said. "Did what?" I ask.
　　—"CONSUMER GUIDE TO M.I.T. MEN," by two women students who rated ex-lovers, four stars to none

Harpists, hairdressers, and cooks: most are women, but the best are men. ... Women contend they have not been given a chance but chances are taken, not given.
—NED ROREM

I go for two kinds of men. The kind with muscles and the kind without.
—MAE WEST

It would be preposterously naïve to suggest that a B.A. can be made as attractive to girls as a marriage license.
—DR. GRAYSON KIRK, former president of Columbia University

Man forgives woman anything save the wit to outwit him.
—MINNA ANTRIM, *Naked Truth and Veiled Allusions*

Women like other women fine. The more feminine she is, the more comfortable a woman feels with her own sex. It is only the occasional and therefore noticeable adventuress who refuses to make friends with us.
—PHYLLIS MCGINLEY, *Some of My Best Friends*

A little woman is a dangerous thing.
—ANON.

THE GUFFAWS OF 1900

His wife just turned forty, and he'd sure like to exchange her
    for a couple of twenties.
I say, Freddie, what do you call a man who's lucky in love?
    A bachelor!
Mumsie says marriage is a wonderful institution. Right. But
    who wants to live in an institution?
Well, here's to our wives and sweethearts—may they never
    meet!
Well, a bachelor never makes the same mistake once.
Tell me, do any of you chaps believe in clubs for women?
    Yes, if every other form of persuasion fails.
Oh, if only there was a way to fall into a woman's arms
    without falling into her hands!

    —EXCERPTS, EVE MERRIAM, *The Club* (A Musical Diversion)

An expert on zoological nomenclature was leading an expedition into the wilds of the upper Nile. One day an underling ran to him in a state of great excitement.

"Professor," he cried, "something dreadful has just happened. Your wife has been swallowed by an alligator."

A deep look of concern came over the professor's face.
"Surely," he said, "you mean a crocodile."
    —ISAAC ASIMOV, *Treasury of Humor*

There are only three things to be done with a woman. You can love her, suffer for her, or turn her into literature.
    —LAWRENCE DURRELL, *Justine*

The Mona Lisa is a woman beyond the reach of my sympathies or the ken of my interests . . . watchful, sly, secure, with a smile of anticipated satisfaction and a pervading air of hostile superiority.
    —BERNARD BERENSON

Ever since my childhood I have nourished a timid feeling of adoration for women, all my life I have remained stunned and stupefied by her beauty, by her place in life, and by my pity of her and fear for her. . . . Since childhood I have gathered pebbles from under her feet on the path she had trodden.
    —BORIS PASTERNAK, in a letter to Nina Tabidze

No man is as anti-feminist as a really feminine woman.
    —FRANK O'CONNOR

I consider that women who are authors, lawyers, and politicians are monsters.
    —PIERRE AUGUSTE RENOIR

Several men I can think of are as capable, as smart, as funny, as compassionate and as confused—as remarkable, you might say—as most women.
    —JANE HOWARD, *Life*

What we owe men is some freedom from their part in a murderous game in which they kick each other to death with one foot, bracing themselves on our various comfortable places with the other.
    —GRACE PALEY

Whether women are better than men I cannot say—but I can say they are certainly no worse.
    —GOLDA MEIR

So this gentleman said, "A girl with brains ought to do something else with them besides think."
    —ANITA LOOS, *Gentlemen Prefer Blondes*

All men are alike in the light.
    —ANON.

Men define intelligence, men define usefulness, men tell us what is beautiful, men even tell us what is womanly.
—SALLY KEMPTON

LASCIVIOUS MAN: I want your body.
WRITER JILL JOHNSTON: You can have it when I'm through with it.
—LETA CLARK, *Women Women Women*

Yo' ain't the man yo' mamma was. . . .
—ANON., heard on a street

So long as a woman is dependent on a man for her self-image or her self-esteem she will remain without any sense of her own worth—can never be a fully realized human being.
—ELEANOR PERRY, in Kay Loveland and Estelle Changas, *Rebirth*

QUESTION: How have most men had sex with you?
ANSWER: Badly.
—SHERE HITE, *The Hite Report*

A mother watched her son as he pushed his way through a group of little girls to get to the swings. "Oh dear," she said, "I'm afraid my son is a male chauvinist sprig."

WOMEN THEN AND NOW

He seems to me just like the gods,
That man who sits opposite you
And, while close to you, listens to
You sweetly speaking
And laughing with love—things which cause
The heart in my breast to tremble.
For whenever I look at you,
I can speak no more.
My tongue freezes silent and stiff.
Light flame trickles under my skin,
I no longer see my eyes.

My ears hear whirring,
Cold sweat covers me, shivering takes
Me complete captive, I become
More green than the grass, near to death
To myself I seem
 —SAPPHO, seventh century B.C., quoted in Sarah Pomeroy,
  Goddesses, Whores, Wives and Slaves

A whole troop of foreigners would not be able to withstand a single Gaul if he called his wife to his assistance, who is usually very strong, and with blue eyes.
 —MYLES DILLON and NORA CHADWICK, *The Celtic Realms*

. . . [Sweete Megg,] men [who] read your writings suspect you to have had help from some man. . . .
 —SIR THOMAS MORE, in a letter to his daughter Margaret

If [early] Christianity turned the clock of general progress back a thousand years, it turned back the clock two thousand years for women.
 —MARGARET SANGER

Women have burnt like beacons in all the works of all the poets from the beginning of time.
 —VIRGINIA WOOLF

One scarcely need be a vocalizing feminist to observe that women—along with blacks, Indians, and to a lesser extent other minorities—have not been given their due sufficiently in American history. More than these other groups, perhaps, women have been not so much misrepresented as missing: their presence cavalierly, boldly omitted.
 —EVE MERRIAM, *Introduction to Growing Up Female in America*

"Why are there no great women artists?" sounds as ignorant of human geography as the query "Why are there no Eskimo tennis teams?"
 —FRANCINE DU PLESSIX GRAY, *NYT*

There have been women in the past far more daring than we would need to be now, who ventured all and gained a little, but survived after all.
 —GERMAINE GREER, *The Female Eunuch*

I took a ride to Cambridge and waited on Mrs. Washington at 11 o'clock, where I was received with that politeness and respect shown in a first interview among the well-bred, and with the ease and cordiality of friendship of a much earlier date. If you wish to hear more of this lady's character, I will tell you I think the complacency of her manners speaks at once of the benevolence of her heart, and her affability, candor, and

gentleness qualify her to soften the hours of private life, or to sweeten the cares of the hero, and smooth the rugged paths of war.
—MERCY WARREN to Abigail Adams (1776)

Betsy Ross sewed the first American flag according to a design approved by George Washington. . . . She "suggested" a five-pointed star because she could make it with a single snip of the scissors.
—THE NATIONAL HISTORICAL WAX MUSEUM, Washington, D.C.

The women of Connecticut will freely talk upon the subjects of history, French, geography, and mathematics. They are great causists and polemical divines; and I have known not a few of them so well schooled in Greek and Latin as often to put to the blush learned gentlemen.
—DESCRIPTION OF NEW ENGLAND WOMEN (1781)

The heroism of the females of the Revolution has gone from memory with the generation that witnessed it, and nothing, absolutely nothing remains upon the ear of the young of the present day.
—CHARLES FRANCIS ADAMS (1840)

Dear Sister . . .
Our kind friend Mr. Carroll, has come to hasten my departure, and in a very bad humor with me, because I insist on waiting till the large picture of General Washington is secured, and it requires to be unscrewed from the wall. It is done and the precious portrait placed in the hands of two gentlemen of New York for safe keeping. And now, dear sister, I must leave this house, or the retreating army will make me a prisoner in it by filling up the road I am directed to take. When I shall again write to you, or where I shall be tomorrow, I cannot tell.

Dolley (Madison)
—Written during the War of 1812. After she left the presidential residence was destroyed by fire.

Why is it that the pages of all history glow with the names of illustrious men, while only here and there a lone *woman* appears, who, like the eccentric comet, marks the centuries?
—SUSAN B. ANTHONY (1857)

The difference between us is very marked. Most that I have done has been in public and I have received much encouragement at every step of the way. You, on the other hand, have labored in a private way. I have wrought in the day, and you in the night. I have had the applause of the crowd and the satisfaction that comes of being approved by the multitude, while the most that you have done has been witnessed by a few trembling . . . bondsmen and women . . . whose heartfelt "God bless you" has been your only reward.
—FREDERICK DOUGLASS to Harriet Tubman

On my underground railroad, I nebber run my train off de track and I nebber los' a passenger.
—HARRIET TUBMAN

I don't know as I am fit for anything and I have thought that I could wish to die young and let the remembrance of me and my faults perish in the grave rather than live, as I fear I do, a trouble to everyone. Sometimes I could not sleep and have groaned and cried till midnight.
—HARRIET BEECHER STOWE, at age sixteen

The last two years has been like a trouble dream to me. It is said Master is in want of monney. If so, I know not what time he may sell me, and then all my bright hope of the futer are blasted, for their has ben one bright hope to cheer me in all my troubles, that is to be with you, for if I thought I should never see you this earth would have no charms for me.
I want you to buy me, for if you do not get me some body else will.
—MRS. NEWBY'S appeal to her husband in a letter, in John Blassingame, *Slave Testimony*

The happiest women, like the happiest nations, have no history.
—GEORGE ELIOT, *The Mill on the Floss*

[Victoria Woodhull] is a spirit to respect, perhaps to fear, certainly not to be laughed at.
—HORACE GREELEY

Fame is a bee.
It has a song—
It has a sting—
Ah, too, it has a wing.
—EMILY DICKINSON

The eye that directs a needle in the delicate meshes of embroidery will equally well bisect a star with the spider web of the micrometer.
—MARIA MITCHELL, mathematician and astronomer (1853)

Social science affirms that woman's place in society marks the level of civilization.
—ELIZABETH CADY STANTON

I began to study Latin, Greek, and mathematics with a class of boys in the Academy. I strove for and took the second [prize in Greek class]. One thought alone filled my mind. "Now," said I, "my father will be satisfied with me."
I rushed breathless into his office, laid the new Greek Testament, which was my prize, on his table and exclaimed: "There, I got it!" He took up the book and, evidently pleased, handed it back to me. Then he kissed

me on the forehead and exclaimed, with a sigh, "Ah, you should have
been a boy!"
　　　—ELIZABETH CADY STANTON, *Eighty Years and More* (1898)

My father told me never to give anyone anything, not even a kindness. I am not a self-made woman. I was born rich. My father was a
millionaire, and so was his father, and all my ancestors have been
rich.
　　　—HETTY GREEN, "Queen of Wall Street," in Ishbel Ross,
　　　Charmers and Cranks

A man with whom [Hetty Green] was negotiating a large loan said to her
on one occasion: "I'm almost afraid to borrow so much and give securities
to a single individual. Suppose you were to die?"
　　"Never mind," Hetty responded. "I'll throw in a couple of cemeteries
as a margin on the securities."
　　　—ISHBEL ROSS, *Charmers and Cranks*

When Queen Victoria had special praise for one of Felix Mendelssohn's
"Songs Without Words," the composer was embarrassed. Fact is, he
wasn't the composer. It was written by his sister, Fanny Hensel. She had
told her brother that she wanted to be a composer, but he said she should
forget such frippery and stick to her husband and children. As a compromise, he agreed to publish some of her songs under his own name. Her
Majesty was applauding the wrong person!
　　　—SCOTT BEACH, *Musicdotes*

I think of you as a figure on a wondrous cinquecento tapestry—and of
myself as one of the small quaint accessory domestic animals, a harmless
worm, or the rabbit who is very proud and happy to be in the same
general composition with you.
　　　—HENRY JAMES, on Mrs. Jack Gardner, patron of arts

[The portrait of Mrs. Gardner was] so imbued with her personality that
if it were cut up into pieces an inch square and the pieces were scattered
on the Charles River, the finder of one piece would know it came from
a portrait of her.
　　　—JOHN SINGER SARGENT, on his painting

There is, I suppose, no girl in the world so perfectly capable of taking care
of herself and doing it well as the American girl. . . . The failings of our
American girls are simply . . . the somewhat troublesome excess of unem-
ployed strength.
　　　—MRS. FRANK LESLIE, writer, publisher, in Ishbel Ross,
　　　Charmers and Cranks

[I often failed to see] the meaning or force of some favorite conception of my own till Mrs. Young had given it back to me.
　　—JOHN DEWEY, speaking of Ella Flagg Young, first woman
　　　　Superintendent of Schools in Chicago (1909)

The history of every country begins in the heart of every man or woman.
　　—WILLA CATHER

In matters pertaining to the care of life there has been no marked gain over Greek and Roman antiquity.
　　—MARY RITTER BEARD, *Understanding Women*

In the Red Scare that followed World War I, women's peace societies were charged with acting as fronts for the Communists . . .

Miss Bolsheviki has come to town
With a Russian cap and a German gown,
In women's clubs she's sure to be found,
For she's come to disarm America.
She uses the movie and lyceum too
And alters text-books to suit her view;
She prates propaganda from pulpit and pew,
For she's bound to disarm America.
　　—*The Dearborn Independent* (1924), in Page Smith,
　　　　Daughters of the Promised Land

I lived in a luxurious home until I was sixteen, and then for years after that had the easy life that immoral living brings, and I just cannot be moral enough to see where drudgery is better than a life of lazy vice.
　　—"MAIMIE," a reformed prostitute and former morphine addict
　　　　(1910) in Sue Davidson and Ruth Rosen, eds., *The Maimie*
　　　　Papers

It was 1926. I had just come back from Samoa. I weighed ninety-eight pounds and I had bobbed hair, which was still unusual for a woman.

As a newly appointed assistant curator of ethnology at the American Museum of Natural History, I was meeting a group of college students in an exhibition hall. Chairs had been set up and, as I was preparing to address the group, a guard approached.

"Does Dr. Mead know you are here?"

"I am Dr. Mead."

He snorted, half incredulously, half contemptuously. "As if we didn't have enough trouble without making *girls* doctors."
　　—MARGARET MEAD

Mrs. [Mary McLeod] Bethune is a great woman. I believe in her because she has her feet on the ground—not only on the ground but in the deep, plowed soil.
> —FRANKLIN D. ROOSEVELT

I wish I knew what people meant when they say they find "emptiness" in this wonderful adventure of living, which seems to me to pile up its glories like an horizon-wide sunset as the light declines. I'm afraid I'm an incorrigible life-lover, life-wonderer, and adventurer.
> —EDITH WHARTON, in R.W.B. Lewis, *Edith Wharton, A Biography*

The past is only the present become invisible and mute; and because it is invisible and mute, its memoried glances and its murmurs are infinitely precious. We are tomorrow's past.
> —MARY WEBB, *Precious Bane*

[I wanted to] leave the world I had been so false in, where I had always been trying to play a part and always feeling unrelated, a dying world with no one appearing who would save it, a decadent unhappy world, where the bright, hot, rainbow flashes of corruption were the only high spots.
> —MABEL DODGE LUHAN, *Intimate Memories* (1927)

I steal from the present and from the glorious past—and I stand in the dark of the future as a glorying and joyous thief—There are so many wonderful things of the imagination to pilfer—so I stand accused—I am a thief—but with this reservation—I think I know the value of that I steal and I treasure it for all time—not as a possession but as a heritage and as legacy—
> —MARTHA GRAHAM, in Nancy Wilson Ross, ed., *The Notebooks of Martha Graham*

Couldn't we end this interview with what I really want to say? That what the world really needs is a real feeling of kinship—everybody: stars, laborers, Negroes, Jews, Arabs. We are all brothers. If we could end this article saying just that, we'd get down to what we should all be talking about.

Please don't make me a joke. End the interview with what I believe.
> —MARILYN MONROE

I'll have no more operas I want to sing in, no more roles I want to do. There are no more opera houses I haven't sung in. I will have recorded everything I ever dreamed of recording. I'll put my voice to bed and go quietly and with pride.
> —BEVERLY SILLS

Today the gifted as well as the deranged among us are struggling to be famous the way earlier Americans struggled to be saved. Not only musicians, actors, athletes—performers in the old sense of the word—but also poets, politicians, scientists, designers, and assassins are spending at least as much time and energy making themselves visible as they are doing their jobs.

> —SUSAN MARGOLIS, *Fame*

Black women have no identity crisis as women. We have not been playthings, idols on pedestals. That's why black professional women tend to have ease of movement.

> —PATRICIA ROBERTS HARRIS, Secretary, Housing and Urban
> Development

I can remember arguing to an imaginary Justice Burger in my mind what it would be like to be pregnant and not want to be. I'm not sure I ever really phrased that in a way I was satisfied with.

> —SARAH R. WEDDINGTON, who successfully pleaded the
> landmark abortion case before the Supreme Court

As the first American-trained woman to be the recipient of a Nobel Prize in any of the sciences I feel that I have a special responsibility. I know very well that this ultimate reward does not make me more competent, more knowledgeable or in any way more worthy than I was before this recognition. However it does make me more visible. Therefore I cannot conform to traditional stands with which I disagree even if it were easier for me to not "make waves." I have decided not to accept the 1978 Woman of the Year Award in the category of New Scientific Community from the *Ladies' Home Journal.* . . . It [is] inconsistent and unwise to have awards restricted to women or to men in fields of endeavor where excellence is not inherently sex-related.

> —DR. ROSALYN YALOW

In Chicago pool halls, one policeman reports, a male officer can start a fight just by asking for identity papers. But when a woman asks to see identification, a quiet "Yes, ma'am" almost invariably follows.

> —"POLICEWOMEN ON PATROL," *Reader's Digest*

Women are forcing their way into a system that has dehumanized men for centuries and calling this a great victory.
—MARION LACHOFF, letter to *NYT*

Each honest calling, each walk of life, has its own elite, its own aristocracy based upon excellence of performance.
—JAMES BRYANT CONANT

There are three ingredients in the good life: learning, earning, and yearning.
—CHRISTOPHER MORLEY, *Parnassus on Wheels*

There are very few jobs that actually require a penis or vagina. All other jobs should be open to everybody.
—FLORYNCE KENNEDY, lawyer

Ideas are power because ideas are money. An idea is probably the most vulnerable property a creative person owns. There are never enough good ideas to go around. That's why uncreative people are so good at swiping them.

The "let's make it work" ploy is a power strategy aimed at appropriating ideas. Here the game is to make Millicent seem like a bright little girl who does, by George, have ideas, though she's not good at getting them to work.

If you come up with a good idea, be mighty careful to claim it yourself before you start yelling, "Eureka!" Sometimes, before you can even attach your own label or flesh the idea out, someone is telling it back to you as news. And this isn't good news for the creator.
—JANE TRAHEY, advertising executive

A friend of my father's gave me a job. Apparently he didn't consult his partners first; one of them refused to speak to me during the entire time I worked there.

At my second job, the senior partner, a man, groaned when he met me: "I don't know why I let them talk me into hiring a girl." But thereafter there was no discrimination—he gave me the same periodic early-morning reports on his sex life he gave the other lawyers on the staff.
—NANCY F. WECHSLER, lawyer, *New Woman*

Whether women's design sensibilities [as architects] are actually different from men's is immaterial; there is more than one way to design a good building. But society has made certain that there is no way for those sensibilities to operate. The record as a whole is pathetic, provocative, and distressing. This is apparently going to be the last "liberated" profession—far behind medicine and the law.
—ALINE SAARINEN, "Architecture Review," *NYT*

An influential woman is one who makes a dent in the pillow next to the leader of the Western world.
> —LOIS GOULD, "Hers," *NYT*

Success is counted sweetest
By those who ne'er succeed.
> —EMILY DICKINSON

Repair programs for women constitute a currently profitable industry: how to be more assertive, how to be a manager, how to communicate more effectively, how to make decisions. None of the personal improvement courses attacks root causes of inequality in the system. Far from it. They confirm the old American notion that money and time are best spent remaking the person.... This reinforces stereotypes about women's need for compensatory education to remedy their deficiencies before they are fit to compete with men.
> —ROSABETH MOSS KANTER, *Men and Women of the Corporation*

[The six women members of the new group of astronauts are] extremely highly qualified and motivated because, unlike previous applicants, many have wanted to become astronauts since they were ten or twelve years old.
> —CHRISTOPHER C. KRAFT, JR., director, Lyndon B. Johnson Space Center

My favorite question that is asked only of women is, "What do you do with yourself all day?" The only possible answer, I have known for some time is, "Make nuclear bombs in my bathroom. Just little ones, though."
> —LOIS GOULD, "Hers," *NYT*

A bee is never as busy as it seems; it's just that it can't buzz any slower.
> —KIN HUBBARD

We've still got to deal with the resistance that comes from the idea of the "strong man in uniform."
> —A WOMAN PARK RANGER

In the old days, people said, "Who is she killing to get this job? What producer is she sleeping with? What makes Barbara run?" Nobody thought, "As long as she's working, maybe she just wants to do good work." ... But do you know what success has done to me? ... I know it sounds crazy. Success in some people breeds a zeal, a desire for much more. But it has made me, well, lazier.
> —BARBARA WALTERS, *Newsweek*

Survival in the sphere of work means maintaining and protecting my home, and providing an income through my profession. The time-old excuse of being a woman, hence frail and afraid, in need of protection and a man's assistance, has no place in an isolated and rustic life-style. I believe a woman can do whatever she sets her mind to, once she's learned how.

    —ANNE LA BASTILLE, *Woodswoman*

I could have been a much better painter and nobody would have noticed me. There's a difference between a painter and a person.

    —GEORGIA O'KEEFE

I can work for days without sleep because I get so caught up with every detail of producing and conducting an opera. Once in a while, when everything is just right, there's a moment of magic. People can live on moments of magic.

    —SARAH CALDWELL, director of the Opera Company of Boston

It has been said of Virginia Johnson, discoverer of the multi-orgasmic woman, that she wouldn't have influenced much without her co-discoverer, Dr. Masters. The same thing was probably said in France about Marie Curie.

    —LOIS GOULD, "Hers," *NYT*

They are a special twentieth-century breed, those ladies who guard the boss's door and fend off the telephone calls and read his mail; women largely without private lives because the real world is right there in the vortex spinning around the great man; women with small fiefdoms of their own encompassing subsecretaries, the Xerox machine, and the messenger service. Selfless, happily job-enslaved, they are the vestal virgins in the temples of business and politics, the Indispensables, the private secretaries.

    —HELEN DUDAR, *N.Y. Post*

It's the coattail theory that operates. You're told to find a bright young man and rise with him. I'm twenty-five years older than those bright young men, and I don't want to take a chance for ten years while they rise. When did I sign a marriage contract? Why is my career advancement tied to my boss's?

    —A SECRETARY FOR TWENTY YEARS

It is hard to be a man in a field dominated by women. Like the token woman, I am under great pressure to be above average.

    —RALPH A. DOWLING, secretary for twenty years

In days of yore, heaven protected the working girl. Nowadays it takes a union, a wage-hour law, unemployment compensation, social security, health insurance, and a pension plan.
—ANON.

It's a recession when your neighbor loses his job; it's a depression when you lose your own.
—HARRY S. TRUMAN

For chipped glasses and nicked plates, change the housemaid instead of the plates. It's less expensive, and good housemaids are easier to find than cherished patterns in china.
—ADV., *NYT* (1911)

You just start right in on the (cutting) block, you start boning, cutting steaks, cutting up chickens, bagging chickens. . . . Your arms really have to get in shape. And *especially* your hands. Boning is what you use your hands for the most. It just takes time and experience to learn how to hang onto the knife. When you wake up in the morning, your hands are curled up like you're *still* hanging onto that knife!
—NANCY KAYE ANDERSEN, butcher, in Terry Weatherby, ed.,
Conversations

[At my firm's convention] the brokerage people would say to him, "Who are you with?" and he'd answer, "Bankers Trust." They'd sort of look at him and say, "What are *you* doing here?" Then he'd say, "I'm with my wife." No one took him seriously.
—CINDY VAUGHAN, first vice-president of an investment banking
firm

Women should insist upon their lovers showing them a fully paid-up union card . . . or show them the door.
—ELEANOR MARX, daughter of Karl Marx, in Yvonne Kapp,
Eleanor Marx

I remember the first sales manager I ever worked for. He had a sign over his desk that read: "Secret of Success. Sell your wristwatch and buy an alarm clock." Another sales manager used to tell me, "Keep your eye on the ball, your shoulder to the wheel, and your ear to the ground." I tried it, but I couldn't ever get any work done in that position. He is the same sales manager who announced a big sales contest one time. He gave everybody goals and quotas and made a stirring sales talk to all of us. He didn't tell us what the prize was, so I asked him. I said, "What does the winner get?" And he said, "The winner gets to keep his job."
—WINSTON PENDLETON, *How to Win Your Audience with
Humor*

I like work; it fascinates me.
I can sit and look at it for hours.
—JEROME K. JEROME

The tall black woman is a successful investment counselor in a Wall
Street brokerage firm, where most of her colleagues are conservative,
middle-aged white men. One day one of them came up to her desk and
blurted, "I don't know why you wear a bra; you don't need to." She said,
"I don't like what you have just said. I have neither business nor friendship to discuss with you at my desk. Will you please leave." The man
stood there, arguing, "I didn't mean to insult you, but I know you don't
wear one sometimes; I know it!"

"I couldn't say what I wanted to say. Like, 'Are you wearing a jockstrap
today?' Then it would be my fault. I would be ugly, awful, not professional. I had to just take it, and go to the ladies' room and run my hands
under the water to calm myself down."

Sexual harassment might be called the taming of the shrew syndrome.
It's a reminder of powerlessness—a status reminder.
—GLORIA STEINEM

I'll tell you why the ancient Egyptians wrote their history on walls. It's
because they were smart enough to know that, if they put it in the files,
it would be lost forever.
—ADV.

If you're hammering nails all day and not carrying lumber, then your
right arm will get big. If you're carrying lumber, your back will get big.
If you're welding, you'll develop other muscles. You develop muscles for
whatever you need them. The stronger you get, the easier it is.
—MARY GARVIN, carpenter

If you fancy yourself an amateur psychologist and if you have a high
capacity for listening to terrible jokes, you might consider becoming a
bartender.

It's a popular job, and it's easy to see why. After all, you are being paid
to mix drinks and be congenial, and you don't have to get up early.
—KATHY MATTHEWS

If I ever was afraid, it was then. I can still feel the way it was in the metal
shop, the presses, the ten-hour day, and the brutal foremen, and the
missing fingers, and the heat, and the headaches, and . . .
—SIMONE WEIL, *La Condition Ouvrière*

Women describe themselves as:
• Waiting to be chosen, discovered, invited, persuaded, asked to accept
a promotion.
• Often feeling conflicted and confused about their own goals.

- Reluctant to take risk.
- Feeling guilty over having a career and trying to be a perfect woman/-wife/mother simultaneously.
  —MARGARET HENNIG and ANNE JARDIM, *The Managerial Woman*

Ruth, our young stock girl, handed in more suggestions than anyone else in the company—for such things as improving procedures and cutting production costs. Not a one was accepted. One morning, though, the personnel manager requested her presence. We thought jubilantly that Ruth had finally made it.

Our girl was glum, however, when she came out of the executive's office. "He admitted that I've been submitting a lot of suggestions," Ruth explained. "But he's beginning to wonder when I find time to do my regular work."

They allow you only four answers: "Yes, sir," "No, sir," "I do not understand, sir," and "No excuse, sir," and not everything fits into those categories. They also say, "I can't hear you," over and over until you are screaming. I never understood why.
  —A WOMAN CADET AT WEST POINT

HAZEL: Listen, Admiral [of a merchant ship], do I look like a sex symbol to you? Do you think for one moment that the men are going to chase me all over the vessel trying to rape me, or else that I'm going to start chasing the men all over the vessel trying to rape *them?* Do you think that's likely to happen?
ADMIRAL: I have no facilities for you.
HAZEL: I've never seen separate toilets for men and women. There were boys and girls in my family and we turned out all right, with only one bathroom. Did *your* mother have a special bathroom for her boys and another for her girls?
  —FIFTY-FIVE-YEAR-OLD HAZEL _____, one of the first women to get a job on a merchant ship, *Working Woman*

After the tactics class, I fall in step beside Joyce, the Californian. "So if I came at you with a knife," I say, half-kidding, "you'd be all ready with one of those 'Kung Fu' chops, right?"

She eyes me, taking in the length of my reach, measuring it against hers. She shakes her head no.

"Why not?" I ask in surprise.

"I'd probably just kick you in the crotch," she says. Then she winks. "My legs are longer than your arms."
  —WOMEN IN THE FBI, *New Dawn*

I want to take you home to meet my mother. If she likes you, maybe she'll give you a job in her company.
  —DAUGHTER TO HER NEW BOYFRIEND

A verbal contract isn't worth the paper it's not written on.
    —SAMUEL ORNITZ

Drive thy business; let not that drive thee.
    —BENJAMIN FRANKLIN

One of the symptoms of approaching nervous breakdown is the belief that one's work is terribly important. If I were a medical man, I should prescribe a holiday to any patient who considered his work important.
    —BERTRAND RUSSELL

To business that we love, we rise betimes, and go to it with delight.
    —SHAKESPEARE

The two leading recipes for success are building a better mousetrap and finding a bigger loophole.
    —EDGAR A. SHOAFF

The main thing to remember is that a drink date is meant to be productive, not social, and should have a clearly defined purpose agreed upon in advance. A lunch can be used to flatter people, buy them off, chat them up, or make contact, but between five and seven, people expect a serious return on the investment of their time, since it is really the executive equivalent of overtime.
    What is started at lunch is usually finished off over drinks, which explains why you so seldom see people reading, signing, or writing anything at lunchtime and so often see the tables covered with papers, documents, and contracts in the early evening. As the sun goes down, the pen is mightier than the swizzle stick.
    —MICHAEL KORDA, *Success*

I like earning money. I like having to face week after week all but impossible deadlines. The fame you earn has a different taste from the fame that is forced on you.
    —GLORIA VANDERBILT, *Vogue*

What would Seventh Avenue designer Kasper advise a woman to wear for a job interview at IBM, say? "That's easy," he replied. "She should wear a machine."
    —GEORGIA DULLEA, *NYT*

Nancy dear,
We were so proud to receive your year-end Business Report. Your father and I can't believe that our little girl is V.P. of such a big company.
    Are you getting plenty of rest and fresh air—and taking your vitamins? And is your husband helping you with the housework?
                        Your loving Mum and Dad

Many people in business—and in life in general—live by win/lose: If someone wins, then someone else must lose. Besides win/lose strategies, there are also strategies for negotiation and for win/win. Win/win means we are both in the same boat. You have an oar and so do I and we want to go to the same place.
　　　—GEORGE PEABODY, *NYT Mag.*

You're right, I *have* slept around to get where I am today. I've slept in planes, on trains, and once I was so exhausted after a big sales meeting that I even fell asleep in a taxi!
　　　—LOUISE M., account executive, *New Woman*

If you have built castles in the air, your work need not be lost; that is where they should be. Now put the foundations under them.
　　　—HENRY DAVID THOREAU

Let not thy will roar, when thy power can but whisper.
　　　—DR. THOMAS FULLER

How many cares one loses when one decides not to be something, but to be someone.
　　　—"COCO" CHANEL

Emotion isn't a sex-linked trait. Both sexes cry, but I think men cry from frustration and women cry over injustice.
　　　—SHIRLEY YOUNG, executive vice-president

If a man mulls over a decision, they say, "He's weighing the options." If a woman does it, they say, "She can't make up her mind."
　　　—BARBARA PROCTOR, advertising agency president

Two can live as cheaply as one—if they both have good jobs.
　　　—DR. LAWRENCE J. PETER

The common idea that success spoils people by making them vain, egotistic, and self-complacent is erroneous; on the contrary, it makes them, for the most part, humble, tolerant, and kind. Failure makes people cruel and bitter.
　　　—FRANCIS BACON

You don't meet famous authors, you get dirty fingernails from opening up book cartons.
　　　—DILYS WINN, writer, on opening a bookstore

She who would thrive, must rise at five;
She who hath thriven, may lie till seven.

 —ANON.

Make the most of yourself, for that is all there is to you.
 —RALPH WALDO EMERSON

Why, yes, I am a "little homemaker"—I'm in the construction business and I build small houses.
 —CARTOON, *Woman's Day*

In my dreams, the ones I have just before I wake up and have to go to work, I see myself on top of my grandmother's favorite mountain, standing as tall as I can on my tiptoes to see more, bowing to no one. A mountain dream like that will carry a person right through a day working at that supermarket.
 —HANNAH MORGAN, working mother, Harlan County, Kentucky,
  in Robert Coles and Jane Hallowell Coles, *Women of Crisis*

A conscious decision to compete with men is essential to a woman's success in almost any job. It seems so obvious: Most good jobs, in blue-collar unions as well as white-collar professions, are held by men. Most hiring is done by men. The situation can only be changed by women who regard themselves and are regarded by others as being plain excellent—not excellent only in comparison to other women.
 —SUSAN JACOBY, "Hers," *NYT*

You have learned to look directly into the eyes of men from whom you want *nothing*—except a serious conversation. You have trained your mind, perfected your style, and you know your rights.

And while you're drinking a toast to yourself, someone starts calling you abrasive. And then someone starts calling you ruthless. A man has got to be Joe McCarthy to be called "ruthless." All a woman has to do is put you on hold.

I believe that any woman who accepts aloneness as the natural by-product of success is accepting a punishment for a crime she didn't commit. And she is not acknowledging one of the most precious lessons of the women's movement, the lesson of community. . . .

We may not be able to tell women that there is safety in freedom. But we certainly can say, with absolute certainty, that for free women, the only safety is in numbers.
 —MARLO THOMAS, from a speech honoring the winners of the
 New York Women in Communications Matrix Awards

""!!!**
WRITERS

UPON THE SAYING THAT MY VERSES WERE MADE BY ANOTHER

The envious age only to me alone,
Will not allow what I do write, my own; . . .
I willingly accept Cassandra's fate,
To speak the truth, although believed too late.

> —ANNE KILLIGREW, seventeenth century

Aunt Jane for various circumstances was not so *refined* as she ought to have been for her *talent.*

> —NIECE OF JANE AUSTEN, in Margharita Laski, *Jane Austen and Her World*

Perhaps when you again appear in print you may chuse to dedicate your volumes to Prince Leopold; any historical romance, illustrative of the history of the august House of Coburg, would just now be very interesting.

> —JAMES STANIER CLARKE, letter to Jane Austen (1816)

Her reply:
I am fully sensible that an historic romance, founded on the House of Saxe-Coburg, might be much more to the purpose of profit or popularity than such pictures of domestic life in country villages as I deal in. But I could no more write a romance than an epic poem. I could not sit seriously down to write a serious romance under any other motive than to save my life, and if it were indispensable for me to keep it up and never relax into laughing at myself or other people, I am sure I would be hung before I had finished the first chapter. No, I must keep to my own style and go on in my own way. . . .

> —JANE AUSTEN

Mr. Thoreau dined with us yesterday. He is a singular character—a young man with much of wild original nature remaining in him. . . . He is a keen and delicate observer of nature—a genuine observer, which, I suspect, is almost as rare a character as even an original poet; and Nature, in return for his love, seems to adopt him as her especial child. . . .

> —NATHANIEL HAWTHORNE, *American Notebooks*

Look sharply after your thoughts. They come unlooked for, like a new bird seen on your trees, and, if you turn to your usual task, disappear; and you shall never find that perception again; never, I say—but perhaps years, ages, and I know not what events and worlds may lie between you and its return.

> —RALPH WALDO EMERSON

To live is war with trolls
in the vaults of the heart and the brain.
To *write:* that is to sit
in judgment over one's self.

> —HENRIK IBSEN

All women love him—all except the Muses.

> —HEINRICH HEINE, about a poet

Persons attempting to find a motive in this narrative will be prosecuted; persons attempting to find a moral in it will be banished; persons attempting to find a plot in it will be shot.

> By Order of the Author,
> Per G. G. Chief of Ordnance
> —MARK TWAIN, *Huckleberry Finn*

THE TURNINGS OF A BOOKWORM

Love levels all plots.
Dead men sell no tales.
A new boom sweeps clean.
Circumstances alter bookcases.
The more haste the less read.
Too many books spoil the trade.
Many hands make light literature.
Epigrams cover a multitude of sins.
Ye can not serve Art and Mammon.
A little sequel is a dangerous thing.
It's a long page that has no turning.
Don't look a gift book in the binding.
A gilt-edged volume needs no accuser.
In a multitude of characters there is safety.
Incidents will happen even in the best regulated novels.
One touch of Nature makes the whole book sell.
Where there's a will there's a detective story.
A book in the hand is worth two in the library.
An ounce of invention is worth a pound of style.
A good name is rather to be chosen than great characters.
Where there's so much puff, there must be some buyer.

> —CAROLYN WELLS (1900)

The money is a lifebelt thrown to a swimmer who has already reached the shore in safety.
—GEORGE BERNARD SHAW refusing the Nobel Prize

The moral of George Sand's tale, the beauty of what she does for us is not the extension she gives to the feminine nature but the richness she adds to the masculine.
—HENRY JAMES

[I am] the Spartacus of women slaves.
—GEORGE SAND

I have just reread my heart's diary, and am much struck by the rapid haphazard gallop at which it swings along, sometimes indeed jerking almost intolerably over the cobbles. Still, if it were not written rather faster than the fastest typewriting, if I stopped and took thought, it would never be written at all. The advantage of the method is that it sweeps up accidentally several stray matters which I should exclude if I hesitated, but which are the diamonds of the dustheap.
—VIRGINIA WOOLF, A *Writer's Diary*

A woman has to sacrifice all claims to femininity and family to be a writer.
—SYLVIA PLATH, in a letter written when a graduate student

Novel writing has to be learned, but it can't be taught. This bunkum and stinkum of college creative-writing courses—writers make their decision to write in secret. The academics don't know that. They don't know that the only thing you can do for someone who wants to write is buy him a typewriter.
—JAMES CAIN, author

Rebelliousness is an essence of [Lillian Hellman's] vitality—that creative sort of dissatisfaction which shouts out, "Life ought to be better than this!" Every great artist is a rebel. The maker's search for new forms—for ways of testing the givens—is in her a fierce rebellion against what has been accepted and acclaimed and taken for granted. And a deep, deep, rebellious anger against the great cheat of human existence, which is death, feeds her love of life and gives bite to her enjoyment of every minute of it.
—JOHN HERSEY, *New Republic*

Homer ... greatest of all storytellers, knew the most difficult secret of his craft: when enough is enough.
—ELEANOR CLARK, *Eyes etc.*

... [H]er lifelong love of words sprang from her early emotional impover-
ishment, and words were a rich bounty that she could absorb with hun-
gering appreciation.
    —CYNTHIA GRIFFIN WOLFF, *The Triumph of Edith Wharton*

It's a book about a man whose mother could not sign her name, written
by a man whose father could not sign his.
    —CARL SANDBURG, on his biography of Lincoln

What is written is merely the dregs of experience.
    —FRANZ KAFKA

The attraction of this way of writing is that it is easier—even quicker,
once you get the habit—to say *In my opinion it is not an unjustifiable
assumption that* than to say *I think.*
    —GEORGE ORWELL

Poetry is an effort to express the inexpressible in terms of the unforgettable.
    —LOUIS UNTERMEYER

Art, it seems to me, should simplify. That, indeed, is very nearly the
whole of the high artistic process; finding what conventions of form and
what detail one can do without and yet preserve the spirit of the whole
—so that all that has been suppressed and cut away is there to the
reader's consciousness as much as if it were in type on the page.
    —WILLA CATHER, "On the Art of Fiction"

It is a real dilemma. What *is* the authentic voice of the woman writer?
Does anyone *know*? Does anyone know what the authentic voice of
woman is? Is it sweet and low, like the voice of Shakespeare's Cordelia;
or is it raging and powerful, like the voice of Lady Macbeth? Is it an
alternation of the two?
    The problem is, I suppose, that women have never been left alone to
be themselves, and to find *out* for themselves.
    —ERICA JONG, *Vogue*

If anyone has an alternative to writing for a living, he should take it.
When I was in the third grade I had a panacean vision that I would one
day sit in front of a typewriter, just stroke the keys and make a living. All
I had to do was talk to my typewriter. I've spent the rest of my life
disabusing myself of that vision. ...
    I do get a kick out of writing—about two minutes a day.
    —JOHN MCFEE, author

The habits of a lifetime when everything else had to come before writing
are not easily broken, even when circumstances now often make it possible for the writing to be first; habits of years: response to others, distracti-

bility, responsibility for daily matters, stay with you, mark you, become you. The cost of "discontinuity" is such a weight of things unsaid, an accumulation of material so great that everything starts up something else in me; what should take weeks, takes me sometimes months to write; what should take months, takes years.

I speak of myself to remind us of those (I so nearly was one) who never come to writing at all.

We who write are survivors.

> —TILLIE OLSEN, in Sara Ruddick and Pamela Daniels, *Working It Out*

The one thing a writer has to have is balls.

> —NORMAN MAILER

I still have that overlag of feeling, that I am *pretending* to be an author.

Perhaps I am a little like my grandson, young Mathew, at two years old, coming down the stairs and reassuring himself by saying, *"This is Mathew coming downstairs!"* And so I . . . said to myself: "This is Agatha pretending to be a successful author, going to her own large party, having to look as though she is someone."

> —AGATHA CHRISTIE, *An Autobiography*

People around town are employing a new gambit for awkward lulls in cocktail and dinner-table conversation. They simply ask, "And how is the book coming?"

> —BARBARA GAMAREKIAN, *Washington Post*

A writer submitted a novel to a publisher. After a month went by without a reply, the writer sent a letter.

"Please report on my manuscript immediately, as I have other irons in the fire," he wrote.

The publisher wrote back, "We have considered your manuscript and advise you to put it with the other irons."

I have a sense of shamelessness as I sit in front of a blank sheet of defenseless paper. The difficulty is not in the writing, it's in the head. Being able to write the words is a reward for the pain and concentration that have gone before.

Poetry and morality are inseparable, and in violating morality you assure your destruction as a poet.

> —BELLA AKMADULINA, Russian poet

"Poetess": It brings to mind something vague and nebulous, rustling with its false wings, touching things in a little album with a golden edge. Akmadulina possesses the full right to be called a poet and not a poetess.

> —YEVGENY YEVTUSHENKO, Russian poet

No one can tell you what it's like to have a human being, helpless as a beached flounder, in a crib in the middle of your own life. An interviewer once faced Gloria Steinem with the key question: Could she have a child and still be the amazing activist journalist? Gloria was certain of it. She would just write when the baby was asleep.

The thing is, babies only sleep for half an hour, and then they're into your sewing box and wrapping thread around your typewriter.
> —GAIL SHEEHY, *Passages*

I thought of myself as a writer, even when I took the job of editor.

I wasn't able to stop. It was for me the most extraordinary way of thinking and feeling—it became the one thing I was doing that I had absolutely no intention of living without. I just wanted to do it better and better. . . .

It stretches you, makes you think the unthinkable, project yourself into people you even dislike. I guess it's like going underwater for me, the danger, yet I'm certain I'm going to come up.
> —TONI MORRISON, author, in interview with Mel Watkins, *NYT*

[Ring] meant it when he complained: "Where do they get that stuff about me being a satirist? I just listen." Most revealing of all was his response to a contention, with only family present, that Dickens was sentimental and sloppy. "How can you write if you can't cry?" he said.
> —RING LARDNER, JR., *The Lardners*

What I think you get from Emily Dickinson is what you get from any great writer—all of life.
> —JULIE HARRIS, actress, in *The Belle of Amherst,* a
>   dramatization of Emily Dickinson's life

If you steal from one author, it's plagiarism; if you steal from many, it's research.
> —WILSON MIZNER

Ilka Chase had recently published her book, *Past Imperfect,* when she encountered a noted Hollywood actress at a party.

"I enjoyed your book," cooed the star. "Who wrote it for you?"

"Darling, I'm so glad you liked it," Ilka replied. "Who read it to you?"

My, but he's brilliant. He hates everything.
> —PETER DE VRIES, *Through Fields of Clover*

The aggressive act of creation; the guilt for creating, I did not want to rival man; to steal man's creation, his thunder. I must protect them, not outshine them.
> —ANAIS NIN

He and I had an office so tiny that an inch smaller and it would have been
adultery.
>—DOROTHY PARKER, on working with Robert Benchley for
>*Vanity Fair*

The black writer has the American experience and he also has the black
experience; so he's very rich.
>—GWENDOLYN BROOKS, *Report from Part One*

Even now we do not fully take women seriously as writers. Success, in us,
is still considered something of a fluke. It is not something we tend to go
after, in the sense that we look for, expect, and organize our lives for it.
The point is that we, ourselves, consider success, when it comes, a gift of
fate. And this is deadly.
>—COLETTE DOWLING, *New York*

An *oeuvre* is a body of work which, like a true body, interacts with itself,
and with its own growth. . . . If a writer's work has a shape to it—and most
have a repetition like a heartbeat—the *óeuvre* will begin to construct
him.
>—HORTENSE CALISHER

The art of writing is the art of applying the seat of the pants to the seat
of the chair.
>—MARY HEATON VORSE

They're fancy talkers about themselves, writers. If I had to give young
writers advice, I would say don't listen to writers talking about writing
or themselves.
>—LILLIAN HELLMAN

I was thirty-seven when I went to work writing the column. I was too old
for a paper route, too young for Social Security, and too tired for an affair.
>—ERMA BOMBECK

It was my turn to be famous and to make money, to get heavy mail, to be
recognized by influential people, to be dined at Sardi's and propositioned
in padded booths by women who sprayed themselves with musk, to buy
Sea Island cotton underpants and leather luggage, to live through the
intolerable excitement of vindication. (I was right all along!) I experienced the high voltage of publicity. It was like picking up a dangerous wire fatal to ordinary folk. It was like the rattlesnakes handled by
hillbillies in a state of religious exaltation.
>—SAUL BELLOW, after winning the Nobel Prize, in Susan
>Margolis, *Fame*

There are nights when one comes home after a cancerously dull party, full of liquor but not drunk, leaden with boredom, somewhere out of Fitzgerald's long dark night. Writing at such a time is like making love at such a time. It is hopeless, it desecrates one's future, but one does it anyway because at least it is an act.

  —NORMAN MAILER

POETRY

. . . nor til the poets among us can be
  'literalists of
  the imagination'—above
    insolence and triviality and can present
for inspection, 'imaginary gardens with real toads in them,'
  shall we have
  it. In the meantime, if you demand on the one hand,
  the raw material of poetry in
    all its rawness and
    that which is on the other hand
      genuine, you are interested in poetry.

  —MARIANNE MOORE

INDEX

jazz, 171, 173
Jenkins, Rhoda, 112
jogging, 209, 210
Johnson, Virginia, 254
Jones, Robert Edmond, 55
journalism, 178
judges, 115, 116
justice, 72, 118

Kearns, Jack, 150
Keller, Helen, 67
Kennedy, Edward M., 177
Kennedy, John F., 235
Kennedy, Rose Fitzgerald, 177
Kerr, Walter, 224
Kiner, Ralph, 215
King, Billie Jean, 215
kitchens, 49
"kooky," 163
Kreps, Juanita, 102–103

LaGuardia, Fiorello, 55
Landers, Ann, 164
language, 107–114
  American English, 108, 110, 112
  blacks' use of, 110
  communication in, 42, 114
  de-sexist thinking and, 108
  euphemisms in, 112, 113
  food and, 49
  gender in, 109, 117
  grammatical grundyism in, 107
  insincerity as enemy of, 109–110
  of law, 115, 116
  of North American Indians, 109
  of Plains English, 108
  pregnancy and, 112
  visual sense and, 67
  women as source of, 208
Lardner, Ring, 266
Lasky, Jesse, 162
law, 115–119
  abuse of, 72, 118
  as exhibitionism, 117
  love vs., 129
  Murphy's, 78
  women and, 115, 118, 119, 131
lawns, 80
lawyers, 115, 116, 117, 118
leaders, 100
learning, 60
Lee, Gypsy Rose, 179
legalese, 115, 116
leisure, 225–230

Levant, Oscar, 125
Leyster, Judith, 26
liberty, 178
life, 77, 119–124, 171, 232, 266
  art and, 28
  effectiveness learned from, 162
  emptiness in, 250
  habit vs. marvel in, 156
  as jest, 124
  as therapist, 193
life-style, 151–156
  of Americans, 154
  contemporary, 155
Lind, Jenny, 11, 166
Liszt, Franz, 168
literature, 238, 243, 264
loneliness, 72, 106, 121, 190
Lopez, Nancy, 216
Los Angeles, 72
love, loving, 106, 124–131, 196
  action vs. language in, 125–126
  admiration vs., 126
  as bad for music, 127
  cooking and, 49, 52
  distance in, 126
  enemies of, 127, 129
  between equals, 128
  infatuation vs., 128–129
  law vs., 129
  like vs., 128
  marriage vs., 132, 133, 138
  of one's keeper, 59
  Platonic, 126
  as sharing of life, 128
  as stronger than hate, 130–131
  wise men in, 124–125
  among women, 125
  women's age in, 130
  work and, 255
Lowrey, Bette, 175
luck, 23
Lucretius, 46

machines, 80
McLuhan, Marshall, 63
manners, 151–156
  emotions and, 154
  for gentlemen, 152, 153
  table, 152
marriage, 131–139, 198, 236, 239
  as acquisition, 128
  in advertising, 14
  as ceremony, 139
  death and, 17, 18, 58

ABOUT THE AUTHOR

Dorothy Uris teaches effective verbal communication at New York University. At the Mannes College of Music and the Manhattan School of Music she has for years trained voice students in English diction. As a speech consultant at General Foods, she sharpened executive speech skills. She has coached the casts of operas and major singers at the Metropolitan Opera, the New York City Opera, and the Santa Fe Opera.

A former actress in theater and some thirty films, she has also staged readings of literary and dramatic materials. Her wide-ranging experiences are reflected in *Say It Again* as well as her previous books, *A Woman's Voice* and *To Sing in English*.